# Good English!

**John Ayto**

OXFORD
UNIVERSITY PRESS

OXFORD
UNIVERSITY PRESS

Great Clarendon Street, Oxford OX2 6DP

Oxford University Press is a department of the University of Oxford.
It furthers the University's objective of excellence in research, scholarship,
and education by publishing worldwide in

Oxford New York
Auckland Bangkok Buenos Aires Cape Town Chennai
Dar es Salaam Delhi Hong Kong Istanbul Karachi Kolkata
Kuala Lumpur Madrid Melbourne Mexico City Mumbai Nairobi
São Paulo Shanghai Taipei Tokyo Toronto

Oxford is a trade mark of Oxford University Press
in the UK and in certain other countries



This edition 2004

First published 1995 as The Oxford School A–Z of English
First published in 2002 as Good English!



British Library Cataloguing in Publication Data available

Part of a 6-part set. Not to be sold separately.
ISBN 0-19-911201-0 (complete set)
ISBN 0-19-911264-9 *Good English!* (when part of this set)

1 3 5 7 9 10 8 6 4 2

Typeset in Utopia
by Pentacor Book Design, High Wycombe

Printed in Great Britain by
Cox & Wyman Ltd, Reading, Berkshire

# Introduction

Do you say *a hotel* or *an hotel*? Do you say *bored with* or *bored of*? What's the difference between *sometime* and *some time*? Is it *two oranges* or *two orange's*? Is it all right to put a preposition at the end of a sentence? How are semicolons used?

**Good English!** will answer questions like these. It's arranged in alphabetical order, so you can easily get to the word or topic you want to find out about. For instance, if you want to know what preposition to use with *bored*, you look at the entry for *bored*. If you want to know whether you make the plural of nouns by adding *s* or *'s*, you look at the entry for *plurals*.

Many of the entries in the book are about facts. It's a fact that British people spell *armour* with a *u*, but Americans spell it *armor*, without a *u*. No one would argue about that. But a lot of the entries are not about facts. They're about conventions: what you should do. Some people spell *all right* as two words, and some people spell it *alright*. Which is right? What should you do? **Good English!** gives you guidance on questions like these.

The entries explain what standard practice is over a whole range of disputed points, from split infinitives and the use of sexist language to the difference in meaning between *disinterested* and *uninterested* and the pronunciation of *controversy*.

This isn't a dictionary. Some entries are concerned with the meaning of words, but most of the entries are to do with some other aspect of language, like syntax or pronunciation. In these cases, the purpose of a definition is simply to introduce the entry, and to make quite clear what word is being discussed. Also, many words have more than one part of speech, but not all of them will be mentioned if they're not relevant to the usage point being discussed.

The pronunciation of words is shown between oblique lines, like this: **ate** /et/. When a word has several syllables, the one that's stressed is printed in thick black letters, like this: **longitude**/**long**-gi-tyood/. Most of the letters used between these oblique lines have their usual sound, but there are some special letters and combinations you need to know:

| | |
|---|---|
| /ə/ | represents the sound that's written as **a** in **along** and as **e** in **given** |
| /th/ | represents the sound of **th** in **thin** |
| /dh/ | represents the sound of **th** in **this** |
| /zh/ | represents the sound of **s** in **pleasure** |
| /oo/ | represents the sound of **oo** in **soon** |
| /uu/ | represents the sound of **oo** in **book** |

**Key to the symbols used in the text:**

- ✔ standard form
- ⚠ non-standard form
- ❗ spelling guide
- 🔊 pronunciation guide

# Aa

## a, an

**A** (or **an**) goes before singular nouns: *a girl, two girls.* You choose between **a** and **an** by the sound, not the spelling of the word that follows. Use **a** before words that begin with a consonant sound, including the sound of *y*: *a drum, a yacht, a university.* Use **an** before words that begin with a vowel sound: *an idiot, an onion.*

In most of the words that begin with the letter *h*, you pronounce the *h* sound, so you use **a** with them: *a hat, a helicopter.* If you don't pronounce the *h* sound, you use **an**: *an honour, an hour.* Today, the standard practice is to pronounce the *h* in the words *habitual, heraldic, hereditary, historian, historic, horrendous, horrific* and *hotel,* so you use **a** with them. In the past it was more usual not to pronounce the *h* in those words. Some speakers continue to do this, thinking it is more 'correct'. They say /ən oh-**tel**/, for example, and write it *an hotel.* This is not 'wrong', but in written work it's best to use **a** in front of these words. When speaking you should avoid saying 'an' and then pronouncing the *h* (/ən hoh-**tel**/).

Before an abbreviation with a vowel sound, use **an**: *an AA member, an MP.* If it's a consonant sound, including *y*, use **a**: *a BBC programme, a UFO.* The same applies to numbers: *an 80 per cent increase, a £200 pay rise.*

**A** and **an** are called 'indefinite articles'.

## abbreviations

Abbreviations are shortened forms of words. They're quicker to write and say than their full forms.

There are two sorts of abbreviation. In the first sort, you just take the first letter of a word, or the first letters of a group of words – for example, *m* for *million*, *N* for *North*, *UN* for *United Nations*, *BBC* for *British Broadcasting Corporation.* When we speak, we don't usually bother to use single-letter abbreviations – we'd probably say 'North' rather than 'N'. But for a group of letters we usually say the letters: *BBC* /bee bee **see**/. There's a special type of abbreviation, called an acronym, where you pronounce the group of letters as if it were an ordinary word, so that *acquired immune deficiency syndrome* becomes *AIDS* /aydz/.

In the other sort of abbreviation, you take the first letter and one or more other letters of a word. For instance, you might take the first two or three letters – *Fr* for *French*, *Col* for *Colonel*. You might take the first and last letters, as in *Mr* for *Mister*; or you might take the first and last letters and a letter in the middle – *Sgt* for *Sergeant*.

To find out about whether to use full stops with abbreviations look at the entry for FULL STOP. For apostrophes and abbreviations see under APOSTROPHE. There's also an entry for E.G. AND I.E. and one for ETC.

## abide *verb*

If you **abide** by a promise or a decision, you keep to it. If you say you can't **abide** something, you dislike it very much. The past form of the verb in both cases is **abided**: *He abided by his promise.*

There's another use of **abide**, meaning 'to live or stay in a place', which is no longer current. Its past form is **abode**.

## -able, -ible *suffix*

If you put **-able** on to the end of a verb, you make an adjective that means 'able to be done'. For example, *bendable* means 'able to be bent', and *repeatable* means 'able to be repeated'.

Some adjectives have **-ible** on the end rather than **-able**. It means the same. It's usually not possible to tell which adjectives these are from the way they're pronounced, so the best way to make sure you get the spelling right is to learn them by heart or check them in a dictionary. These are the main **-ible** adjectives:

accessible
admissible
audible
collapsible
combustible
compatible
comprehensible
contemptible
convertible
corruptible
credible
defensible
destructible
digestible
discernible
divisible
edible
eligible
expressible
fallible
feasible
flexible
forcible
gullible
incorrigible
indelible
inexhaustible
intelligible
invincible
irascible
irrepressible
irresistible
legible
negligible
perceptible
permissible
plausible
possible
reducible
reprehensible
responsible
reversible
sensible
susceptible
tangible
visible

For some adjectives you can use either **-able** or **-ible**. The main ones are *collectable/collectible, extendable/extendible, includable/includible* and *preventable/preventible.*

## about see AROUND

## abridgement, abridgment *noun*

An **abridgement** or **abridgment** of a book is a shortened version of it. Both spellings are correct, but **abridgement** is commoner in British English.

a

## **accede** *verb* and **exceed** *verb*

If you **accede** /ək-**seed**/ to someone's request, you agree to do what they've asked you to do. **Accede** is quite a formal word.

Remember the spelling of **accede**, with two **c**s.

When one thing **exceeds** /ik-**seedz**/ another, it's larger, higher, etc.: *Today the temperature exceeded 30°C.* **Exceed** is a fairly formal word too. In ordinary writing it's often better just to say *is more than* or *is over*.

Remember the spelling of **exceed**, with a **c** after the **x**.

## **accept** *verb* and **except** *preposition, verb*

**Accept** /ək-**sept**/ is a verb. It means 'to agree to receive': *I accepted her apology.*

**Except** /ek-**sept**/ is mainly a preposition, meaning 'not including': *I've tried all the flavours except strawberry.* It can also be a verb, meaning 'to leave out': *I except Shirley from all my criticisms.* This is a very formal way of using the word. It's usually better to say something like *I don't include* or *I leave out*: *I don't include Shirley in my criticisms.*

Remember the spelling of **except** – there's a **c** between the **x** and the **e**.

## **access** *noun, verb* and **accession** *noun*

If you have **access** to something, you can get into it or use it: *Ramps enable people in wheelchairs to have access to public buildings.* You can also use **access** as a verb, meaning 'to get into a computer file'.

The **accession** of a king or queen is when they begin their reign.

**accommodate** *verb*, **accommodation** *noun*

To **accommodate** someone or something is to find a suitable place for them. **Accommodation** is the place where they stay.

❶ Remember the spelling of **accommodate** – two **c**s, two **m**s and two **o**s.

**accomplice** *noun*

An **accomplice** is someone who helps you do something bad, such as a crime. 🔊 The standard British pronunciation of the word is /ə-**kum**-pliss/, but /ə-**kom**-pliss/ is also acceptable.

**accomplish** *verb*

To **accomplish** something is to finish it or succeed in doing it. 🔊 The standard British pronunciation of the word is /ə-**kum**-plish/, but /ə-**kom**-plish/ is also acceptable.

**accuse** *verb*

If you **accuse** someone, you say that you think they've done something bad or illegal. The preposition that goes with **accuse** is **of**: *The manager accused him of stealing.*

**acknowledgement, acknowledgment** *noun*

An **acknowledgement** or **acknowledgment** is a sign that you recognize, accept or have received something. Both spellings are correct, but **acknowledgement** is commoner in British English.

❶ Remember the **c** before the **k**.

**acquaint** *verb*, **acquaintance** *noun*

If you **acquaint** yourself with *something*, you find out about it. If you are **acquainted** with *someone*, you know them, but not well. An **acquaintance** is someone you know, but not as closely as a friend. This is a rather formal word, and can sound stilted. It's often better to use simpler alternatives, such as *know* and *find out*.

❶ Remember the **c** before the **q**.

**acquire** *verb*

**Acquire** is a rather formal word meaning 'to get possession of': *From somewhere he'd acquired a rather battered old top hat. These offices have been acquired for Fred Bloggs Ltd.*

❶ Remember the **c** before the **q**.

**acquit** *verb*

If you **acquit** someone **of** a crime, you say officially that they're not guilty of it.

❶ Remember the **c** before the **q**. When you're adding **-ing** and **-ed** to **acquit**, you double the **t**: **acquitting**, **acquitted**.

**acronym** see ABBREVIATION, FULL STOP

**active** see CLEAR WRITING, VERBS

**acute** *adjective*

When **acute** is used of something bad, it shows that it's very serious or extreme (*acute embarrassment*) and often also that something needs to be done about it quickly (*in acute danger*). It's also applied to diseases that develop very quickly (see CHRONIC).

❶ Remember the spelling – there's only one **c**.

**AD**

AD is used with dates to denote a year of the modern era, after the birth of Christ (in contrast with *BC* 'before Christ'). It's short for Latin *anno domini*, which means 'in the year of the Lord'. It used to be put in front of the date (*AD 1520*), but it's now far commoner to put it afterwards, like BC (*1520 AD*), and this is now regarded as acceptable. More information about dates can be found under CENTURY.

## adjectives

Adjectives describe things, places or people (*green, old, funny, difficult*). They can go before a noun (*green paint*) or after a verb (*That was funny*).

You compare things by adding *-er* to an adjective or by using *more* with it: *She's older than me. That was more difficult than I expected.* This is called the **comparative**. To find out more about it, look at the entry for DOUBLE COMPARATIVES.

You say that things are the best, worst, biggest, smallest, etc. by adding *-est* to an adjective or by using *most* with it: *That was the funniest joke I've ever heard.* This is called the **superlative**.

## admission *noun* and admittance *noun*

**Admission** and **admittance** both refer to going in or letting in, but they're used in slightly different ways. **Admittance** is a formal word for 'going in'. It's often found on notices saying that you're not allowed in: *No admittance except on business.*

**Admission** is the more usual word for 'permission to go in': *Men without ties were refused admission to the restaurant.* It also refers to the money you have to pay to go in: *Admission £8.*

**Admission** also means 'confession': *his admission of guilt.*

a

**admit** *verb*

❶ When you add **-ing** and **-ed** to **admit**, you double the t: **admitting, admitted**.

**adopt** *verb*, **adapt** *verb* and **adept** *adjective*

If people **adopt** a baby or a young child, they take it to live with them as their own child, often because it hasn't got any parents of its own. You can **adopt** a thing, too, in the sense of 'taking it up' or 'accepting it': *The council have adopted a plan to paint all the lamp-posts blue.* This is a rather formal use of the word.

To **adapt** something is to change it so that it's more suitable for what you want to do with it: *a stage play adapted for television.*

If you're **adept** at something, you're clever at doing it: *Joe's adept at finding excuses for not giving his work in on time.* **Adept** is quite a formal word, mainly used in writing.

🔊 When you say **adopt** and **adapt**, you put the main stress on the second part of the word: /ə-**dopt**/ and /ə-**dapt**/. For **adept** most people put the main stress on the first part: /**ad**-ept/, but /ə-**dept**/ is also correct.

**adopted** *adjective* and **adoptive** *adjective*

If people adopt a child, the child who has been taken into a new family is described as an **adopted** child. Its new parents are called its **adoptive** parents.

**advance** *noun* and **advanced** *adjective*

An **advance** is a forward movement, usually to a better position. If you do something **in advance**, you do it beforehand. You can also use **advance** in front of other nouns, meaning 'done beforehand'. For example, if you give someone *advance warning* of something, you warn them about it well before it happens.

Something that's **advanced** is very highly developed, not simple or basic: *an advanced computer design*. Don't use **advanced** to mean 'done beforehand'. ⚠ *An advanced warning* is not standard English.

## advantageous *adjective*

Something that's **advantageous** is to your advantage – it puts you in a better position than you would have had without it.

❶ Remember the spelling, which keeps the **e** of **advantage**.

## adverbs

Adverbs add to the meaning of other words (*slowly, incredibly, very, unfortunately*). They can add to the meaning of verbs (*The time goes slowly*), of adjectives (*That was incredibly funny*), and even of other adverbs (*The time goes very slowly*).

Adverbs can also add to the meaning of whole sentences: *Unfortunately, no one was at home*. To find out more about this, look at the entry for SENTENCE ADVERBS.

***Where to put adverbs***

The same set of words can often mean something different depending on how we say it. For example, if we say *There you are* with the main stress on *there*, we mean 'I've found you', but if we say it with the main stress on *are*, we mean 'That proves that I was right'. If we say *She won't accept any excuse* with the main stress on *excuse*, we mean 'She'll accept no excuse', but if we say it with the main stress on *any*, we mean 'The excuse will have to be a good one for her to accept it'.

When we speak, we can make these differences clear by the way we say the words. But when we write, we can't do this. Usually the context or the punctuation will

a

show what's meant, but if they don't, it may be necessary to alter the sentence. In some cases, changing the position of an adverb in a sentence will change the sentence's meaning. For instance, *I've only dusted the table* could imply 'I haven't polished it', whereas *I've dusted only the table* could imply 'I haven't dusted the chairs'. To find out more about this, look at the entries for ALSO, EVEN, NOT, NOT ONLY ... BUT ALSO and ONLY.

## **adverse** *adjective* and **averse** *adjective*

**Adverse** means 'harmful': *She ate a whole pie all on her own, but it didn't seem to have any adverse effect on her.* **Adverse** can also mean 'critical': *He made a few adverse comments about my work.*

**Averse** is followed by **to**. It means 'opposed to, against', but it's almost always used with **not**, to show that you're in favour of something: *I'm not averse to a bit of fun occasionally* (it would sound less formal to say *I like a bit of fun occasionally*). It goes with nouns, and with -**ing** forms (*She's not averse to lying when it's really necessary*), but not with verbs.

## **advice** *noun* and **advise** *verb*

**Advice** is a noun. It means 'what you tell someone who needs to know what to do or how to act': *Don't go out with Dave again – that's my advice.* 🔊 It rhymes with *price.*

**Advise** is a verb. It means 'to tell someone what you think they ought to do': *I'd advise you not to go out with Dave again.* 🔊 It rhymes with *prize.*

## adviser, advisor *noun*

An **adviser** is someone who gives you advice: *Before signing any documents you should consult your financial adviser.*

❶ **Adviser** is the standard spelling, but **advisor** is an acceptable alternative.

## aesthetic, esthetic *adjective*

**Aesthetic** means 'connected with the judgement of beauty, especially in art, literature, etc.' **Aesthetic** is the British spelling. American English uses both spellings, but mainly **esthetic**.

## affect *verb* and effect *noun, verb*

The verb **affect** 🔊 /ə-**fekt**/ has two main meanings. It can mean 'to have a result on, to make a difference to': *The dog had swallowed some poisoned meat, but it didn't seem to affect him.* It can also mean 'to pretend': *She affected not to care about it, but we all knew she really did.* This is a formal use of **affect**.

The noun **effect** 🔊 /i-**fekt**/ means 'what happens to someone as a result': *The dog had swallowed some poisoned meat, but it didn't seem to have any effect on him.*

The verb **effect** 🔊 /i-**fekt**/ means 'to cause to happen' or 'to bring about': *We plan to effect several changes in the timetable.* This is a very formal use, and it's best to avoid it in ordinary speech and writing. Instead, you could say *We plan to make several changes …*

## affection *noun* and affectation *noun*

**Affection** is a feeling of fondness for someone: *He had a great affection for his old dog.*

An **affectation** is a strange and unnatural way of behaving, put on to impress people: *He hasn't really got a lisp – it's just an affectation of his to talk that way.*

a

## affinity *noun*

An **affinity** is a relationship between two people, or between a person and a thing, or between two things, in which they seem to belong together naturally because there's something that links them: *There's an affinity between cheese and wine* (= they go well together). *I can feel some affinity with her because I find spelling difficult too.*

Sometimes the link is that you like someone or something: *He's got an affinity for jazz music* (= he likes it). People used to object to this use of **affinity** meaning 'liking', with the preposition **for**, but it's now established in the language, and can be regarded as standard.

## afflict *verb* and inflict *verb*

You use **afflict** when something bad is happening to someone: *a disease which particularly afflicts the elderly.* You use **inflict** when someone does something bad to someone else: *He seems to enjoy inflicting pain on people.*

## Afro-American, Afro-Caribbean see RACES AND PEOPLES

## afterward *adverb* and afterwards *adverb*

**Afterwards** is the usual British form. Americans use **afterward**.

## aged *adjective*

🔊 If you say that someone is *aged 24*, meaning '24 years old', you pronounce **aged** as /ayjd/, with just one syllable. But if you talk about an **aged** man, meaning an 'old man', you pronounce **aged** as /**ay**-jid/, with two syllables.

**ageing, aging** *present participle, adjective, noun*

Both spellings are correct, but **ageing** is commoner in British English: *You could see the problems of his job were ageing him.* Americans tend to use **aging**.

**aggravate** *verb*

If you **aggravate** a problem, an injury, a situation, etc., you make it worse. But that's quite a rare use of the word. It's more often applied to people, when it means 'to annoy': *He's got a really aggravating habit of clicking his false teeth when he talks.* Some people object to this use of **aggravating** for 'annoying', but it's perfectly correct English, and there's no good reason to avoid it.

**ago** *adverb* and **since** *conjunction*

**Ago** and **since** don't go together. A sentence like ⚠ *It's ten years ago since I saw them* is not standard English. Either follow **ago** with **that**: ✔ *It was ten years ago that I saw them*; or use **since** on its own: ✔ *It's ten years since I saw them.* These two sentences don't mean quite the same. If you say *It was ten years ago that I saw them*, you're simply saying when in the past you saw them. If you say *It's ten years since I saw them*, you're drawing attention to the period of time that's gone by since you saw them.

**agreement** see PERSON AGREEMENT, SINGULARS AND PLURALS

**ain't**

**Ain't** means the same as **am not**, **are not** and **is not** (as in *Ain't it a shame?*) and as **has not** and **have not** (as in *You ain't seen nothing yet*). It's common in certain varieties of English – for example, in several British dialects and in very informal American English – but it's not part of standard English. ▲ Don't use it in writing unless you're actually representing someone speaking in one of these varieties of English.

❶ Remember where the apostrophe goes – between the **n** and the **t**, taking the place of the missing **o**.

## alibi *noun*

If someone accuses you of doing something wrong, and you can prove that you were somewhere else at the time it was done, you have an **alibi** for it: *His alibi for the night of the robbery won't stand up in court.*

You can also talk about having an **alibi** for something, or more usually for not doing something, when you simply mean 'an excuse': *What's your alibi for not doing that piece of work I set you?* Some people dislike this use, but it's well enough established to be regarded as standard English.

## all *adjective, noun*

Should you use **all** or **all of**? In front of a pronoun, you have to have **all of**: *All of us think he's brilliant.* In front of a noun, you can use either **all** or **all of**, but **all** is more generally accepted as standard in British English: *All my brothers and sisters have blue eyes.* **All of** is more common in American English: *All of my brothers and sisters have blue eyes.*

## allot *verb*

If you **allot** something to someone, you give it to them as their share.

❶ When you add -**ing** and -**ed** to **allot**, you double the **t**: **allotting, allotted**.

**allow** *verb*

You can say *The facts allow only one explanation* or *The facts allow of only one explanation*. They mean the same: the facts can only be explained in one way. **Allow of** is more formal than **allow** on its own.

**all right** *adjective, adverb*

*Are you feeling all right? It's expensive all right.* The standard accepted spelling for the adjective and the adverb is **all right**. You'll sometimes see another spelling, ⚠ *alright*. But this is not generally considered acceptable in standard English, so avoid it.

**allude** *verb* and **elude** *verb*

If you **allude** 🔊 /ə-**lood**/ to something, you mention it, usually in a rather indirect way: *I think he was alluding to the size of my stomach.*

If something **eludes** 🔊 /i-**loodz**/ you, you fail to get it or catch it: *She had always wanted the job, but it had always eluded her.*

❗ Remember the spelling: **allude** has two **lls**, **elude** has one.

**almost** *adverb* and **all most**

**Almost** and **all most** are nearly opposite in meaning, so don't confuse them. *It was all most amusing* (= very amusing) is a compliment, but *It was almost amusing* (= not actually amusing) definitely isn't.

**alone** *adjective, adverb*

**Alone** can have a different meaning depending on where you put it in a sentence. If you say *I can do it alone*, you mean that you can do it on your own, without anyone else's help. If you say *I alone can do it*, you mean that you are the only person who can do it.

a

## **already** *adverb* and **all ready**

**Already** means 'by now' or 'before now'. It has nothing to do with being 'ready'. If you say *They're already on stage,* you mean that they'd arrived on the stage before anyone had asked about them. But if you say *They're all ready on stage,* you mean that everyone on stage is ready.

## **also** *adverb*

**Also** can go in different positions in a sentence. Usually it doesn't make any difference to the meaning. There are times, though, when the meaning of a sentence can change according to where you put the **also**. For example, *I've also cleaned the car* probably just means 'I've cleaned the car (as well as doing various other things, not connected with the car)', and you could equally well say *I've cleaned the car also.* But it might mean 'I've cleaned the car (as well as repairing it)' or 'I've cleaned the car (as well as the bike)'.

When you speak, you can make clear what you mean by the way you say the words. But when you write this is not possible, so you must make sure you put **also** in the right place to express what you mean.

In writing, it's not good style to use **also** as if it were the same as **and.** ⚠ *I bought some cherries and peaches, also a mango* isn't acceptable in standard written English. Write either ✔ *I bought some cherries and peaches, and also a mango,* or simply ✔ *I bought some cherries and peaches, and a mango.* See also NOT ONLY ... BUT ALSO.

## **alter** *verb* and **altar** *noun*

To **alter** something is to change it: *We had to alter our plans at the last minute.*

An **altar** is a sort of table at which religious ceremonies are performed in a church or other holy place.

**alternate** *adjective, verb* and
**alternative** *adjective, noun*

**Alternate** the adjective is pronounced 🔊 /awl-**tern**-ət/. It means 'once in every two': *We have swimming on alternate Tuesdays* (= one Tuesday we have it, then the next we don't, then the next we do, etc.).

**Alternate** the verb is pronounced 🔊 /**awl**-tə-nayt/. It means 'to take turns in coming after each other': *Periods of sunshine alternated with heavy showers. He alternated between joy and depression.*

An **alternative** is one of the things you can choose, especially instead of another: *If you don't want to see a film, there are several alternatives – we could go skating, or go to a disco, or just stay in.*

As an adjective, **alternative** means 'that can be used instead': *If the car breaks down, have you got an alternative means of transport?* American English uses **alternate** in this sense.

**although** see THOUGH

**altogether** *adverb* and **all together**

❶ Don't confuse **altogether** and **all together**. **Altogether** has nothing to do with the idea of being 'together'. It means 'completely' or 'in total': *I wasn't altogether happy about it.* **All together** means 'all at the same time or in the same place': *The team arrived at the ground all together.* If you say *There were six books altogether on the top shelf,* you mean that there was a total of six books. If you say *There were six books all together on the top shelf,* you mean that all six books were in the same place, next to each other, on the top shelf.

a

**aluminium, aluminum** *noun*

**Aluminium** is a kind of metal. 🔊 **Aluminium** /al-ə-**min**-i-əm/ is the British name for it. Americans call it **aluminum** /ə-**loo**-mi-nəm/.

**amateur** *noun, adjective*

An **amateur** is someone who does something for pleasure, without being paid for it (as opposed to a professional, who is paid to do it): *an amateur golfer.*

🔊 The standard pronunciation is /**am**-ə-tə/ or /am-ə-**ter**/, but /**am**-ə-chə/ is also correct.

**ambiguous** *adjective* and **ambivalent** *adjective*

If something's **ambiguous**, it has more than one possible meaning, and it's easy to mistake one for another. For example, *an American football player* is ambiguous – it could mean 'a player of American football' or 'an American player of football'.

If you're **ambivalent** 🔊 /am-**biv**-ə-lənt/ about something, you have mixed feelings about it, or you can't decide about it. You may not be sure whether you like it or hate it, whether you approve of it or disapprove of it, etc.: *I've got the chance of a job in Australia, but I'm ambivalent about it* (= I can't decide whether to take it or not).

**amiable** *adjective* and **amicable** *adjective*

**Amiable** and **amicable** both have to do with being pleasant, but they're used in slightly different ways. **Amiable** is applied to people who are friendly and likeable, and don't make you feel uncomfortable in any way: *He had a rather fierce reputation, but he turned out to be quite an amiable old man.*

**Amicable** is a formal word, applied to situations or events where people are friendly towards each other, not quarrelling: *We settled our disagreement and parted on amicable terms.*

**amoeba, ameba** *noun*

An **amoeba** is a tiny one-celled animal that lives in water. **Amoeba** is the British spelling. In American English, the word is spelled **ameba**.

The usual plural form of the word is **amoebas**, but in scientific writing **amoebae** /ə-**mee**-bee/ is also used.

**amok, amuck** *adverb*

If a person or animal **runs amok**, they rush around wildly, damaging things. Both spellings, **amok** and **amuck**, are correct, but **amok** is more common. The standard pronunciation is /ə-**muk**/, but /ə-**mok**/ is also acceptable.

**among, amongst** *preposition*

There's no difference in meaning or use between **among** and **amongst**. Use either.

**among(st)** *preposition* and **between** *preposition*

When you're talking about only two things or people, you must use **between**: *Divide the cake between Sophie and George.* But when there are more than two, you can choose either **among(st)** or **between**.

It's traditional to use **among**, but **between** is very common, and is now fully accepted: *Divide the cake among/between Sophie, George and Derek.*

**amuck** see AMOK

## anaemia, anemia *noun*

**Anaemia** is a disease of the blood, which makes you feel weak or tired. **Anaemia** is the British spelling. The word is spelt **anemia** in American English.

## anaesthetic, anesthetic *noun*

An **anaesthetic** is something used to stop people feeling pain, especially during an operation. **Anaesthetic** is the British spelling. The word is spelt **anesthetic** in American English.

## analyse, analyze *verb*

To **analyse** something is to examine it to see what it's made of. **Analyse** is the British spelling, **analyze** the American spelling.

## and *conjunction*

***'And' at the beginning of a sentence***

There's no good reason not to start sentences with **and**. There's an old-fashioned 'rule' which says that it's bad English to do this, but it's a perfectly natural part of the way we speak English. There's no logic in trying to ban it from writing. And it can often be a useful way of drawing attention to a new point. Don't overdo it, though. It gets distracting if it's repeated too often.

***'And' joining unlike things***

The words and phrases joined by **and** need to have an equal role in the sentence. For instance, in *I like burgers and milkshakes, burgers* and *milkshakes* are equal, because they play the same part in the sentence – they're objects of the verb *like*. In *I do all the cooking, cleaning and sewing and make all the beds, cooking, cleaning* and *sewing* are equal – they're all objects of *do*; and *do* and *make* are equal – they're both verbs that go with *I*. In quite long lists like this, it's easy to forget which bits are equal, and leave out an **and**: ⚠ *I do all the cooking, cleaning, sewing and make all the beds.* This is not accepted in standard written English, so try to avoid it.

It's also easy to miss out an **and** in a list of things where you change prepositions before the end: ⚠ *on land, sea and in the air.* In standard written English this should be ✔ *on land and sea and in the air.*

The same goes for *or*: ✔ *on land or sea or in the air* is accepted in standard written English, ⚠ *on land, sea or in the air* isn't.

***'And' before 'who', 'which', 'where', etc.***

It sounds very awkward to put **and** in front of relative pronouns like *who, which* and *where*: *He's an actor famous for playing monsters, and who often appears in horror movies.* It's much better to write *He's an actor famous for playing monsters, and often appears in horror movies,* or *He's an actor famous for playing monsters, who often appears in horror movies.* The only time it's all right to follow **and** with *who*, etc. is when there's already a *who* earlier in the sentence: *He's an actor who is famous for playing monsters, and who often appears in horror movies.*

***'And' and the verb that comes next***

Words joined by **and** usually show that there are two or more things, so you use a plural verb with them: *The sparrow and the thrush are birds.* But sometimes you think of the things joined by **and** as a single unit. In that case, it's all right to use a singular verb: *Soap and water is the only thing for a dirty face like that.*

On the use of the comma with **and**, see COMMA.

a

**and/or** *conjunction*

*Shirley and/or Yasmin* means 'Shirley, or Yasmin, or Shirley and Yasmin'. **And/or** covers three possibilities. Where there are only two possibilities, just use **or** or **and**.

**annual** *adjective* and **perennial** *adjective*

Something that's **annual** happens once a year. Something that's **perennial** lasts for several years. In particular, **annual** plants have to be grown from seed every year as they die each winter, but **perennial** plants live for several years.

**antenna** *noun*

**Antenna** has two different plurals. When it means 'an insect's feeler', its plural is **antennae** /an-**ten**-ee/. When it means 'an aerial' its plural is **antennas**.

**anticipate** *verb*

**Anticipate** has two meanings. It can mean 'to expect': *I don't anticipate any difficulties.* It can also mean 'to take action in advance': *I anticipated her request by putting a cup of tea on her table* (= I got her some tea before she could ask me for it).

These are both standard usages in modern English, and there's no good reason for saying the first meaning, 'to expect', is 'incorrect', as some people still do. However, it is a rather formal word to use, and *expect* or *foresee* are often preferable: *I don't expect/foresee any difficulties.*

**antisocial** *adjective*, **unsocial** *adjective* and **unsociable** *adjective*

Someone who's **antisocial** does things that are unreasonably annoying or embarrassing to other people in general: *It's very antisocial to rev engines and slam car doors at one o'clock in the morning.*

**Unsocial** hours are working hours that are awkward because they're at a time when most people aren't working – for example, in the middle of the night.

Someone who's **unsociable** doesn't like mixing with other people, and prefers to be alone.

## any *pronoun*

Do you use a singular verb or a plural verb after **any**? It depends on whether the noun it refers to is singular or plural: *Is any of that soup left?* (*soup* is singular, so use a singular verb). *Are any of your friends here?* (*friends* is plural, so use a plural verb).

It's also possible to use a singular verb when the noun is plural if you mean **any** to refer to an individual person or thing (as in *Is any of your children interested in horse-riding?*), but this tends to sound old-fashioned or formal.

## any more, anymore

*Would you like any more tea? I won't have any more, thank you. She doesn't live here any more.* In the last of these sentences, where **any more** means 'any longer', in American English it would be written as one word, **anymore**: *She doesn't live here anymore.* But in British English it's standard to write it as two words.

## apostrophe

An apostrophe is a mark like a comma, but up above the line (').

It has three uses in English:

***Possessive***

If something belongs to someone, you show it with an apostrophe and an *s* – *Diane's watch* is the watch that belongs to Diane.

a

When a noun ends in an *s*, you still add an apostrophe and then an *s* – *the boss's daughter* is the daughter of the boss.

With plural nouns with an *s* on the end, you put the apostrophe after the *s* – *the teachers' room* is the room used by the teachers.

For plural nouns that don't end in an *s*, you add an apostrophe and then an *s* – *the children's toys* are the toys that belong to the children.

When a short phrase comes after the noun, you add the apostrophe *s* to the end of the phrase: *the chairman of the company's office* (the office belongs to the chairman, not to the company).

To find out more about the possessive, look at the entry for POSSESSIVES.

### *Leaving letters out*

When we write words to show how they're actually pronounced, we often have to leave letters out. We put in an apostrophe to take the place of the letters.

For example, when we say *is not*, it usually sounds like /**iz**-ənt/, not /iz not/. We can write this as *isn't*. The apostrophe shows that the *o* has been left out. Other examples are *mustn't* for *must not*, *I'm* for *I am*, *they'll* for *they will* and *would've* for *would have*.

To find out more about these words look under CONTRACTIONS.

### *Odd endings*

It can be awkward to add the plural *-s* or verb endings – for example to numbers or abbreviations. You can use an apostrophe to help you do this: *Three 8's are 24. She OK'd the changes.*

**appal, appall** *verb*

If something **appals** you, it's so bad that you're shocked or disgusted by it: *What an appalling smell!* **Appal** is the British spelling, **appall** the American.

❗ When you add **-ing** and **-ed** to **appal**, you double the **l**: **appalling**, **appalled**.

**appendix** *noun*

**Appendix** has two different plurals: **appendixes** and **appendices** 🔊 /ə-**pen**-di-seez/. When it means 'a small organ inside your abdomen', you usually use **appendixes** as the plural. But when it means 'an extra section at the end of a book', you can use either **appendices** or **appendixes**.

**appraise** *verb* and **apprise** *verb*

When you **appraise** something, you make a judgement about how good or valuable it is: *The report appraises the department's work over the past year* (= says whether it's been good or bad).

If you **apprise** someone of something, you tell them about it: *I shall keep you fully apprised of all developments* (= I'll tell you about them).

These are both formal words. **Appraise** is suitable mainly for serious writing. **Apprise** is very formal. It's better to avoid it altogether, and use a more straightforward word such as *tell* or *inform*.

**archaeology, archeology** *noun*

**Archaeology** is the study of people who lived long ago by examining the remains they left behind them. **Archaeology** is the standard British spelling, but **archeology** can also be used. **Archeology** is the main American spelling.

a

**ardour, ardor** *noun*

**Ardour** is very strong passionate feeling, especially of love or enthusiasm. **Ardour** is the British spelling, **ardor** the American.

**aren't**

**Aren't** means the same as **are not** (as in *They aren't here*). It's also used in **aren't I?**, meaning 'am I not?' (as in *Aren't I clever?*). This is standard English, and completely acceptable.

❶ Remember where the apostrophe goes – between the **n** and the **t**, taking the place of the missing **o**.

**arise** *verb* and **arouse** *verb*

If something **arises**, it happens: *If any difficulties arise, let me know.* This is a rather formal word. Its past tense is **arose** and its past participle is **arisen**.

If your suspicions are **aroused**, you become suspicious. If something **arouses** your anger, you become angry. To **arouse** someone can also mean to wake them up, but it's more usual to use *rouse* in this sense.

**aristocrat** *noun*

An **aristocrat** is a member of the nobility, such as a lord, a duke or a countess. 🔊 The standard British pronunciation of the word is /**ar**-is-tə-krat/. American English uses /ə-**ris**-tə-krat/, and this is also sometimes used in British English.

**armour, armor** *noun*

**Armour** is a strong protective covering made of metal. **Armour** is the British spelling, **armor** the American.

**around** *adverb, preposition* and
**about** *adverb, preposition*

**Around** and **about** overlap in meaning. They can both mean 'in the general area': *There was no one around/about*; and 'here and there': *I wandered around/about for hours*. They can both also mean 'approximately': *I'll be back around/about 10 o'clock*. American English uses **around** in this sense. British English traditionally uses **about**, but **around** is now very common.

**around** *adverb, preposition* and
**round** *adverb, preposition*

**Around** and **round** mean more or less the same. Most American speakers use only **around**. But in British English, things aren't quite so simple. There's a trend to use only **around**, but many people use both **around** and **round**, and make a difference between them. When there's the idea of going in a curve or revolving, they use **round**: *I drove round the corner*. But when there's the idea of a general area, they use **around**: *Do you live around here?* Both **around** and **round** are acceptable in either case. ⚠ Don't use **round** to mean 'approximately' (see AROUND AND ABOUT).

**arouse** see ARISE

**artefact, artifact** *noun*

An **artefact** is something that someone has made. The word is mainly applied to objects such as tools, weapons and ornaments found by archaeologists when they dig up ancient sites. **Artefact** is the main British spelling. **Artifact** is the main American spelling, and it's becoming more common in British English.

a

## articles

The **definite article** is *the* and the **indefinite article** is *a* or *an*. They are both types of DETERMINER. You can find out more about them in the entries for A and THE.

## artist *noun* and artiste *noun*

An **artist** is someone who paints, draws, makes sculptures, etc. An **artiste** (🔊 /ah-**teest**/) is someone who performs on stage, in a circus, etc. **Artiste** is now a rather old-fashioned word, and **artist** is widely used instead: *one of our most promising young recording artists.*

## as *adverb, conjunction* and *preposition*

***as ... as***

*You're not as tall as me. We can be just as successful as them.* In sentences like these it's best to use *me, him, her, us* and *them* after the **as**.

Some people still keep to the old rule that you should use *I, he, she, we* and *they* after **as** (*We can be just as successful as they*). This is based on the idea that they're short for *I am, he is, she is, we are* and *they are* (*We can be just as successful as they are*). It's perfectly correct to do this, but it can sound rather artificial.

Sometimes, sentences with this **as ... as** construction can be ambiguous. For example, if you say *I don't think you like me as much as Ben,* it might mean 'Ben likes me more than you do' or 'You like Ben more than you like me'. When you speak, you can usually make clear which you mean by the way you say it. But when you write, if the meaning isn't clear from the context, it would be better to rephrase the sentence – for instance, *I don't think you like me as much as Ben does.*

a

***'As' followed by a verb***
**As** is the standard word to use in sentences like *You played brilliantly, as you always do.* ⚠ *Like* is commonly used instead (*You played brilliantly, like you always do*), but it's not yet generally accepted as standard English. In writing, use **as**. (Before a noun, you do use *like*: *She crept up on him stealthily, like a cat.* See LIKE.)

***Other uses of 'as'***
**As** can mean 'because': *As I was cold, I put on a sweater.* It can also mean 'while' or 'when': *As I was looking out of the window, I saw someone walk up the path.* Just occasionally, it can mean either: *As she was leaving, she said goodbye.* In writing, if it's not clear whether **as** means 'because' or 'while', it's better to write the sentence another way: *Since she was leaving, she said goodbye,* or *As she left, she said goodbye.*

You can find more information on **as** in the entries for AS SUCH, AS TO and AS X AS OR XER THAN.

**ascent** *noun* and **assent** *noun, verb*

**Ascent** and **assent** are pronounced the same, but they mean quite different things.

An **ascent** is when you climb up something, such as a mountain: *the ascent of Everest.* The verb that goes with it is **ascend**: *We ascended the stairs.* They're quite formal words. In ordinary speech or writing you'd be more likely to use *climb, climb up* or *go up.*

If you give your **assent** to something, you agree to allow it. **Assent** can also be used as a verb: *I reluctantly assented to their request.* It's a formal word, usually found only in serious writing.

**Asian** see RACES AND PEOPLES

a

## aside *adverb* and a side

**Aside** means 'to the side' or 'on one side': *I stepped aside to let him pass.* Don't confuse it with **a side**, in sentences like *To give everyone a game, we agreed to play thirteen a side,* where it means 'on each side'.

## assent see ASCENT

## assignment *noun* and assignation *noun*

An **assignment** is a piece of work which you're given to do. An **assignation** is a secret meeting that has been arranged between people, especially a man and a woman.

## as such

**As such** can mean 'in itself' or 'in the strict meaning of the word': *There will be no inspectors as such, but occasional unofficial checks will be made.* The phrase is sometimes used without any real meaning, because the writer thinks it sounds impressive: *They have no rights as such, and are liable to be imprisoned at any time.* Try to avoid doing this.

## assure *verb*, ensure *verb* and insure *verb*

If you **assure** someone, you try to convince them that something's true: *I assure you I've never seen her before in my life.*

If you **ensure** /in-**shor**/ that something happens, you make certain that it does: *Please ensure that all the lights have been turned off before you leave the building.* (In American English, **insure** is often used with this meaning.)

If you **insure** /in-**shor**/ something, you make a legal agreement that if it's damaged or destroyed, you'll be paid money to compensate you for it: *This painting's insured for £100,000.*

**as to** *preposition*

When **as to** is used to mean 'about', it usually sounds uncomfortably formal and stiff: *Can you give me any information as to the whereabouts of the sports centre?* It would be much clearer and more straightforward to say *Can you tell me where the sports centre is?* Often, you can simply replace **as to** (*I have doubts as to his honesty*) with *about* (*I have doubts about his honesty*). Before *whether* (*I'm not certain as to whether I can make it*), it's better to leave it out altogether (*I'm not certain whether I can make it*).

**astrology** *noun* and **astronomy** *noun*

**Astrology** is foretelling the future from the way the stars and planets move in the sky. **Astronomy** is the scientific study of stars, planets and all the other objects and events in space.

**as X as or Xer than**

*She's as old as or older than me.* When you talk, it's quite common to miss out the second **as**, especially in long sentences: *These plastic ones are as cheap or cheaper than the sort made out of real wood.* ⚠ But this is not regarded as acceptable in standard English, so always take care to include the second **as** when you write. This can sound rather formal, and if it's not suitable for what you're writing, you can try changing the sentence round: *She's as old as me, or older.*

**attribute** *noun, verb*

When **attribute** is a noun it's pronounced 🔊 /**at**-rib-yoot/, with the main emphasis on the first syllable. It

a

means a particular quality or feature that a thing has and that is typical of it.

When **attribute** is a verb it's pronounced /ə-**trib**-yoot/, with the main emphasis on the second syllable. It means 'to suggest that someone has a particular quality, did a particular thing, etc.': *This painting has been attributed to Rembrandt* (= it's claimed that he painted it, but it's not certain).

**aural** *adjective* and **oral** *adjective*

**Aural** and **oral** sound the same, but they're used about different parts of the body.

**Aural** refers to the ears, and particularly to the power of hearing – for example, an *aural check-up* would test your hearing.

**Oral** refers to the mouth – for example, *oral hygiene* includes cleaning your teeth properly.

**auxiliary verb** see VERBS

**averse** see ADVERSE

**await** *verb* and **wait** *verb*

The difference between **await** and **wait** is that **await** has to have an object after it (*We are awaiting your reply*) but **wait** doesn't (*Don't keep us waiting*). If you want to have an object with **wait**, you have to use the preposition **for**: *How long have you been waiting for me?*

**Await** is a very formal word. In ordinary speech and writing it's usually better to use **wait for**.

**awake** *adjective, verb*, **awaken** *verb*, **wake** *verb* and **waken** *verb*

The usual past tense of **wake** is **woke**, and its usual past participle is **woken**. For **awake**, the past forms are always **awoke** and **awoken**. The past forms of **waken** and **awaken** are **wakened** and **awakened**.

All these verbs can be used in the same way, either intransitively, without an object (*I woke at 7 o'clock*), or transitively, with an object (*Mum woke me at 7 o'clock*). **Wake** is the most commonly used of the four in speech and writing. It's often followed by **up**: *The alarm bell rang and I woke up.* **Awake**, **awaken** and **waken** are more formal. They're used mainly in writing.

When you're comparing an action to waking someone up, though, it's usual to use **awake** or **awaken**: *We must awaken the country to the need for immediate action.* **Awake** is also an adjective: *Are you awake?*

**axe, ax** *noun, verb*

**Axe** is the British spelling, **ax** is the American spelling.

# Bb

**backward** *adjective, adverb,* **backwards** *adverb*

**Backwards** is the usual British form. Americans use **backward**. (In British English **backward** is mainly an adjective: *a backward step.*)

**bad** *adjective* and **badly** *adverb*

**Bad** is an adjective. It goes in front of nouns: *a bad teacher.* It also goes after the verbs *be, become, get, go, look, remain, seem, smell, sound, stay, taste* and *turn*: *Things are/look/sound bad.* With other verbs you use the adverb **badly**: *We haven't played so badly for months.* With the verb *feel* you can use either **bad** or **badly**. If you say you *feel bad* you mean either that you feel ashamed or regretful, or that you feel ill. If you say you *feel badly about something* you mean that you feel ashamed or regretful.

Be careful how you use **badly** with *want.* If you say *I want to do it badly* you may give the wrong impression. It would be clearer to say *I badly want to do it* if you mean **badly** in the sense 'very much'.

**bail** *noun, verb* and **bale** *noun, verb*

**Bail** is money paid to a court to allow an arrested person to be released until their trial. If you **bail** someone **out**, you pay this money.

The **bails** are the two small pieces of wood on top of cricket stumps.

If you **bail out** or **bale out** a boat, you scoop water out of it. If you **bale out** or **bail out** of an aircraft, you jump out of it with a parachute.

A **bale** is a large bundle of hay or straw.

**base** *noun*, *verb*, *adjective* and **bass** *noun*

A **base** is the bottom part of something, on which it stands: *At the base of the cliff there's a rocky beach.* A **base** is also a place where a military group is stationed: *Several US air force bases are being closed down.* **Base** can also be a verb, meaning 'to fix or establish' (*We had nothing to base our suspicions on*) or 'to put in a headquarters' (*Our firm's based in Birmingham*). And it can be an old-fashioned adjective meaning 'wicked' or 'cowardly'.

A **bass** (🔊 rhyming with *base*) is a man with a low singing voice, or a stringed musical instrument that plays low notes (called in full a *double bass*). A **bass** (🔊 rhyming with *gas*) is a type of fish.

**basically** *adverb*

**Basically** means 'at the simplest or most fundamental level': *An oven is basically a metal box with a heating element.* Some people use it as a way of introducing and emphasizing what they're saying: ⚠ *Well, basically, I think their latest album's rubbish.* This has not become accepted as part of standard English, so you should avoid it in writing.

**bass** see BASE

**bath** *noun*, *verb* and **bathe** *verb*

**Bath** 🔊 /bahth/ is mainly a noun, but in British English it can also be used as a verb, meaning 'to have a bath' or, more usually, 'to wash someone in a bath': *Fred was bathing the baby.*

Americans use the verb **bathe** 🔊 /baydh/ to mean 'to have a bath'. It also means, in both British and American English, 'to swim in the sea or a pool' and 'to wash a part of the body or a wound'.

b

## because *conjunction*

**Because** means 'for the reason that': *I've come indoors because it's too hot in the garden.*

Sometimes, when it's used with *not*, it can produce sentences that are ambiguous. For example, if you say *I didn't criticize him because he's young*, you could mean 'The reason why I didn't criticize him is that he's young' or 'The fact that he's young is not what I criticized him for'. When you speak, you can make clear what you mean by the way you say it, but in writing it's better to rephrase the sentence.

The role of **because** is to give explanations, and for that reason it's unnecessary to use it with nouns that already include the idea of 'explanation'. For example, ⚠ *The reason I left was because I was feeling tired* isn't standard English. The way to express it in writing is ✔ *The reason I left was that I was feeling tired.*

In serious writing you shouldn't use sentences like *Just because they're economically powerful (it) doesn't mean they can order other countries about.* Instead, write something like *The fact that they are economically powerful does not mean that they can order other countries about*, or *Although they are economically powerful, they should not order other countries about.*

## beg the question

Originally, **to beg the question** meant 'to assume that something is true without showing any proper proof'. For example, if someone said 'He must be brainy because he wears glasses', you could accuse them of **begging the question**.

It's also come to mean 'to avoid giving a direct answer to a question'. People often accuse politicians of **begging the question**. This usage has become very common, and it's now generally accepted in standard English.

A more recent new meaning of the expression is 'to seem to invite an obvious question': ⚠ *Your development plans sound very impressive, but they beg the question, how is it all going to be paid for?* This hasn't yet become established in standard English, and it's best avoided.

## behalf *noun*

**On behalf of** means 'representing' someone else: *I'm speaking on behalf of my brother.* You can also say **on** someone's **behalf**: *I'm speaking on my brother's behalf.* American English uses **in behalf of** instead.

**On behalf of** is also sometimes used as if it meant the same as *by*: ⚠ *That was a terrible mistake on behalf of the Liverpool defence.* This is not accepted as part of standard English, so you should avoid it in serious writing.

## behaviour, behavior *noun*

**Behaviour** is the way someone or something behaves. **Behaviour** is the British spelling, **behavior** the American.

## beloved *adjective, noun*

**Beloved** is a rather old-fashioned or literary word meaning 'much loved' or, as a noun, 'much loved person'. When it's a noun (*My beloved is sad*) or an adjective in front of a noun (*my beloved son),* it's pronounced 🔊 /bi-**luv**-id/. But when it's an adjective after a verb (*He was greatly beloved*) it's pronounced 🔊 /bi-**luvd**/.

b

## **beside** *preposition*, **besides** *adverb, preposition*

**Beside** is a preposition. It means 'next to': *Come and sit beside me.* It's also used in the expression *beside the point,* meaning 'irrelevant'.

**Besides** can be either an adverb or a preposition. As an adverb it's used to introduce something additional that you want to say: *I don't want to go out. It's raining, and besides I've got a lot of work to do.* As a preposition it means 'in addition to' (*There are a lot of people besides you who want to go*) and 'except for' (*I don't think anyone besides you likes him*).

## **bet** *verb*

To **bet** is to risk money on the result of something. The usual past form is **bet**: *I'd have bet anything they didn't see me.* There is another past form, **betted**, but it's quite rare. It's mainly used without an object: *I haven't betted since I lost £100 on a single race.*

## **between** *verb*

**Between** usually comes before a plural noun (*the path between the trees*) or before a pair of nouns linked by *and* (*She held it up between her finger and her thumb*). When you have long groups of words it's easy to forget this and use another word, especially *or*: ⚠ *I had to choose between going to university or looking for a job.* But this is not considered to be acceptable standard English, so you should stick to *and*.

Another tempting thing to do when the first part of the pair is very long and contains an *and* is to repeat the **between**: ⚠ *There's a lot of difference between flying a plane with an instructor there to help you and encourage you and between flying one on your own.* Again, this is not acceptable standard English.

Prepositions, including **between**, are followed by the object form of the pronoun (*me, her, them*, etc.): *There wasn't much to choose between them.* But when there are two pronouns, people tend to put the second into the subject form, especially with *I*: ⚠ *Between you and I, I think it's awful.* Although this is very common it's still not considered standard English, so you should avoid it. Use ✔ *between you and me, between her and him*, etc.

On the difference between **among** and **between** see AMONG(ST).

**biannual** *adjective* and **biennial** *adjective*

Something that's **biannual** happens twice a year: *We hold our biannual art exhibition in April and October.*

Something that's **biennial** happens once every two years: *She won the biennial piano competition in 1982 and 1984.*

**bias** *verb*

To **bias** something is to arrange it unfairly: *The system of elections is biased in favour of the larger political parties.*

❗ When you add **-ing** and **-ed** to it, you can either use a single **-s-** or a double **-ss-**: **biasing**, **biassing**; **biased**, **biassed**. The single **-s-** is commoner than the double.

**bid** *noun, verb*

Newspapers often use the noun **bid** in headlines to mean 'an attempt', because it take up less room than *attempt*: *Brave rescue bid fails.* But it sounds out of place when you use it in ordinary writing, so try to avoid this use.

The main past form of **bid** is **bid**: *She bid £600 for a silver tray.* But there are old forms of the past tense (**bade**, pronounced either 🔊 /bayd/ or /bad/) and the past participle (**bidden**) that are still sometimes used

when **bid** means 'to command' or 'to invite': *He courteously bade me enter.*
❶ The **-ing** form of the verb **bid** has two **ds**: **bidding**.

**biennial** see BIANNUAL

**billion** *noun, adjective*

Most people now use **billion** to mean a thousand million – 1,000,000,000. But in the past in British English it meant a million million – 1,000,000,000,000. In recent years British English has increasingly used it for a thousand million, which is what it has always meant in American English – but in older texts you should bear in mind that it could mean 'a million million'.

**bisect** see DISSECT

**black** see RACES AND PEOPLES

**bloc** *noun* and **block** *noun*

A **bloc** is a grouping of nations, political parties, governments, etc. The word was used especially to refer to the countries of Eastern Europe when they were controlled by the Soviet Union: *the Eastern bloc, the Communist bloc.* All other words pronounced 🔊 /blok/ are spelt **block**: *a block of wood, an office block, a block in the pipe.*

**blond** *adjective, noun* and **blonde** *adjective, noun*

**Blond** and **blonde** refer to fair or light-coloured hair. As an adjective, **blond** is used of men with this hair colour and **blonde** of women. The noun **blonde** means 'a blonde woman'. The noun **blond** means 'a blond man'.

**boat** *noun* and **ship** *noun*

Many seafarers insist that there's a difference between a **boat** and a **ship** – a boat is a small vessel, such as a rowing boat, and a ship is a large vessel, such as an oil tanker. But the word **boat** is much more widely used for a vessel of any size – for example 'crossing the Atlantic by boat', referring to a liner and this is accepted usage. A **ship**, though, is always a large **boat**.

**bored** *adjective*

You're **bored with** something or **bored by** something: ✔ *I'm bored with this game.* ⚠ **Bored of** is not acceptable, so don't use it in writing.

**born** *adjective* and **borne** *past participle*

**Born** is an adjective. It means 'given birth to': *I was born in London.* **Borne** is the past participle of the verb *bear* in all its meanings, from 'to carry' (*He was borne across the water in a leaky boat*) to 'to give birth to' (*She had borne him two daughters*). People often use **born** when talking about someone who has changed his or her name: *Jasper Carrott, born Robert Davies.* This has become common as we avoid making assumptions about someone's religion by saying 'christened' (see *christen*). But clearly no one is 'born' with a first name so it's best to avoid this. Instead, you could say 'whose original name was'.

**borrow** *verb* and **lend** *verb*

To **borrow** something is to take it for a period with its owner's permission, with the intention of returning it. ⚠ Don't confuse it with **lend**, which means just the opposite – 'to give something to someone for a period, with the intention of getting it back'.

b

✔ You **borrow** something **from** someone: *I borrowed this tennis racquet from my brother.* ⚠ To **borrow** something **off** someone is not acceptable in standard written English.

**both** *adjective, pronoun, adverb*

**Both** refers to two things, so don't use it for more than two – ⚠ *She can both sing, dance and play the piano* isn't good English. It's best, too, not to use it with other words that have the idea of 'two' in them, such as *alike, equal* and *identical.* For example, there's no point in saying ⚠ *We were both equally sorry.* It's simpler to say ✔ *We were equally sorry*, which means exactly the same.

*And* is the word that joins the two things referred to by **both**: ✔ *I was both surprised and delighted by the news.* ⚠ Don't use any other joining words, such as *as well as.*

**Both** can cause confusion if you're not careful with it. For example, does *Both teachers and the chair of the governors support the changes* mean that all teachers support them and the chair of governors does too, or that the two teachers and the chair of governors support them? In cases like this it's best to rewrite the sentence to make the meaning clear.

In writing, it's best to put **both** immediately in front of the pair of things it refers to. For example, ✔ *She writes both songs and stories* is acceptable standard English, but ⚠ *She both writes songs and stories* isn't good style. You can write either ✔ *He played for England at both cricket and football* or *He played for England both at cricket and at football,* but preferably not ⚠ *He played for England both at cricket and football.* We all use sentences like this every day when we speak, but it's still best to avoid them in writing.

You can use either **both** or **both of** in front of nouns (*Both (of) my sisters went to that school*), but before a pronoun you can only use **both of** (*Both of us saw him do it*).



**bought** *past tense and participle* and
**brought** *past tense and participle*

Don't get **bought** mixed up with **brought**. **Bought** is the past form of *buy*: *I bought four oranges for £1*. **Brought** is the past form of *bring*: *Have you brought your umbrella with you?*

## brackets

You put brackets ( ) round a part of a sentence that adds information to the sentence but isn't fully a part of what the sentence is about: *James Skinner (not his real name) says he found the coins in a field with a metal detector.*

Punctuation that belongs to the main part of the sentence goes *outside*, not inside, the brackets: *She gave it to her brother (an old friend of my father), who then gave it to me. Have you seen my glasses (not that I need them yet)?*

Punctuation that belongs to the additional part of the sentence goes *inside* the brackets: *Simon (silly idiot!) had forgotten to put the handbrake on.*

A whole sentence can be in brackets, if it adds extra information to a paragraph: *You need the best steak for this recipe. (I'm a vegetarian myself, incidentally.) Cut the meat into small chunks ...*

It's not good style to use lots of brackets. Only use them when the part of a sentence you're adding is really separate from the main part of the sentence. If it's only slightly separate, you should use commas or dashes instead: *My gran, who's a bit deaf, didn't hear what he said.*

You also use brackets round dates, page numbers and other references like that: *Charles Dickens (1812–70).*

b

*The life cycle of the wasp is described in more detail in Section 10 (p. 7).*

In American English, brackets are called *parentheses.*

**breach** *noun, verb* and **breech** *noun*

A **breach** is a breaking of the law (*a serious breach of regulations*), a gap made in something (*Their bombardment had made a breach in our defences*) or an end of friendship between people. To **breach** an agreement is to break it, and to **breach** a wall is to make a gap in it.

A **breech** is the rear part of a gun barrel. **Breeches** is an old word for 'trousers', especially short ones fastened just below the knee.

**breath** *noun* and **breathe** *verb*

**Breath** /breth/ is a noun: *I'm out of breath!* **Breathe** /breedh/ is a verb: *Breathe deeply.*

**broadcast** *verb*

To **broadcast** something is to transmit it by radio or television. The past participle of the verb is **broadcast**. For the past tense you can use either **broadcast** or **broadcasted**, but **broadcast** is more widely accepted.

**broke** *past tense, adjective* and
**broken** *past participle, adjective*

**Broke** is the past tense of *break* (*When she fell she broke her arm*) and **broken** is the past participle (*I've broken my arm*).

Both words can be used as adjectives. **Broken** just takes the literal meaning of *break*: *a broken arm*. **Broke** is an informal word meaning 'having no money': *After spending all that money on clothes I'm completely broke.*

**brought** see BOUGHT

**budget** *noun, verb*

A **budget** is an amount of money available or, in Britain, the annual estimate of the amount of money the government is going to need and spend.

❶ When you use **budget** as a verb, meaning 'to arrange to have money available', you don't double the **t** when you add **-ing** and **-ed**: **budgeting, budgeted**.

**burn** *verb*

The verb **burn** has two past forms, **burnt** and **burned**. When the verb has an object, **burnt** is commoner in British English (*I burnt my finger*) and **burned** is commoner in American English (*I burned my finger*). When it doesn't have an object, both British and American English prefer **burned**: *The great fire burned for five days.*

**Burnt** is also used as an adjective: *There were a few burnt bits in the bottom of the pan.*

**bus** *noun, verb*

The main plural form of **bus** in Britain is **buses**. Americans use either **buses** or **busses**, but **busses** is rare in Britain.

You can use **bus** as a verb, meaning 'to transport by bus': *We'll bus the children to the station.* ❶ When you add **-es**, **-ing** and **-ed** you can either keep a single **s** or double it to **ss**: **buses** or **busses**, **busing** or **bussing**, **bused** or **bussed**.

**but** *conjunction, preposition*

***'But' at the beginning of a sentence*** There's no good reason not to start sentences with **but**. There's an old-fashioned 'rule' which says that it's bad English to do this, but it's a perfectly natural part of the way we speak English. There's no logic in trying to ban it from writing. If you use it too often it gets distracting. But it can be a useful way of drawing attention to a contrasting point.

***'But' as a preposition before pronouns*** **But** as a preposition means 'except'. The standard rule for prepositions usually applies – a following pronoun is in the object form: *Everyone had gone home but her.* However, when you switch this sort of sentence round, so that the pronoun comes before the verb, it can produce a result that some people find odd: *Everyone but her had gone home.* It makes them uncomfortable to say *her had*, so they change the pronoun to the subject form: *Everyone but* ***she*** *had gone home.* (Strangely, no one seems to object to *Everyone except her had gone home.*) Standard English allows either the subject form or the object form when the pronoun comes before the verb, but bear in mind that the object form is more common in ordinary speech, and the subject form can sound rather formal.

**by** *preposition, adverb* and **bye** *noun, interjection*

❶ **Bye** is the spelling for the noun, meaning 'a run in cricket from a ball not hit by the bat' or 'free passage into the next round of a sporting competition', and for the interjection, short for *goodbye.* For the preposition and the adverb, **by** is the spelling. In the expression *by the by(e)*, meaning 'incidentally', the first word is always **by** and the second can be either **by** or **bye**.

❶ The prefix **by-** 'secondary', as in *byline* and *by-product,* is usually spelt without an *e*, but *by-election* and *by-law* can also be spelt *bye-election* and *bye-law.*

# Cc

## **calendar** *noun*

A **calendar** is a set of diagrams which show the months and days of the year.

❶ Remember the spelling: **-dar**.

## **calibre, caliber** *noun*

The **calibre** of a gun is the width of the inside of its barrel. The **calibre** of a person is the quality of their character. **Calibre** is the British spelling, **caliber** the American spelling.

## **can** *verb* and **may** *verb*

The verb can has two main meanings: 'to be able to' (*I can swim*) and 'to have permission to' (*Can I come in?*). Some people get very annoyed by the second meaning. They say you should only use **may** for 'to have permission to'. If you ask them 'Can I come in?', they'll say sarcastically 'Don't you mean "May I come in?"' But there's really very little reason to prefer **may**. **Can** is very widely used in this sense, and has been for a long time. It's extremely unlikely that you'd ever misunderstand **can** as 'be able to' when it was meant to mean 'have permission to'. **May** is appropriate in formal or official writing, but elsewhere it can sound too formal. (See under MAY for more on **may**.)

The negative form of **can** is **cannot**. In speech **cannot** is usually shortened to **can't**. You can use this in ordinary writing too, but it's not appropriate for formal writing.

C

## cannon *noun, verb* and canon *noun*

A **cannon** is a large gun. A **canon** is a type of clergyman. It's also a rule or law, especially a religious one, a type of musical composition, and all the works of a particular writer, composer, etc.

You can use **cannon** as a verb. It means 'to collide': *Just as I was turning the corner he cannoned into me.*

## can't help

*I can't help laughing when I think of it.* In standard English, **can't help**, and **couldn't help**, are followed by the -**ing** form of a verb. An alternative is to follow it with **but** and the infinitive form of the verb – *I can't help but laugh when I think of it.* In the past, this has not been accepted as standard, but now the objections to it seem to have faded away.

## canvas *noun* and canvass *verb*

**Canvas** is a sort of strong coarse cloth, used for painting pictures on, among other things. To **canvass** people or an area, or to **go canvassing**, is to go around an area asking people to vote for you, or for the person you support, in an election that's about to happen.

## capital letters

A capital letter is used at the start of a sentence, like this one.

Names of people, places and things begin with a capital letter: *Jenny*; *Sandy Baxter*; *Brighton*; *South America*; *the River Amazon*; *Sunday*; *February*; *Christmas*; *the Daily Telegraph*; *the Ritz Hotel*; *Cambridge University*; *Stanwell Road*; *Serbo-Croat.* Adjectives referring to places and people also begin with a capital letter: *German*; *Australian*; *Liverpudlian*; *Shakespearian.*

Titles of people begin with a capital letter: *King James*; *President Lincoln*; *Uncle Fred*. In the same way titles of books, plays, films, pieces of music, paintings, sculptures, etc. begin with a capital letter. It's usual to give a capital letter to the first and last words, and to all the other words unless they're *a, an, the, and, but, or* and short prepositions such as *in* and *to*: *The Lord of the Rings*; *The Merchant of Venice*; *Snow White and the Seven Dwarfs*; *West Side Story*; *Girl on a Swing*.

Words made from the first letters of other words are usually written all in capital letters: *EU* (standing for 'European Union'); *ITV* (standing for 'Independent Television'); *UN* (standing for 'United Nations'); *VHF* (standing for 'very high frequency').

## carcass, carcase *noun*

A **carcass** is a dead body, especially of an animal to be cut up for meat. The word can also be spelt **carcase** in British English, but in America **carcass** is the only spelling.

## careen *verb* and career *noun, verb*

To **careen** a ship is to turn it over on its side to clean its bottom or repair it. This is a rather rare, technical word, used mainly by people who deal with ships.

A **career** is the jobs people have during their life. **Career** is also a verb. It means 'to move along quickly, often swerving about dangerously as if out of control': *The runaway cart came careering down the hill, scattering pedestrians on either side.*

In American English, **careen** is used with the same meaning as the verb **career**: *We were careening along at 80 miles an hour.* Some British people use it in this way too, but it hasn't yet become part of standard British English.

## Caribbean

The **Caribbean** is a sea to the west of the Atlantic, between the southern part of Mexico and the north coast of South America, with the islands of the West Indies at its edge. In Britain **Caribbean** is pronounced /ka-rə-**bee**-ən/, with the main stress on the third syllable. That is a common pronunciation in America too, but many Americans say /kə-**rib**-i-ən/, with the main stress on the second syllable.

Remember the spelling – one **r**, two **b**s and **ean** at the end.

## case *noun*

*Is it the case that duck-billed platypuses lay eggs? It has been said that I was angry, but that was not the case.* This use of **the case** to mean 'what is true' usually sounds very wordy. It would have been better to say *Do duck-billed platypuses lay eggs?* and *... but I wasn't.*

You also need to take care when you use *in the case of X* to mean 'as far as X is concerned'. *In the case of Sally, she could be asked to stay later* is very long-winded. *In the case of Sally, you could ask her to stay later* is a bit better – because *Sally* isn't immediately repeated as she in the next clause – but not much. It would be much more straightforward to say *You could ask Sally to stay later.*

## castor, caster *noun*

A **castor** is a small swivelling wheel fixed to the underneath of a piece of furniture, to enable you to move it around. It's also a small container with holes in the top for sprinkling sugar. **Castor** is the main spelling, but you can also use **caster**. The same applies to *castor sugar* or *caster sugar*, which is a sort of fine-grained sugar. But *castor oil*, a type of oil used as a medicine, can only be spelt with an **o**.

**cauldron, caldron** *noun*

A **cauldron** is a large deep pot for boiling things in. **Cauldron** is the main spelling in British English, but Americans mainly use the spelling **caldron**.

**cease** *verb*

This is a very formal word. Unless you're writing something deliberately solemn or dignified, it's better to use *stop*.

**Celsius** see CENTIGRADE

**censor** *noun, verb* and **censure** *noun, verb*

If you **censor** something, such as a book or film, you take out the parts you don't approve of. A **censor** is someone who does this.

If you **censure** someone or something, you criticize them strongly: *The committee officially censured the chairman, but didn't require him to resign.* **Censure** is criticism of this sort: *None of the group escaped censure in the report.*

So **censor** is about taking things out, and **censure** is about criticizing. But the adjective **censorious**, which looks as though it ought to be closer in meaning to **censor** than to **censure**, means 'making harsh criticisms'.

**centenary** *noun* and **centennial** *noun*

Both these words mean 'the hundredth anniversary': *The year 1974 was the centenary of Winston Churchill's birth* (= he was born in 1874). **Centenary** is much more common in British English, and **centennial** is much more common in American English. The main pronunciation of **centenary** in Britain is /sen-**teen**-ə-ri/, in America /sen-**ten**-ə-ri/.

C

## centigrade *noun* and Celsius *noun*

**Centigrade** and **Celsius** both refer to a temperature scale in which water freezes at 0 degrees and boils at 100 degrees. **Centigrade** is the commoner term in general English. **Celsius** used to be used mainly by scientists writing for other scientists, but it has become more widespread – weather forecasters on radio and television often use it. You can use either.

## centre, center *noun, verb*

**Centre** is the only spelling used in British English. Americans almost always use **center**.

## centre (a)round *verb* and centre on *verb*

*Most of the opposition to the new road is centred on its cost. The story centres (a)round a parrot which escapes from its cage.* **Centre** is used as a verb with both **on** and **(a)round**. The meaning is the same – 'to be about', or more precisely, 'to have as its main subject or concern'. Most of the opposition to the road is because of its cost. The story is mainly about the parrot.

There are people who get annoyed by this use of **(a)round** with **centre**. They say that the centre of something is the middle of it, and that it's not logical to talk about the middle being 'round' something else. But language doesn't necessarily work by logic. **Centre (a)round** is widely used and widely accepted, and there's no good reason not to regard it as part of standard English.

## centrifugal *adjective*

**Centrifugal** is a scientific word meaning 'moving outwards from a centre'. 🔊 In Britain its main pronunciation is /sen-tri-**few**-gəl/, but it's also pronounced /sen-**trif**-yə-gəl/, which is also the way it's pronounced in America.



## century *noun*

If something happened in the eighteenth **century**, it happened between 1700 and 1799. Another way of saying it would be that it happened in the seventeen hundreds (the 1700s). If someone describes Charles Dickens as a nineteenth-century writer, it means that he lived at some time between 1800 and 1899. The ordinal number (with a *-th*) before **century** is always one ahead of the actual dates in the century you're referring to.

The same thing happens with BC dates, but we count the year BC (= before Christ) backwards from 1 BC – so the ninth century BC is the years 899 to 800 BC.

Traditionally, centuries have been counted from the number 1. According to that way of doing it, the nineteenth century started in 1801 and ended in 1900. But in modern usage it's far more common to start from the number 0, and it avoids a lot of confusion to stick with this method.

## cereal *noun* and serial *adjective, noun*

**Cereal** and **serial** are pronounced the same, but their meanings are completely different. A **cereal** is any sort of grain that's eaten, such as wheat or maize. It's also a breakfast food made from one of these. A **serial** is a story that's told in several parts over a period of time. **Serial** is also an adjective, meaning 'following one after another, as in a series'.

## character *noun*

*Our talks were of a constructive character. The food was quite different in character from what we had expected.* It would be much simpler and clearer to say *Our talks were constructive* and *The food was quite different from what we had expected*. Using **character** in this general way, to mean 'type', almost always sounds wordy. It's best avoided. See also NATURE.

C

## charge *noun, verb*

*He's in charge of a nurse and three assistants*. British people would say this meant that he controls the nurse and the other people. But it could also mean exactly the opposite – that the nurse and the assistants control him. In British English you would usually say this as *He's in the charge of a nurse and three assistants*, but in American English it would be quite normal to say it as *He's in charge of a nurse and three assistants*. Usually it's clear which you mean from the rest of what you say, but if there's any doubt, try to express it another way.

If you want to use **charge** in the sense 'to accuse officially', the preposition to use is **with**: *He was charged with murdering his wife*.

## check *noun, verb* and cheque *noun*

A **check** is a quick examination to see if everything's all right. It's also a position threatening the king in chess and a pattern of small squares, and in America it's a bill in a restaurant. To **check** something is to examine it or make sure about it, and it can also be to hold it back: *The bad weather checked the progress of the building work*.

In British English a **cheque** is a piece of paper used for payment, on which you write the amount to be paid. Americans spell this **check**.

## childish *adjective* and childlike *adjective*

Both these words mean 'like children', but they're used in very different ways. If you describe something as **childlike**, you mean that it has some of the good qualities that people associate with childhood, such as innocence, simplicity and happiness: *He took a childlike delight in watching the monkeys scampering about.* But if you say that someone or something is **childish**, you mean that a grown-up person is behaving in a silly way, like a child: *He stamped on the floor in childish fury when she wouldn't do what he wanted.*

## chord *noun* and cord *noun*

A **chord** is a combination of musical notes. A **cord** is a piece of string or electric flex, or a part of the body that is long and thin like this, such as the umbilical cord or the vocal cords.

## christen *verb*

To **christen** someone is to give him or her one or more Christian names at a religious ceremony. Like *Christian name* itself, this implies that the person belongs to the Christian religion, so it's best not to use **christened** to mean 'given a name' (for example, when talking about someone who has changed their original name) if you're not certain whether they are a Christian or not. See also BORN.

## Christian name *noun*

The traditional term in English-speaking countries for the name someone is given soon after they're born (such as *Caroline* or *Stephen*) is **Christian name**. But in modern times, when many people in these countries belong to religions other than Christianity, or don't belong to any religion at all, it's not always appropriate to refer to a 'Christian' name. To people from other religions it may well be offensive. The best term to use is *first name*. In American English, *given name* is a common alternative. There's also *forename*, but this is a rather formal word, used on official documents, forms, etc. If there are other names that come before the surname you can use *middle name*.

C

## chronic *adjective*

The word **chronic** is used of bad things, and means that they last a long time. It was originally applied to illnesses (*chronic bronchitis*), where it contrasts with *acute*, which means 'getting bad very quickly'. But it's now also used of other conditions that could be thought of as illnesses (*chronic unemployment*).

It's also used to mean 'very bad' (*I thought her performance was really chronic*), but this is extremely informal, so you shouldn't use it in serious writing.

## chute see SHOOT

## circumlocution

Circumlocution is using more words than are necessary to say what you mean.

Often there's a good reason for doing this. For instance, if you want to be polite, it might be better to say *I wonder if you'd mind closing the window* than *Please close the window* (or, ruder still, *Close the window!*).

But usually, using too many words gets in the way of your message. And it can sound pompous too. For example, why say *with the exception of* when you could say *except*, or *on account of the fact that* when you could say *because*? Why say *The outcome was of a surprising nature* when you could say *The outcome was surprising*?

✔ Be simple and straightforward. There's no harm in using circumlocutions from time to time, but if your writing becomes full of them, people may fail to understand what you mean, or even stop trying to. They could also come to the conclusion that you're trying to sound impressive in order to cover up the fact that you haven't anything important to say.

To find out more about this, look at the entries for CASE, CHARACTER, EXCEPT, MOMENT, NATURE and SITUATION.



## **circumstances** *noun*

Both **in the circumstances** and **under the circumstances** mean 'in the conditions as they now exist': *I think that in/under the circumstances, it would be better if we left now.* There's an old objection to using *under*, which some people still cling on to. There's no good reason for it, though, and *under* is perfectly correct and acceptable.

## **classic** *adjective, noun* and **classical** *adjective*

The adjective **classic** is applied to a piece of work done by someone in the past that has come to be seen as of very high quality and lasting value: *Von Frisch's classic study of the way bees dance to show their companions where to find pollen.* It's also used of something that's very typical of its kind: *She shows all the classic symptoms of chickenpox.* It's applied to things that are elegant and well-proportioned, simple and without a lot of extra decoration: *the classic lines of a Jaguar car.* And in particular it's used of clothing that's simple and elegant and therefore stays in fashion all the time: *She wore a classic black dress.*

A **classic** is an outstanding or typical example of its kind: *'The Hobbit' is one of the classics of children's literature.* If you study **classics** at university, you study ancient Greek and Roman language and culture.

**Classical** is used of ancient Greece and Rome, or the study of their culture and language: *classical antiquity; a classical education.* Applied to music, it means anything that is 'serious' or has an intellectual content, as opposed to light music or pop music – a pretty loose category which has fuzzy edges. In the arts in general, including painting, literature and architecture as well as music, it refers to a style which is formal and restrained, and based on rules and ideas, as opposed to romantic art, which is based on feelings and emotions.



## clauses

Clauses are the building blocks of sentences. They consist of a verb and usually its subject, and often other words as well. There are two types of clause:

***Main clauses***

A main clause can stand on its own, as a complete sentence. For example, the sentence *I resign* consists of a main clause. Its verb is *resign,* and its subject is *I. She stroked the cat* is a main clause too.

***Subordinate clauses***

A subordinate clause can't stand on its own. You have to put it with a main clause to make a sentence. For example, you wouldn't say *where I put it,* but if you join it to the main clause *I'd forgotten* you get the complete sentence *I'd forgotten where I put it.*

Subordinate clauses that begin with words like *that, which, what, who, when* and *how* are called **relative clauses**. The words *that, which, what, who, when* and *how* are called **relative pronouns**.

There are two types of relative clause. The first sort is called a **restrictive relative clause** or a **defining relative clause**. You use it to say which particular thing or person you're talking about. For example, if you say *The trifle which I like has lots of sherry in it,* you mean that there are several different sorts of trifle, but your particular favourite is the one with lots of sherry.

The other sort is called a **nonrestrictive relative clause** or a **nondefining relative clause**. You use it to add extra information that isn't strictly necessary to complete the sentence. For example, if you say *The trifle, which*

*I liked, had lots of sherry in it,* your main message is that the trifle had lots of sherry, but you're also saying that you liked it.

You can use words like *which, what* and *who* in both types of clause, but *that* can only be used in restrictive clauses. Nonrestrictive clauses usually have commas round them, but restrictive clauses don't.



## clean *adjective, adverb* and
## cleanly *adjective, adverb*

As an adverb, **clean** usually means 'completely': *I clean forgot.* It's best not to use it as an adverb in any of the main senses of the adjective **clean** – ⚠ *He didn't fight clean,* for example, isn't standard English. **Cleanly** is the adverb to use: ✔ *He struck the black ball cleanly into the top pocket.*

The adverb **cleanly** is pronounced 🔊 /**kleen**-li/. But the adjective **cleanly** is pronounced 🔊 /**klen**-li/. It means 'always clean and tidy', and is rare. Much more common is the noun **cleanliness** 🔊 /**klen**-li-nəs/: *High standards of cleanliness are essential in school kitchens.*

## clear writing

When you write, it's polite to make your meaning as clear as possible to the people who read it, and to write in a style suited to your audience.

Here are some ideas to help you do this:

***Be simple***: don't use long or formal words when shorter or more straightforward ones will do just as well. Usually, *try* is better than *endeavour, find out* is better than *ascertain, poor* is better than *impecunious,* and so on.

Don't use difficult technical terms if the people who are going to read what you write are unlikely to know what they mean. If you can't avoid using them, make sure you explain their meaning.

C

***Don't use lots of words*** when fewer will do just as well (look at the entry for CIRCUMLOCUTION to find out more about this).

***Use short sentences:*** don't use long sentences with lots of clauses. Readers may lose their way before they get to the end. It's usually better to break a long sentence up into two or more shorter ones.

For instance, *Because not all the questionnaires were returned, we had to do our analysis on incomplete data, which was not ideal, since it altered the proportion of age groups we had planned* rambles on for a long time. The sentence would be better as *Because not all the questionnaires were returned, we had to do our analysis on incomplete data. This was not ideal, since it altered the proportion of age groups we had planned.*

***In long sentences*** it's better to put the main verb near the beginning. For instance, *Confidence in the new system, which has been in operation for three months now, is growing* would be better as *Confidence is growing in the new system, which has been in operation for three months now.*

***For verbs***, prefer the active (*He hit the ball*) to the passive (*The ball was hit by him*). Unless there's a particular reason for using the passive, it's better to use the active. It's more direct and it's often easier to understand. For instance, *Paper bags are to be found in the pocket of the seat in front of you* is rather stiff. It would be more straightforward to say *You can find paper bags in the pocket of the seat in front of you*, or even just *Paper bags are in the pocket of the seat in front of you.*

*Positive sentences* are better than negative ones. Sentences with a lot of negative words in them can be difficult to understand. For example, *You wouldn't deny that he's not the world's greatest guitar player* takes quite a lot of working out. It would be less confusing to say something like *You have to admit he's not the world's greatest guitar player.*



## clerk *noun*

In Britain, **clerk** is an old-fashioned word. It used to mean 'a low-ranking office worker', but this has gone out of use. It survives in various official titles – the *clerk of the course*, for instance, is in charge of a horse-racing course. In America the word is still commonly used for a shop assistant: *a sales clerk.*

🔊 British speakers pronounce the word as /klark/, Americans as /klerk/.

## clothes *noun* and cloth *noun*

🔊 When we're being careful we usually pronounce **clothes** as /klohdhz/. But most of the time, when we're just talking normally, we say /klohz/, rhyming with *hose.* In America this is regarded as completely ordinary and acceptable, but in Britain it tends to be disapproved of (even though the people who disapprove of it do it all the time). So it's best to keep to /klohdhz/ on formal occasions.

⚠ Don't confuse **clothes** with **cloths** 🔊 /kloths/, which is the plural of **cloth**: *I bought a packet of three washing-up cloths.*

## coco *noun* and cocoa *noun*

⚠ Don't confuse **coco** and **cocoa** (both pronounced 🔊 /**koh**-koh/). The **coco** is a palm tree on which **coconuts** grow. **Cocoa** is a brown powder used for making a chocolate-flavoured drink.

## colon

The colon is a punctuation mark consisting of two dots, one above the other (:). These are the ways it's used in English:



***For joining***

A colon joins together two parts of a sentence that could each be a sentence on its own, but which you feel belong together in some way.

The part after the colon can explain the part before: *I do feel ill: it's as if someone were sticking a knife in my stomach.*

It can interpret the reason for the part before: *I do feel ill: it must have been something I ate.*

Or it can add something further to the part before: *I do feel ill: you'd better call the doctor.*

***For lists***

A colon can introduce lists of things and examples of things. In the description of the use of the colon for joining, the three examples of how the colon can be used are each introduced by a colon. And at the beginning of this entry, the list of all the ways in which colons can be used is introduced by a colon – like this: *These are the ways it's used in English:*

***With numbers***

A colon comes between the chapter and verse numbers in giving Bible quotations (Deuteronomy 1:22–46) and between the act and scene numbers in plays (*Macbeth* II:i).

***For times***

In American English, colons are used between hours and minutes in writing the time (2:30) (British English uses a full stop (2.30)).

**coloration, colouration** *noun*

An animal's **coloration** is the natural colour or pattern of colours of its fur, feathers, skin, etc. **Coloration** is the only common 'colour' word that can be spelt without a **u** in British English. The alternative **colouration** is available in British English, but **coloration** is the only American spelling.

**colour, color** *noun, verb*

The word is spelt **colour** in British English and **color** in American. The same applies to most words formed from **colo(u)r** – **colourful** and **colourless** in Britain, for instance, and **colorful** and **colorless** in America. But see COLORATION.

**combat** *verb*

To **combat** something is to oppose it or fight against it. ❶ In British English, when you add **-ing** and **-ed** to it, there's only one **t**: **combating, combated**. In American English you can double the **t**, but it's more usual not to: **combating, combatting; combated, combatted**.

**comic** *adjective, noun* and **comical** *adjective*

The adjective **comic** means 'connected with comedy' or 'intended to make you laugh': *a fine comic actor; a comic film.* **Comical** means 'funny, making you laugh, often unintentionally': *He was a comical sight, standing there with his trousers around his ankles.*

A **comic** is a comedian, or a magazine containing strip cartoons.

**comma**

The comma (,) marks off the separate sections of a sentence, generally in places where we'd make a slight pause if we were speaking the sentence. These are its main uses:



***To join two parts of a sentence*** that are linked by a word such as *and, but, or* or *so*: *It's a charming little house, and it's very near the station.*

Remember, you can only do this when *and, but,* etc. are present. ⚠ It's not acceptable in English to write *It's a charming little house, it's very near the station.* If you don't want to use the *and* here, you either have to use a semicolon instead of the comma, or you have to make the two parts of the sentence into separate sentences.

***To show that one part of a sentence is separate*** and different from another: *When you leave, don't forget to turn out the lights.*

When this separate part comes in the middle of a sentence, remember that you need a comma in front of it and a comma after it: *Charlie, however, wanted to stay at home.*

You usually put a comma before a nonrestrictive relative clause, but not before a restrictive relative clause (to find out more about this, look at the entry for CLAUSES).

***To separate items in a list:*** *a chicken, some ham, strings of sausages, a big pork pie.*

When *and* or *or* comes before the last item, it's common in British English to leave out the comma (*a chicken, some ham, strings of sausages and a big pork pie*), but some publishers like to keep it, and you will find a comma before the *and* in their books. In American English it's standard to keep it.

In the same way you can use a comma to make your meaning clear when you're using a list of adjectives to describe something. For example, in *I saw a green, winged insect*, the comma shows that you're writing about an insect that had wings and was green, rather than one that had green wings.

***To make the meaning of a sentence clear,*** if there's a possibility that it could be misunderstood.

For example, there's a big difference between *The government will do nothing to calm the situation down* (= The government isn't taking any action that will calm the situation down) and *The government will do nothing, to calm the situation down* (= In order to calm the situation down, the government will do nothing). But a comma should only be a last resort in cases like this. It's much better to rewrite the sentence so that it can't be misunderstood.

***To separate the parts of big numbers.*** For numbers with more than four figures, it's usual to divide the figures into groups of three. This is traditionally done with commas (*1,000,000*), but it's now becoming more common to do it with spaces (*1 000 000*).

For numbers with four figures, you can either use a comma (*3,759*) or not (*3759*). But for four-figure dates, house numbers and room numbers, it's standard not to use a comma.

## commence *verb*

**Commence** is a very formal way of saying 'to start'. In speech and ordinary writing it's better to use *start* or *begin*.

## commit *verb*

To **commit** a crime or sin is to do it: *He'd committed several murders*. If you **commit** yourself, you give a firm undertaking to do something, support something, etc.: *They asked me to join, but I wasn't willing to commit* *myself without finding out more about it.* If you commit something to someone, you give it to them for some purpose: *She committed the valuable painting to his care.*

❶ When you add **-ing** and **-ed** to **commit**, you double the **t**: **committing, committed**.

## committal *noun* and commitment *noun*

**Committal** and **commitment** both come from the verb commit, but they have different meanings. **Committal** means sending someone to be tried in court, or putting them in prison or a mental hospital. A **commitment** is something you have to do (*With all my other financial commitments I can't afford a holiday this year*), or something you've made a firm undertaking to do or support (*No one can doubt the strength of her commitment to the cause*).

## common *adjective*

The main meaning of **common** is 'occurring a lot': *The sparrow is a common bird.* But it can also be used to mean 'shared': *The British and the Americans have a common language – English.* You can use the preposition **to** with it, to mean 'shared by': *A problem that's common to both schools is truancy.* In this use, it's very close in meaning to *mutual*, and it's easy to get the two words mixed up – see MUTUAL.

## common noun see NOUNS

## comparable *adjective*

🔊 The standard pronunciation is /**kom**-pə-rə-bəl/, with the main stress on the first syllable, but /kəm-**pa**-rə-bəl/ is also quite widely used and perfectly acceptable.

You can use either **to** or **with** after **comparable**, although **to** is commoner. Both **comparable to** and **comparable with** generally mean 'quite similar to': *The new Mark IV prototype is comparable in performance to/with the best of the foreign competition.*



## comparative *adjective* and comparatively *adverb*

These words are commonly used in a very general way to mean 'quite' or 'rather': *She was a comparative stranger.* But in writing it's best to use them with at least some suggestion that you're comparing something with something else: *The weather was terrible yesterday, but today it's comparatively good.*

For the comparative of adjectives and adverbs, look at the entry for DOUBLE COMPARATIVES, and under ADJECTIVES and AS X OR XER THAN.

## compare *verb*

When **compare** is used with an object, it can be followed by either **to** or **with**: *Compared to/with our swimming pool, theirs is quite small.* It's common to use **to** and **with** interchangeably like this, but there is a difference between them. Traditionally, **to** is used when you're pointing out a similarity between two things: *He compared the soup to washing-up water* (= *he said the soup was like washing-up water*). **With** is used when you're trying to find out how one thing is like another: *If you compare this year's results with last year's, you'll find that this year's are much more consistent.* Sometimes the meaning of a sentence can depend on which you use. For instance, *The report compared current British methods to those being used in America ten years ago* suggests that the British methods are like the American ones. But *The report compared current British methods with those being used in America ten years ago* simply says that the report showed in what way the British and American methods were alike and in what way they were different.

C

When **compare** doesn't have an object, you can only use **with** with it: *These little yellow plums can't compare with the big juicy red ones* (= the red ones are much better).

Remember to use the preposition that expresses what you mean – and if there's any possibility of confusion, rewrite the sentence in a different way.

## compass *noun* and compasses *noun*

A **compass** is an instrument which shows where north, south, east and west are. It's also (but rarely) an instrument for drawing circles. A pair of **compasses** is only an instrument for drawing circles.

## compel *verb*

If something **compels** you to do something, it makes you do it: *The new law compels newspapers to reveal the sources of their information.*

❶ Remember, when you add **-ing** and **-ed** to **compel**, you double the **l**: **compelling, compelled**.

## complement *noun, verb* and compliment *noun, verb*

A **complement** is something that, when added to something else, makes a perfect whole, especially by being different: *Mike's aggressive, attacking style of play is a perfect complement to his partner Raymond's more subtle defensive approach.* You can use **complement** as a verb with the same meaning: *Mike's style of play perfectly complements Raymond's.* A **complement** is also the complete quantity of something: *The ship set sail with a full complement* (= it had all the crew members that it needed). To find out about the meaning of **complement** as a grammatical term, look at the entry for VERBS.

A **compliment** is something you say to someone to praise them: *He said my cooking was wonderful, which was a very generous compliment.* You can use it as a verb too: *He complimented me on my cooking.*

C

## complex *adjective* and complicated *adjective*

**Complex** and **complicated** are very close in meaning. They both mean 'having a lot of different parts connected in an intricate way'. The difference between them is that **complex** is usually a neutral or even approving word, but **complicated** is a disapproving word. For example, a *complex poem* is probably subtle, with lots of different meanings interacting with each other. To call it 'complex' is a compliment. But a *complicated message* is difficult to understand, probably because its many different parts are expressed in a confusing way. To call it 'complicated' is usually a criticism.

## compliment see COMPLEMENT

## compose *verb*

If you **compose** music or poetry you invent it and write it down.

You can also use **compose** to mean 'to form or make up': *Eleven players compose a football team.* It's usual to put **compose** in the passive (*be composed of*) in this meaning: *A football team is composed of eleven players.*

To find out how to use two other words with similar meanings, look at the entries for COMPRISE and CONSIST.

C

**compound nouns** see PLURALS

**compound words** see HYPHEN

**comprehensible** *adjective* and
**comprehensive** *adjective*

If something is **comprehensible**, you can understand it: *What he said was barely comprehensible* (= you could hardly understand it). If something is **comprehensive**, it includes everything: *She gave us a comprehensive account of her adventures up the Amazon* (= she told us every detail about them).

**comprise** *verb*

The standard meaning of **comprise** is 'to consist of': *The sports complex comprises a running track, an all-weather pitch, squash courts and a gymnasium.*

There are two other ways of using **comprise**, that aren't generally accepted as part of standard English. The first is to use **comprised of** to mean 'consisting of': ⚠ *The sports complex is comprised of a running track, an all-weather pitch, squash courts and a gymnasium.* The similar word *compose* is all right like this in standard English (look at the entry for COMPOSE), but **comprise** isn't. The second is to use **comprise** to mean 'to form when taken all together': ⚠ *A running track, an all-weather pitch, squash courts and a gymnasium comprise the sports complex.*

Both of these usages, and especially the first, are common in informal spoken English, but it's best to avoid them in writing.

To find out how to use two other words with similar meanings, look at the entries for COMPOSE and CONSIST.

**concave** *adjective* and **convex** *adjective*

A curved surface that's **concave** goes inwards, like a cave. The inside of a hollow ball is **concave**.

A curved surface that's **convex** bulges outwards, like a pimple on the skin. The outside of a ball is **convex**.

**concur** *verb*

**Concur** is a very formal word meaning 'to agree'.

❶ When you add **-ing** and **-ed** to it, you double the **r**: **concurring, concurred**.

**conducive** *adjective*

Something that's **conducive** helps to bring something else about or make it possible. The word is almost always used with **to**: *This dreadful noise isn't conducive to calm thought* (= makes it difficult to think calmly).

**confer** *verb*

If you **confer** something, you give it in a formal or official way: *The degree of Bachelor of Arts was conferred on her.* If you **confer with** someone, you have discussions with them.

❶ When you add **-ing** and **-ed** to **confer**, you double the **r**: **conferring, conferred**.

**confidant** *noun* and **confident** *adjective*

**Confident** 🔊 /**kon**-fi-dənt/ is an adjective. It means 'self-assured' or 'certain, sure'.

**Confidant** 🔊 /**kon**-fi-dant/, a much rarer word, is a noun. It means 'a person you're willing to tell your secrets to'. There's an alternative spelling **confidante**, which can be used when referring to women.

C

## conform *verb*

To **conform to** or **with** a regulation, guideline, etc. is to do what it says: *Your kitchens don't conform to the hygiene regulations – you'll have to clean them up.* **To** is commoner than **with**, but both are standard English.

## conjunctions

A conjunction links clauses or words together. For example, *although* is a conjunction in *I'll come, although I don't want to*, and *or* is a conjunction in *sink or swim*.

## connection *noun*

A **connection** is a joining between two things, or a link.
❶ **Connection** is the main spelling in British English, and the only spelling in American English. There is an alternative British spelling, **connexion**, but this is now rather old-fashioned.

## consensus *noun*

A **consensus** is the way most people think about a matter, or a general agreement between most people involved: *The consensus of opinion seems to be that she was wrong to do it.*
❶ Remember the spelling, with an **s** after the **con-**. It has nothing to do with a *census*, which is a survey to count how many people live in a country.

## consist *verb*

If you say that your meal **consisted of** pasta, a salad and some fruit and cheese, you mean that pasta, a salad and some fruit and cheese were, taken together, the things that made up your meal.

If you say that politeness **consists in** having consideration for the feelings of others, you mean that consideration for the feelings of others is the essential characteristic of politeness. This is a rather formal usage, found mainly in serious writing.

**Consist of** refers to things, solid objects, etc. **Consist in** refers to abstract qualities.

To find out how to use two other words with similar meanings, look at the entries for COMPOSE and COMPRISE.



## consonant doubling

If a word of one syllable ends in a consonant which is preceded by a single vowel letter, you double the consonant when you add an ending that begins with a vowel. For example, if you add *-ed*, *-er* and *-ing* to *fit*, you get *fitted*, *fitter* and *fitting*. But if you add *-ment*, which doesn't begin with a vowel, you get *fitment*. And if you add endings to *foot*, which has *two* vowel letters, you get *footed*, *footing*.

An exception to this is *wool*. American English usually follows the rules and has *woolen*, *wooly*, but British English uses *woollen* and *woolly*.

The same thing happens to words of more than one syllable, as long as the main stress when you say them comes on the last syllable: *regret*, *regretted*, *regretting*.

If the main stress comes on the first syllable, you don't double the last consonant: *wallop*, *walloped*, *walloping*.

There's an important exception to this in British English: words of more than one syllable with the stress on the first syllable *do* double the last consonant if it's *l*: *travel*, *travelled*, *travelling*. American English usually doesn't double the *l*: *traveled*, *traveling*.

Other exceptions are *leap-frog*, which gives *leap-frogged*, *leap-frogging* in both British and American English, and *kidnap* and *worship*, which give *kidnapped*, *kidnapping* and *worshipped*, *worshipping* in British English but also *kidnaped*, *kidnaping* and *worshiped*, *worshiping* in American English.

Words ending in *c* get a *k* if you add on an ending that begins with a vowel: *picnic, picnicked, picnicking, picnicker.*

C

## constable *noun*

A **constable** is a police officer of the lowest rank. The main standard British pronunciation of the word is /**kun**-stə-bəl/, but /**kon**-stə-bəl/ is also widely used and perfectly acceptable.

## consult *verb*

When British people **consult** their doctor or their lawyer, they go to see them to ask for their advice. In the same circumstances, American people **consult with** their doctor or their lawyer.

British English doesn't use **consult with** like this, but it does use it to mean 'talk to someone in order to give them information about something, find out their opinion about it, etc.': *We will consult with all our allies before starting the attack.*

## contemporary *adjective, noun* and
## contemporaneous *adjective*

**Contemporary** has two meanings. It can mean 'happening or existing now': *the problems of contemporary society*. It can also mean 'happening or existing at the same time': *Robin Hood's story was told in contemporary songs* (= songs sung at the time when Robin Hood supposedly lived). Sometimes it's not easy to see which meaning was intended. For instance, does *a performance of Beethoven using contemporary instruments* mean 'instruments of Beethoven's time' or 'modern instruments'? When there's some doubt about what's meant, it's best to rewrite the sentence in another way.

C

**Contemporary** can also be used as a noun, meaning 'someone living at the same time as another': *As she'd grown up, she'd lost touch with her contemporaries at school.*

**Contemporaneous** has only one meaning, 'happening or existing at the same time': *Napoleon and Nelson were contemporaneous.* It's a formal word, and much less common than **contemporary**.

## contemptible *adjective* and
## contemptuous *adjective*

Someone or something **contemptible** is so bad or worthless that you feel contempt for them: *Stealing the poor old man's money was a contemptible thing to do.*

If you're **contemptuous of** someone or something, you feel contempt for them: *I'm contemptuous of someone who could steal a poor old man's money.*

## continual *adjective* and continuous *adjective*

Something that's **continual** keeps on happening or happens all the time, usually with intervals in between each occurrence: *Your continual complaints are beginning to get on my nerves.*

Something that's **continuous** goes on and on without a break: *Water gushed out of the hole in the tank in a continuous stream.*

## contractions

Words like *I've, you'll, won't* and *shouldn't* are a way of putting in writing how we usually say *I have, you will, will not* and *should not.* The apostrophe (') shows where letters have been missed out (to find out more about this, look at the entry for APOSTROPHE).

These words are called **contractions**. It's perfectly acceptable to use them in ordinary writing, but if you're writing a very formal letter or an official document, you should use the full forms of the words.

C

## contribute *verb*

To **contribute** something, such as money, is to give it for a particular purpose. The standard pronunciation of the word is 🔊 /kən-**trib**-yoot/, with the main stress on the second syllable. Another pronunciation, ⚠ /**kon**-tri-byoot/, is quite common, but it's not accepted as part of standard English. The noun **contribution** is pronounced 🔊 /kon-tri-**byoo**-shən/.

## controversy *noun*

A **controversy** is public or general disagreement over something. For example, there's a **controversy** in Britain over how to pronounce the word **controversy**. The traditional standard pronunciation is 🔊 /**kon**-trə-ver-si/, with the main stress on the first syllable. Many people strongly believe that this is the way the word should be said. But there is another way of pronouncing it – 🔊 /kən-**trov**-ə-si/. This is now more common than the traditional pronunciation, and it's generally regarded as an acceptable standard alternative to 🔊 /**kon**-trə-ver-si/. In American English, /**kon**-trə-ver-si/ is the only pronunciation.

The adjective **controversial** is pronounced 🔊 /kon-trə-**ver**-shəl/.

## conversion

Conversion is changing a word's grammatical role – for instance, using a noun as a verb. To find out about it, look at the entry for PARTS OF SPEECH.

**convex** see CONCAVE

**cooperate, co-operate** *verb*

To **cooperate** with someone is to work together with them in a friendly or helpful way.

❶ **Cooperate** is the standard spelling, but **co-operate** is also quite widely used in British English.

**coordinate, co-ordinate** *verb, noun*

To **coordinate** things is to bring them together in such a way that they work well with each other. **Coordinates** are a set of numbers used to describe a position on a map. They're also matching clothes designed to be worn together.

❶ **Coordinate** is the standard spelling, but **co-ordinate** is also quite widely used in British English.

🔈 The verb **coordinate** is pronounced /koh-**or**-di-nayt/, the noun /koh-**or**-di-nət/.

**copula** see VERBS

**cord** see CHORD

**corn** *noun*

**Corn** means different things to British people and Americans. In Britain it's a grain crop such as wheat or barley, but in America it's maize. Australians use **corn** to mean 'maize' too.

**coronary** *adjective, noun*

As an adjective, **coronary** refers to the arteries that take blood to the heart. As a noun it's short for *coronary thrombosis*, which means 'heart attack'.

Its standard pronunciation is /**ko**-rən-ri/, with the main stress on the first syllable.

## **corps** *noun* and **corpse** *noun*

A **corps** is an organized group of people, especially soldiers. You don't pronounce the **-ps** on the end (/kor/), and you use a singular verb with it (*The Marine Corps has launched an attack on enemy positions*).

Its plural (*two corps*) is spelt the same as the singular, but you *do* pronounce the **s** (/korz/) and you use a plural verb with it (*The two corps are to be combined into one*).

A **corpse** /korps/ is a dead body.

## **could** *verb* and **might** *verb*

**Could** and **might** both express possibility: *You might be right* and *You could be right* both mean 'It's possible that you're right.'

Sometimes it's not entirely clear that this is what's meant. For example, *The train could/might be delayed* could mean 'It's possible that the train's delayed', but it could also mean 'We are able to delay the train'. If there's a serious possibility of confusion, write the sentence in another way – for instance, *Perhaps the train's delayed*.

**Could** and **might** are used as the past forms of *can* and *may*. As with *can* and *may* themselves (see the entry for CAN), there's no need to try and make a difference between **could** for 'was able to' and **might** for 'had permission to'. **Could** can be used for both, as in *I couldn't hear* and *She said we could leave*.

## council *noun* and counsel *noun, verb*

A **council** is a group of people who control or govern a particular area or organization – for instance, in Britain the people elected to govern the town you live in are the local council.

**Counsel** is 'advice' (*Thank you for your wise counsel*), and a **counsel** is a barrister, a lawyer who speaks in court. To **counsel** someone is to advise them. **Counsel** is a rather formal or technical word. In ordinary writing it's better to use a more straightforward word, like *advice*.

✔ But **counsel** is the word to use for advice about problems in your personal life given by trained people, as in *marriage-guidance counsel*.

❶ When you add **-ing** and **-ed** to **counsel**, you double the **l** in British English (**counselling, counselled**), but not in American English (**counseling, counseled**).

## coup de grâce *noun*

A **coup de grâce** is a final decisive action which puts a stop to something that had been failing anyway. It's a French expression that's been used in English since the 17th century. 🔊 It's pronounced ✔ /koo də **gras**/, not ⚠ /koo də **grah**/.

## couple *noun*

Although **couple** is a singular noun, it's standard to use a plural verb with it when it means 'two people': *If that young couple come back, tell them the house is sold.*

**A couple of ...** usually takes a plural verb too: *A couple of cars were parked by the gate.* But when you're using it with units of time, you can use a singular verb instead: *A couple of years hasn't made any difference to his bad temper.*

C

## cousin *noun*

Your **cousin** is the son or daughter of one of your parents' brothers or sisters – that is, of your uncle or aunt.

There are some specialized terms for other sorts of cousins, which can be rather confusing. A *first cousin* is exactly the same as a cousin. A *second cousin* is the son or daughter of one of your parents' cousins. Your *first cousin once removed* is either the son or daughter of your cousin, or it's one of your parents' cousins (although you might regard them as your aunt or uncle). Your *second cousin once removed* is the son or daughter of your second cousin, or one of your parents' second cousins.

Informally you might call any of these simply a cousin, and in many cultures the word **cousin** is used much more generally for a wide range of close and distant relatives.

## credence *noun* and credibility *noun*

**Credence** is 'willingness to believe something'. If you say *I don't give his story any credence*, you mean you don't believe it. But it's a very formal word, and it would usually be better to say simply *I don't believe his story.*

**Credibility** is a quality which something or someone has that makes you believe them – in other words, 'convincingness': *For me, her claim to have eaten six hamburgers all at one go lacks all credibility* (= I don't believe it).

## credible *adjective* and credulous *adjective*

If something's **credible**, it's easy to believe – but mostly the word is used in rather negative situations, when you want to say that you don't believe something: *I find it scarcely credible that he could be so selfish* (= I can hardly believe it).

Someone who is **credulous** believes anything you tell them, however silly or unlikely it is: *She's so credulous that it's easy to trick her.*



## crescendo *noun*

The original meaning of **crescendo** is 'a musical passage that gradually gets louder'. It's also used more generally to refer to anything that gradually gets more intense: *There's been a crescendo of criticism about the decision to build the new road.*

It's quite common for **crescendo** to be used for a 'climax': ⚠ *Criticism of the plans for the new road rose to a crescendo.* But this is still not generally accepted as part of standard English. It's best to keep **crescendo** for the build-up. For what happens at the end of it use *climax* or *peak*.

## criterion *noun*

**Criterion** is a singular noun. It means 'a standard for judging things by': *The price of something is not necessarily a criterion of quality.* Its plural is **criteria**: *My main criteria for judging a dictionary are – does it have all the words I want and does it have definitions I can understand?*

⚠ Remember – don't use **criteria** as if it were singular.

## curb *noun, verb* and kerb *noun*

British people call the stone edging to a pavement a **kerb**. Americans use the same word, but they spell it **curb** (the spelling **curb** is sometimes used in British English too).

In both Britain and America a **curb** is a strap attached to a horse's bit to control it. And to **curb** something is to restrain it or keep it in check: *When I heard the new* *teacher had arrived, I couldn't curb my curiosity – I had to go and have a look.*



**currant** *noun* and **current** *adjective, noun*

A **currant** is a small dried grape. You can also get *blackcurrants* and *redcurrants,* which are small berry-like fruits.

A **current** is a flow of water in the sea, in a river, etc. It's also a flow of electricity. The adjective **current** means 'happening now': *In the current season he's already scored 15 goals.*

**cymbal** *noun* and **symbol** *noun*

A **cymbal** 🔊 /**sim**-bəl/ is a musical instrument consisting of a large metal plate that makes a ringing sound when you hit it. ⚠ Don't confuse it with a **symbol** 🔊 /**sim**-bəl/, which is something that represents or stands for something else: *Red is a symbol of danger.*

# Dd

## **dairy** *noun* and **diary** *noun*

A **dairy** 🔊 /**dare**-i/ is a place where milk is processed or sold. *Dairy cattle* are cows kept for the milk they produce, and *dairy products* are milk, cream, yoghurt, cheese, etc.

A **diary** 🔊 /**dire**-i/ is a book in which you write down what happens to you each day, or make a note of your future appointments.

## **dangling participles**

Present participles (ending in *-ing*) and past participles (usually ending in *-ed*) can be used on their own in phrases, without a subject and another verb. For example, *Turning the corner, I spotted Kemal at the bus-stop* and *Excluded from the official club, they decided to form one of their own.*

You can see that the subject in the main part of these sentences belongs with the participle. It was *I* who was *turning the corner*, and *they* who were *excluded.* If you wanted, you could rewrite the sentences *As I turned the corner, I spotted Kemal at the bus-stop* and *Since they'd been excluded from the official club, they decided to form one of their own.*

You sometimes find participles used in this way even if they don't belong to the subject in the main part of the sentence. For example, in *Turning the corner, Kemal came into view at the bus-stop*, it obviously can't be Kemal who's turning the corner, because he's at the bus-stop. But this sort of sentence, where the participle (known as a **dangling participle**) doesn't belong with the subject of the main part of the sentence, isn't regarded as acceptable in standard English, so it's best to avoid it. Besides being not acceptable in standard English, it can often sound ridiculous: *Standing on one leg in the middle of the lake I saw a flamingo.*

You could rewrite the last sentence about Kemal as *As I turned the corner, Kemal came into view at the bus-stop.*



## dare *verb*

To **dare** to do something is to be brave enough to do it, if it's something you're afraid of, or rude enough to do it, if it's something that offends people.

When you put another verb after **dare**, you can do it in two ways. You can either put **to** in front of the other verb: *I didn't dare to speak.* Or you can just use the other verb on its own: *I didn't dare speak.*

If you do it the first way, **dare** behaves like an ordinary verb. But if you do it the second way, you don't add-**s** to it in the third person singular form: *he dare, she dare.* And with this second method, you only use it in negative sentences and questions: *She daren't contradict him in case he shouts at her. How dare he talk to me like that?*

**I dare say** or **I daresay** is used when talking about something which you think is probable: *I dare say/daresay you'd like a cool drink after running around in the hot sun.*

## dash

A dash is a short line (–) separating two words. It's used in three ways:

***A pair of dashes*** – like this – can be used to separate a phrase – such as a comment – from the main part of a sentence. It's like using a pair of commas or a pair of brackets, but it marks a stronger separation than commas and a weaker separation than brackets.

***For lists*** A dash can come before a list of things: *Here's what you'll need for the recipe – tomatoes, onions, aubergines and some minced lamb.* It works in the same way as a colon, but it makes a sharper break between the two parts of the sentence.

You can also put a dash after a list, and before a comment on the list: *Sue, Bob, Mike, Helen, Wilma – they were all there.*

***For a pause*** A dash can also show a strong pause, often followed by a very emphatic comment: *If you're not in bed in ten minutes there'll be trouble – and you'd better believe it!*

To find out the difference between a dash and a hyphen, look at the entry for HYPHEN.

## data *noun*

**Data** is information, especially detailed information, facts, statistics, etc. used for making calculations or decisions: *The result of the experiment isn't what I expected at all – I'd better check my data again.*

Originally **data** was a plural noun: *These data are all wrong.* But it's now widely used as a collective singular noun: *Let me know when all this data has been entered in the computer.* Both usages are acceptable in standard English. The singular is becoming more common than the plural, and it's the standard usage in the field of computers.

🔈 The usual pronunciation is /**day**-tə/ (rhyming with *later*) but /**dah**-tə/ (rhyming with *garter*) is also acceptable.

## dates

The usual way of writing a date, for example at the top of a letter, is like this: *4 March 1973*. You can also write *4th March 1973*, but this is less common than it used to be.

In America, the name of the month is usually written before the number of the day, like this: *March 4, 1973.*

You can use a number for the month too: *4/3/73*, or *4-3-73* or *4.3.73*. But remember, an American would probably interpret this as *3 April*. Don't use numbers for months if they could confuse someone who's likely to read them.

To name decades, you put an *s* on the end of a date ending in 0: *the 1860s*. There's no apostrophe before the *s*. To abbreviate the date, you can replace the first two figures with an apostrophe: *the '60s.* But make sure there's no doubt what century you're talking about before you do this.

⚠ Don't write *between 1250–1350* or *from 1979–1994*. It should be ✔ *between 1250 and 1350* and *from 1979 to 1994.*

To find out how to use AD and BC with dates, look at the entry for AD. To find out how to use the word *century*, look at the entry for CENTURY.

## dear *adverb* and dearly *adverb*

**Dear** as an adverb means 'at a high price'. It's used in expressions like *I'll make him pay dear for that* (= I'll make him suffer for it) as well as in talking about money. **Dearly** means 'with great affection' (*I love you dearly*) and 'with great eagerness and seriousness' (*She'd dearly like to accept* (= she'd very much like to), *but she feels she should refuse*). It's also used in the same way as **dear**: *Their decision to sell their house last year has cost them dearly – if they'd waited till this year they could have got £10,000 more for it.*

## debar *verb* and disbar *verb*

To **debar** someone is to prevent them from doing something: *Anyone who has a criminal record is debarred from holding office in the society.*

To **disbar** a barrister is to take away from him or her the right to do the job of a lawyer.

❶ When you add **-ing** and **-ed** to **debar** and **disbar**, you double the **r**: **debarring**, **debarred**; **disbarring**, **disbarred**.



## decade *noun*

A **decade** is a period of ten years. The standard British pronunciation of the word is /**dek**-ayd/. Some people pronounce it /di-**kayd**/, rhyming with *decayed*, but this has not become generally accepted as standard English.

## decided *adjective* and decisive *adjective*

**Decided** means 'clear and definite, unmistakable': *There was a decided smell of rotting meat coming from the dustbin.*

**Decisive** means 'making quick and effective decisions' (*Never the most decisive of managers, she agonized for days over whether she should sack him*) and 'putting things beyond any doubt' (*6–0 is a pretty decisive victory*).

## decimate *verb*

To **decimate** something is to destroy large parts of it: *The coastal forests have been decimated by a plague of caterpillars.*

Originally, **decimate** used to mean 'to kill one in every ten', and some people think that that's how it should still be used, and that you shouldn't use it to mean 'to destroy large parts of'. But in practice, 'destroy large parts of' is what **decimate** does mean, and it's perfectly acceptable in standard English.

d

**decisive** see DECIDED

**defective** *adjective* and **deficient** *adjective*

Something that's **defective** doesn't work properly: *The train had to be withdrawn from service because of defective brakes.*

Something that's **deficient in** something hasn't got enough of it: *A diet deficient in vitamins causes health problems.*

**defence, defense** *noun*

**Defence** is the action of defending or a means of defending. **Defence** is the British spelling, **defense** the American.

❶ The adjectives **defensible** and **defensive** are spelt with an **s** in Britain and America.

**defer** *verb*

If you **defer** something, you put it off till later. And if you **defer to** someone, you submit to what they want or what they think.

❶ When you add **-ing** and **-ed** to **defer**, you double the **r**: **deferring, deferred**.

**defining relative clauses** see CLAUSES

**definite** *adjective* and **definitive** *adjective*

Something that's **definite** is exact or firm, not vague: *Don't just say maybe – give me a definite answer.*

Something that's **definitive** is complete and authoritative and can't be improved on: *Von Hakkenbakker has published the definitive work on the anatomy of the elephant.*

## definite article see ARTICLES

## defuse *verb* and diffuse *verb, adjective*

If you **defuse** a bomb you take its fuse out so that it doesn't blow up. And if you **defuse** a situation, a crisis a difficulty, etc., you make it less tense or dangerous.

Something that **diffuses** or is **diffused**, spreads out widely in all directions: *Television is a powerful means of diffusing knowledge.* **Diffuse** is an adjective too. It means 'spread out thinly' or 'rambling': *It was a diffuse and wordy speech, and I'm afraid I went to sleep halfway through.*

🔊 The verb **diffuse** is pronounced /di-**fewz**/. The standard pronunciation of **defuse** is /dee-**fewz**/. It's often pronounced /di-**fewz**/, but as this can sometimes lead to confusion with **diffuse**, it's best to stick to /dee-**fewz**/. The adjective **diffuse** is pronounced /di-**fewss**/.

## deity *noun*

A **deity** is a god. There are two ways of pronouncing the word – 🔊 /**day**-ə-ti/ and /**dee**-ə-ti/. /**day**-ə-ti/ is probably commoner, but both are perfectly acceptable in standard English.

## delusion *noun* and illusion *noun*

A **delusion** is a false belief. If you say *He suffers from the delusion that he's a horse,* you mean that he thinks he's a horse, even though he isn't, and you probably think he's mad.

An **illusion** is something you think you see, hear, feel, etc., which isn't really there (*Was that a real ghost or an optical illusion?*), or an idea you have that turns out not to be true (*I always thought that Father Christmas was real. You've really shattered my illusions!*)

d

## demeanour, demeanor *noun*

Someone's **demeanour** is the way they behave, especially if it shows you how they're feeling: *I could tell from his jaunty demeanour that the news was good.*

**Demeanour** is the British spelling, **demeanor** the American.

## dependant *noun* and
## dependent *adjective, noun*

If you have **dependants**, you have people who rely on you, especially to provide them with a home, food, money, etc. **Dependant** is the only British spelling of the noun, but Americans spell it either **dependant** or **dependent**.

❶ The adjective is **dependent** in both British and American English: *The outcome of the game is dependent on* (= depends on) *the weather.*

## deprecate *verb* and depreciate *verb*

If you **deprecate** 🔊 /**dep**-rə-kayt/ something, you say that you think it's bad or that you disapprove of it: *I strongly deprecate the council's decision to delay the election.*

If you **depreciate** 🔊 /di-**pree**-shee-ayt/ something, you belittle it or say that you think it's worthless: *Without wishing to depreciate Mrs Inkpen's sterling efforts, I think her energies might have been better expended in other areas.*

Both words are formal and should be used with care. It's easy to get them mixed up, and in fact the adjective *self-deprecating* has come to mean 'belittling or undervaluing yourself'.

d

**derisive** *adjective* and **derisory** *adjective*

**Derisive** laughter is mocking laughter. If something's so ridiculous that you feel contempt for it, you laugh at it in a derisive way.

An amount that's **derisory** is so small that you feel insulted by it: *They offered us a derisory two per cent pay increase.*

**descendant** *noun* and **descendent** *adjective*

Someone's **descendants** are the people who are descended from him or her. For example, if you say you're a **descendant** of William the Conqueror, you mean that you can trace back a family link between you and him.

**Descendent** is a rare adjective. It means 'going downwards' or 'descended from an ancestor'.

**desert** *noun, verb* and **dessert** *noun*

A **desert** 🔊 /**dez**-ət/ is a large dry area, usually hot and covered with sand. **Desert** 🔊 /di-**zert**/ is also a verb, meaning 'to go away from someone or something and give them up': *She's deserted all her old friends now that she's going round with him.*

Someone's **deserts** 🔊 /di-**zerts**/ are what they deserve – usually something bad: *It served him right when they excluded him – he got his just deserts.*

A **dessert** 🔊 /di-**zert**/ is the part of a meal after the main course, such as a pudding or some fruit.

**despatch** see DISPATCH

**deter** *verb*

To **deter** someone is to stop them doing something by making them anxious about what might happen if they did: *The thought of climbing all those flights of steps deters me from going to see her.*

❶ When you add -**ing** and -**ed** to **deter**, you double the **r**: **deterring, deterred.**

d

## deteriorate *verb*

Something that **deteriorates** gets worse: *Your spelling's deteriorated this term, Mark.*

🔊 **Deteriorate** is quite commonly pronounced ⚠ /di-**teer**-ee-ayt/, but this is not generally accepted as a standard pronunciation. The standard pronunciation of the word is ✔ /di-**teer**-ee-ə-rayt/.

## determiners

Determiners come in front of a noun and specify what it's referring to in some way. For example, *this* is a determiner in *I don't like this bread,* and *some* is a determiner in *There are some people to see you.* When there's an adjective in front of the noun, it comes after the determiner: *I don't like this stale bread.* See also ARTICLES.

## detract *verb* and distract *verb*

If something **detracts** from something else, it makes it seem less good than it would otherwise have been: *She got low marks for geography, but that doesn't detract from the overall high quality of her exam results.*

If something **distracts** you, it takes your attention away from what you were doing: *I was distracted by what was going on at the side of the road, and nearly drove into a lamp-post.*

**develop** *verb* and **development** *noun*

If something **develops**, it changes or comes into existence over a period: *Paul's developed into a useful young striker.*
❶ When you add -**ing** and -**ed** to **develop**, you don't double the **p**: **developing**, **developed**. Also remember the spelling of **development** –there's no **e** after the **p**.



**device** *noun* and **devise** *verb*

A **device** 🔊 /di-**vyss**/ is a piece of equipment: *He'd invented a device for resealing half-empty drink cans.*
To **devise** 🔊 /di-**vyz**/ something is to think it up: *I've devised a cunning plan to get our money back.*

**dial** *verb*

Old telephones had a dial that was turned to select the number you wanted. Although we now press buttons to select the number, we still use the verb **dial**.
❶ When you add -**ing** and -**ed** to **dial**, you double the **l** in British English (**dialling**, **dialled**), but you don't double it in American English (**dialing**, **dialed**).

**diarrhoea, diarrhea** *noun*

**Diarrhoea** is an illness in which you have to keep emptying your bowels.

**Diarrhoea** is the main spelling in British English and **diarrhea** the main spelling in American English, but each variety occasionally uses the other form.
❶ Remember the double **rr** and the **h**.

**diary** see DAIRY

**dice** *noun*

A **dice** is a small cube with spots from 1 to 6 on its sides. The plural of **dice** is the same as the singular: *two dice.*

A **dice** used to be called a **die** (with **dice** the plural), but this is no longer current in standard English.

d

**die** see DYE

**different** *adjective*

There are three prepositions that you can use after **different – from**, **than** and **to**.

The best one to use, especially in writing, is ✔ **from**: *Your coat's a different colour from mine.* No one has any objections to it, and it's equally acceptable in British and American English.

The other two, **than** and **to**, express the same meaning equally well, but not everyone likes them, and there are differences between their use in Britain and America.

**Than** is common in American English: *Your coat's a different color than mine.* It hasn't become standard in British English, but it's the only option if you want to follow **different** with a clause rather than with a noun or a pronoun: *The items in the programme were in a different order than they are in the Radio Times.*

**To** is common and perfectly acceptable in British English: *Your coat's a different colour to mine.* Americans rarely use it, however.

**diffuse** see DEFUSE

**dilapidated** *adjective*

**Dilapidated** means 'in such bad condition that it's practically falling apart': *I don't know how that dilapidated old car of his ever passed its MOT.*

Because it comes from a Latin word meaning 'stone', there are some people who think that **dilapidated** should only be used about stone structures falling down. They get annoyed when it's applied to other things collapsing.

But the fact is that in standard English, **dilapidated** *is* used as a general word for disrepair or ruin, and it's pointless to try to insist that it means something which it doesn't.



## dilemma *noun*

If you're in a **dilemma**, you're faced with a difficult choice between unpleasant alternatives: *Should we invite Richard and risk upsetting Linda, or not invite him and risk upsetting Richard himself? It's quite a dilemma.*

In that sentence, the choice is between two things – and because **dilemma** comes from a Greek word meaning 'two', some people think that it should only be used of a choice between two. However, it's quite normal in standard English to apply it to more than two things. There should be some idea of 'choosing' about it, though. Using **dilemma** to mean simply 'a problem' or 'a difficult situation' hasn't yet become generally accepted in standard English.

**Dilemma** can be pronounced either /dy-**lem**-ə/ or /di-**lem**-ə/.

## dinghy *noun* and dingy *adjective*

A **dinghy** /**ding**-i or **ding**-gi/ is a small boat.

Something that's **dingy** /**din**-ji/ is unpleasantly dark and dirty-looking: *He lived in a dingy basement flat.*

## diphtheria *noun*

**Diphtheria** is a serious disease which causes inflammation of the throat.

The standard pronunciation of **diphtheria** is 🔊 /dif-**theer**-i-ə/. It's quite difficult to say /f/ and /th/ together, and because there's a *p* in the spelling many people pronounce it /dip-**theer**-i-ə/ instead, but when you're speaking carefully try to keep to /dif-**theer**-i-ə/.



❶ When spelling the word, remember that there's an **h** between the **p** and the **t**.

## diphthong *noun*

A **diphthong** is either a sound made up of two vowel sounds (like the sound /oy/ in *boy*), or it's two letters that represent this sound (like the *oy* in *boy*) or that represent a single vowel sound (like *ea* for /ee/ in *seat*).

The standard pronunciation of **diphthong** is 🔊 /**dif**-thong/. The pronunciation /**dip**-thong/ is becoming increasingly common, but it's not accepted by everyone as standard English.

❶ When spelling the word, remember that there's an **h** between the **p** and the **t**.

## direct speech see INVERTED COMMAS

## disappoint *verb*

If you're **disappointed**, something you'd hoped for or expected has failed to happen.

❶ Remember the spelling – one **s** and two **p**s.

## disbar see DEBAR

## disc, disk *noun*

A **disc** is a thin flat circular object. **Disc** is the way the word's spelt in British English, except when it refers to a storage device for computer information – then, it's usually spelt **disk**. **Disk** is the usual American spelling of the word in all its senses.

## discomfit *verb* and discomfort *noun, verb*

Someone who's **discomfited** is disconcerted or put out, made to feel embarrassed and annoyed: *He didn't appear at all discomfited when his colleagues contradicted all he'd said.*

Something that **discomforts** you makes you feel uneasy: *She had the discomforting feeling that someone else was in the room with her.* **Discomfort** is more usually a noun. It's a polite word for 'pain': *You may feel some discomfort when the needle goes in.*

## discover see INVENT

## discreet *adjective* and discrete *adjective*

Someone who's **discreet** is very tactful in what they say, and can be relied on not to give away your secrets to other people.

**Discrete** means 'separate': *It looks like a shapeless mass, but viewed under the microscope it can be seen as a set of discrete dots.*

**Discrete** is quite a rare word, so if you get confused by the two spellings, **discreet** is likely to be the one you want. ✔ Don't forget, for 'tactful' use -**eet** not -**ete**.

## dishevel *verb*

Someone who is **dishevelled** has very untidy hair, and is often generally untidy and scruffy.

❗ When you add -**ing** and -**ed** to **dishevel**, you double the **l** in British English (**dishevelling**, **dishevelled**) but not in American English (**disheveling**, **disheveled**).

**disinterested** *adjective* and **uninterested** *adjective*

If you're **uninterested** in something, it doesn't interest you. It may even bore you: *Several members of his large but uninterested audience had already fallen asleep.*

The standard meaning of **disinterested** is 'not having any personal advantage to gain from something, and therefore impartial': *You won't get disinterested advice from salesmen, because they're always trying to sell you something.*

In modern English, **disinterested** is also very commonly used to mean 'not interested', like **uninterested**. This use is still not generally accepted as part of standard English, but it does mean that if you use **disinterested** in its standard sense 'impartial', there may be times when people will misunderstand you, because they think you meant 'not interested'. For this reason, it's probably better to use a word like *impartial, unbiased* or *unprejudiced* when you mean 'impartial'.

**disk** see DISC

**disorient** *verb* and **disorientate** *verb*

If you feel **disoriented**, or **disorientated**, you feel confused and you're not quite sure where you are. Both verbs are standard English. **Disorient** is rather commoner in American English. **Disorientate** is the main British form, although **disorient** is becoming more frequent in Britain.

**dispatch, despatch** *verb, noun*

To **dispatch** something is to send it off somewhere, and a **dispatch** is an official message, or a report sent from abroad. **Dispatch** is also used to mean 'promptness'.

**Dispatch** is the main spelling, but **despatch** can also be used.

## dispel *verb*

To **dispel** something is to get rid of it because you don't think it should exist: *We must dispel these old myths about male superiority.*

❶ When you add -**ing** and -**ed** to **dispel**, you double the **l**: **dispelling**, **dispelled**.

## dispute *noun*, *verb*

A **dispute** is a disagreement or quarrel: *He got into a dispute with his neighbour over who owned the fence.*

🔊 There are two possible pronunciations of the word. The commoner is /diss-**pyoot**/, but /**diss**-pyoot/ is also perfectly acceptable in standard English.

To **dispute** something is to question the truth or accuracy of it: *I dispute those figures you've just given.* There's only one pronunciation of the verb – 🔊 /diss-**pyoot**/.

## dissect *verb* and bisect *verb*

When biologists **dissect** a specimen, they cut it up so that they can examine its parts. The standard pronunciation of the word is 🔊 /di-**sekt**/. It has nothing to do with 'cutting in two', so it's best to avoid the pronunciation ⚠ /dy-**sekt**/, which suggests 'two'.

Bisect 🔊 /by-**sekt**/ does mean 'to divide something into two halves': *The village is bisected by a busy main road.*

## distil, distill *verb*

To **distil** a liquid is to purify it by heating it up until it turns to vapour, and then cooling it down again. **Distil** is the British spelling, **distill** the American.

❶ When you add -**ing** and -**ed** to **distil**, you double the **l**: **distilling, distilled**.

## distinct *adjective* and distinctive *adjective*

d

Something that's **distinct** is clear and easy to see: *And there, distinct on the horizon, was the wicked queen's castle*. And things that are **distinct** from each other are clearly and completely different: *The flavour of this strawberry ice cream is quite distinct from the flavour of the other company's strawberry ice cream.*

Something that's **distinctive** is different from others, even unusual, and therefore noticeable: *She has her own distinctive way of writing the letter g – you can't mistake it.*

## distract see DETRACT

## distribute *verb*

To **distribute** something is to give it out amongst a lot of people. The standard pronunciation of the word is 🔊 /diss-**trib**-yoot/. The alternative /**diss**-tri-byoot/ is very common in Britain, although it hasn't become fully part of standard English.

## do *verb*

When we talk, we quite commonly use the verb **do** to avoid repeating another verb we've just used: *You work harder than I do. I don't go there as often as I used to do. 'Is he cleaning those windows?' 'He was doing, but now he seems to have gone off somewhere.'* But in serious writing, this **do** should be left out after *used to* and when it's in the form **doing** after the verb *to be*: ✔ *I don't go there as often as I used to. 'Is he cleaning those windows?' 'He was, but now he seems to have gone off somewhere.'*

There used to be a strong difference between British and American English in sentences such as: (British)

*Have you got a pen?* / (American) *Do you have a pen?* But now it's quite common for British speakers to use **do** in this way.

## dogged *adjective, past tense* and *past participle*

When **dogged** is an adjective, meaning 'persistent', it's pronounced 🔊 /**dog**-id/. But when it's the past form of the verb **dog**, meaning 'to pursue', it's pronounced 🔊 /dogd/.

## don't *verb*

**Don't** is the standard way of writing our usual pronunciation of *do not,* with *do* and *not* run together as /dohnt/. In formal writing, it's better to use *do not.*

⚠ Avoid using sentences like *It don't matter,* as it's not standard English to use **don't** instead of *doesn't* for the third person singular.

## double comparatives

The comparative form of adjectives and adverbs is used to express a greater amount of the quality shown by the adjective or adverb. To make it, you either put *-er* onto the end of the adjective or adverb or you use the word *more.*

For adjectives and adverbs with only one syllable, you usually add *-er*: *She's bigger than me.* For some with two syllables you add *-er* (*That's much tidier*), but for others you use *more* (*I've never seen a more handsome man*). For a word with three or more syllables, you usually use *more*: *Today's performance was more impressive than yesterday's.*

⚠ It's not acceptable in standard English to use *-er* and *more* with the same word. Don't say things like *This is much more better* or *He's a more kinder man*; use *much better* or *a kinder man.*

## double negatives

⚠ It's not acceptable in standard English to use two or more negative words together. In some varieties of spoken English it's fine to say things like *I don't want no more coffee* and *I never said nothing about him coming with us*, but in standard English it's not. Say ✔ *I don't want any more coffee* and *I never said anything about him coming with us.*

This doesn't just apply to negative words like *not* and *nothing*. It also covers words like *hardly, barely* and *scarcely*. You should say ✔ *I could hardly see anything,* not ⚠ *I couldn't hardly see anything.*

Be careful, too, not to use an unnecessary extra negative word after you've started a sentence with *I wouldn't be surprised if* or *I shouldn't wonder if.* You should say ✔ *I wouldn't be surprised if it rained,* not ⚠ *I wouldn't be surprised if it didn't rain.*

It *is* all right, though, to see a negative word with a word that has a negative prefix, like *un-* or *dis-*: ✔ *The overall effect was not unattractive.*

## doubling letters in spelling see CONSONANT DOUBLING

## doubt *noun, verb*

There are three conjunctions that can be used after **doubt** – *if, that* and *whether.*

When **doubt** is used with a negative, **that** is the only one you can use: *I don't doubt that he's sincere. There's no doubt that she meant what she said.* (In ordinary speech and informal writing, the *that*'s usually left out: *I don't doubt he's sincere.*)

Otherwise, you can use all three. But there is a slight difference between them. If you say *I doubt whether* or *if they'll hear us,* you mean you don't think they'll hear us but it's possible they will. If you say *I doubt that they'll hear us*, you mean you think it's very unlikely that they'll hear us.



**dour** *adjective*

Someone who's **dour** is very stern and determined and doesn't smile. The standard pronunciation of **dour** is 🔊 /**doo**-er/, rhyming with *tour*, but /**dow**-er/ (rhyming with *hour*) is also acceptable.

**downward** *adjective, adverb* and
**downwards** *adverb*

**Downward** is the adjective: *the downward path*. As an adverb, you can use either **downward** or **downwards**: *The burning plane plunged downward(s)*. **Downwards** is the main British form.

**draft** *noun, verb* and **draught** *noun, verb*

British English uses the spelling **draft** for these meanings: an early version of something: *the first draft of chapter 1*; a written order to pay money: *a banker's draft*; to write an early version of: *They stayed up until dawn drafting the treaty*.

For everything else pronounced 🔊 /drahft/, British English uses the spelling **draught**: a current of air: *There's an awful draught in here*; a type of beer: *Draught beer is beer served from the barrel*; and pulling: *a draught-horse is a horse that pulls loads*.

The board game played with two sets of twelve circular pieces is spelt **draughts**.

American English spells everything pronounced 🔊 /draft/ as **draft**. And in America the game of draughts is called *checkers*.

d

**drawing** *noun, present participle*

The standard pronunciation of **drawing** is 🔊 /**draw**-ing/. ⚠ Putting an /r/ in the middle of it, /**draw**-ring/, is not standard English. (To find out more about this /r/, look at the entry for INTRUSIVE R.)

**dream** *verb*

The verb **to dream** has two past forms: **dreamed** and **dreamt** 🔊 /dremt/: *I dreamed/dreamt a horrid dream last night.* Both are commonly used in British English, but in America **dreamed** is the usual word.

**drier** *adjective, noun* and **dryer** *noun*

**Drier** means 'more dry': *Further inland they have a drier climate.*

A **drier** or **dryer** is a machine for drying things: *a hair-drier.*

**drily, dryly** *adverb*

**Drily** (or **dryly**) means 'with dry humour' or 'sarcastically': *'I'm sure they're doing their best,' he remarked drily.* **Drily** is the main spelling in British English, but American English prefers **dryly**.

**drink** *verb*

The past tense of the verb **to drink** is **drank**: *She drank a whole can of Coke at one go.* The past participle is **drunk**: *Have you drunk your tea yet?* ⚠ Don't get the two mixed up. See also DRUNK, DRUNKEN.

**drivel** *verb*

To **drivel** is to talk nonsense: *He was drivelling on about some pathetic film he'd seen.*

d

❶ When you add -**ing** and -**ed** to **drivel** you double the **l** in British English: **drivelling, drivelled**. But in American English you usually don't double the **l**.

**drunk** *past participle, adjective, noun* and **drunken** *adjective*

**Drunk** is the past participle of the verb *to drink*: *Have you drunk your tea yet?* (see DRINK).

It can be used as an adjective, meaning 'suffering from the effect of drinking too much alcohol': *Champagne always makes me drunk*.

**Drunk** can be used as a noun too, meaning 'a person who is drunk'.

The adjective **drunken** means the same as the adjective **drunk**. The difference between them is that **drunken** is used before nouns (*a drunken sailor*) but **drunk** is used after verbs (*Sailor, you're drunk!*).

**dryer** see DRIER

**dryly** see DRILY

**duel** *verb* and **dual** *adjective*

To **duel** is to fight a contest with weapons against someone in order to settle a quarrel.

⚠ Don't confuse **duel** with **dual**, which means 'double': *a car with dual controls*.

❶ When you add -**ing** and -**ed** to **duel**, you double the **l** in British English: **duelling, duelled**. But in American English, you usually don't double the **l**.

**due to** *preposition*

**Due to** means 'as a result of'. It's used in two ways: after a noun and (usually) the verb *to be*: *His absence is due to*

d

*illness*; and after a complete clause: *The train was delayed due to leaves on the track.*

The second of these two uses has traditionally been regarded as incorrect, and old grammar books recommend that you should use *owing to* instead: *The train was delayed owing to leaves on the track.* You can certainly use *owing to*, or *because of* or *as a result of* if you prefer. But **due to** is now so widely used in this way and generally accepted that there's no reason not to treat it as standard English.

Try to avoid *due to the fact that*, which is very long-winded. Use *because* instead.

## duly *adverb* and dully *adverb*

**Duly** 🔊 /**dew**-li/ means 'in a way that is appropriate or might be expected': *Australia duly recorded their third successive win over England today* (= everyone expected Australia to win, and that's just what they did). Don't confuse it with **dully** 🔊 /**dul**-li/, which means 'in a dull way': *The armour gleamed dully in the candlelight.*

❶ Remember the spelling of **duly**. There's no **e**, even though it comes from *due*.

## duplication *noun* and duplicity *noun*

**Duplication** is doing something twice or making a copy of something: *All this duplication of effort is rather wasteful. One person could do it just as well.*

**Duplicity** is deceitfulness: *He accused the other side of duplicity in evading the terms of the agreement.*

## dwarf *noun*

**Dwarf** has two plurals: **dwarfs** and **dwarves. Dwarfs** is the traditional plural, and it's best to stick with it when the word means 'an animal or plant of a smaller than normal size' or 'a small dense star'. It's the plural that goes with the meaning 'an abnormally short person' too, but as this use of **dwarf** can offend short people, it's best to avoid it altogether. When **dwarf** means 'a small supernatural person', you can use either **dwarfs** or **dwarves** as the plural.



## dye *verb* and die *verb*

To **dye** something is to change its colour by means of a dye. The present participle is **dyeing**, with an **e**: *I'm thinking of dyeing this skirt blue.*

To **die** is to stop living. The present participle is **dying**, without an **e**: *There's a boy dying in there.*

# Ee

**each** *pronoun, adjective*

Do you use a singular or a plural verb after **each**?

When **each** comes after a plural noun or a plural pronoun, it has a plural verb: *The children each have a room of their own.*

When **each** is the subject of a sentence on its own, it has a singular verb: *There are 150 rooms in the hotel. Each has its own television set and an en suite bathroom.*

When **each** is followed by **of** and a plural noun or a plural pronoun, it can have either a singular verb or a plural verb. The traditional usage is to have a singular verb: *Each of the rooms is painted a different colour*. But it's increasingly common to use a plural verb, especially when you want to avoid using *his* afterwards to refer to women as well as men: *Each of the seven winners have received their own personally inscribed medal.* This is well enough established, and useful enough, to count as standard English.

**each other** *pronoun* and
**one another** *pronoun*

Both **each other** and **one another** refer to one person, animal, etc. doing something to one or more others, and the other(s) doing it back: *They promised each other/one another they wouldn't tell anyone what they'd been doing.*

There's a tradition that you should use **each other** for two people and **one another** for more than two, but there's no good reason for it, and people have never paid much attention to it anyway. It's perfectly standard to use **each other** and **one another** in both ways, although **each other** is commoner.

Remember, when you add the possessive **'s** to them, you put it on the end of **other**: *We try to understand each other's problems.*

e

## earn *verb*

To **earn** something is to get it by working for it or deserving it: *She earns $50 000 a year.*

Its past form is **earned** /ernd/. It's quite common in British English to pronounce this as /ernt/, but it's *not* acceptable in standard English to spell it with a **t**. (It's not like *learn*, whose past form does have the two spellings *learned* and *learnt.*)

## earth, Earth *noun*

When you use **earth** or **the earth** to name the world we live on, you can spell it with either a small **e** (*the biggest show on earth*) or a capital **E** (*The burning spacecraft plunged towards the Earth*). When you use it together with the names of other planets, such as Mars and Jupiter, use a capital **E**.

## easy *adjective, adverb* and easily *adverb*

When you want to make an adverb out of the adjective **easy**, the usual thing to do is to put -**ly** on the end and make **easily**: *It was an easy question. I answered it easily.*

But there are just a few expressions where you can use **easy** itself as an adverb: *easier said than done*; *easy come, easy go*; *go easy*; and *take it easy.*

## eat *verb*

The past tense of the verb **to eat** is **ate**. The standard British pronunciation of this is /et/, but /ayt/ is also very common and perfectly acceptable. In American

English it's /ayt/ that's the standard pronunciation, and /et/ is not considered to be good English.

The past participle of **eat** is **eaten**.

**eatable** *adjective* and **edible** *adjective*

e

If you say that something's **eatable**, you mean it's fit to be eaten, either because it tastes reasonably good, or because it hasn't actually gone off. It's usually used in a negative way: *This meat's so tough it's hardly eatable. This disgusting stew's uneatable – bring me an omelette.*

**Edible** is used like this too, but it has another meaning as well – 'able to be eaten without danger': *'Is this plant edible?' 'No, it's poisonous.'*

**economic** *adjective* and **economical** *adjective*

**Economic** means 'connected with economics', which is the study of money and the way it's made and used by people: *Britain has severe economic problems.* It also means 'likely to make a profit': *If they don't charge an economic price for their goods, they'll go out of business.*

**Economical** means 'not spending money carelessly or being wasteful with things': *We've had to be more economical since Dad lost his job.*

**edible** see EATABLE

**effect** see AFFECT

**efficient** *adjective* and **efficacious** *adjective*

Someone who's **efficient** gets things done quickly and with minimum effort: *It was very efficient of you to get all those envelopes addressed in an hour.* **Efficient** is also used about machines and processes.

**Efficacious** means 'producing the necessary effect': *If you suffer from wind, you will find this medicine most* *efficacious* (= it'll cure you). It's an unnecessarily formal word, and is best avoided. *Effective* is usually a perfectly acceptable alternative.

**e.g.** *abbreviation* and **i.e.** *abbreviation*

**E.g.** is short for *exempli gratia,* which is Latin for 'for the sake of example'. It's used to introduce one or more examples of what you've been talking about: *a plant of the brassica family, e.g. cabbages, cauliflowers and Brussels sprouts.*

⚠ Don't get it mixed up with **i.e.**, which is used to introduce an explanation or simplification of what you've just said: *a plant of the brassica family, i.e. the cabbage family.* It's short for *id est,* which is Latin for 'that is'.

**egoist** *noun* and **egotist** *noun*

The main meaning of **egoist** is 'someone who thinks of their own well-being all the time, and doesn't bother much about other people'. The main meaning of **egotist** is 'someone who thinks they are very important, and keeps talking about what they've done, how clever they are, etc.'. These meanings are close together, and keep sliding into each other. It's common to find both words used as a general term of disapproval for a 'self-centred person'.

🔊 For both words, the standard pronunciation of the **e-** is /ee/ (/**ee**-goh-ist/ and /**ee**-gə-tist/). But /e/ is very common, and perfectly acceptable (/**eg**-oh-ist/ and /**eg**-ə-tist/).

**-ei-** see -IE-

**either** *adjective, pronoun, adverb, conjunction*

Do you use a singular or a plural verb after **either**?

When **either** is the subject of a clause, the answer is easy – use a singular verb: '*Should I pay in dollars or pounds?*' '*Either is acceptable.*'

When **either** is followed by **or**, it can make the choice more difficult. When a singular noun comes second, use a singular verb: *I think either Sammy or Teresa has your book*. When a plural noun comes second, use a plural verb: *If either she or any of her friends want to come, they'd be most welcome.*

When you use **either** ... **or** about a man and a woman, or a boy and a girl, it's neater to use a plural verb and the plural pronoun *they* afterwards, in preference to the long-winded *he or she*: *If either Zoe or Liam phone, tell them I'll be back after lunch.*

Put **either** as close as you can to the part of the sentence it refers to. For instance, *I'll have either the cod or the skate, whichever's cheaper* (**either** refers to the two nouns, so it goes in front of them); *Either say what you mean or keep quiet* (**either** refers to the two clauses, so it goes in front of them).

✔ It's perfectly acceptable in standard English to use **either** to mean 'each': *The road is closed at either end.*

🔈 The main British pronunciation of **either** is /**I**-dhə/, but some people say /**ee**-dhə/. In America, it's the other way round – /**ee**-dhər/ is the main pronunciation, and /**I**-dhər/ is rare.

## **elder** *adjective* and **older** *adjective*

The normal word for saying that someone or something is 'more old' is **older**. And the normal word for saying that someone or something is 'most old' is **oldest**: *the oldest man in the world.*

There's another pair of words you can use when you're talking about closely related members of a family: **elder** and **eldest**: *my elder sister, his eldest son.* But this usage is becoming less common. The modern tendency is to use **older** and **oldest** for family members too, and this is perfectly acceptable in standard English.

With **than**, you can only use **older**. *My sister's two years older than me.*

**electric** *adjective*, **electrical** *adjective* and **electronic** *adjective*

**Electric** denotes something that's powered by electricity: *an electric toaster.*

**Electrical** means 'relating to electricity': *an electrical fault; the electrical activity in the brain.*

**Electronic** refers to equipment or systems that work by means of transistors, microchips, etc.: *The new electronic scoreboard puts the score up in just a couple of seconds.*

**eligible** *adjective* and **illegible** *adjective*

If you're **eligible** /**el**-i-jə-bəl/ for something, or to do something, you're entitled to get it or do it: *Anyone over the age of 18 is eligible to enter the competition.*

Writing that's **illegible** /i-**lej**-ə-bəl/ is so bad or damaged that you can't read it.

**else** *adverb*

When you want to add the possessive **'s** to expressions like *no one else* and *somebody else*, put it on the **else**: *That's someone else's problem.*

When you use **else** to compare things, you can use **but**, **except** or **than** with it; *Who else but/except/than Mark would have said something as stupid as that?*

**elude** see ALLUDE

**embarrass** *verb*

If you're **embarrassed**, you feel awkward or self-conscious or ashamed.

❶ Remember the spelling – there are two **rs** and two **ss**.



**emigrant** *noun* and **immigrant** *noun*

**Emigrants** are people who leave the country they're living in and go to live somewhere else. The verb for what they do is **emigrate**: *There are no jobs in this country. I'm thinking of emigrating.*

**Immigrants** are people who've come from one country to live in another: *Thousands of immigrants arrived in New York from Europe each week.*

At the start of their journey, when they leave their original country, the people are **emigrants**. At the end of it, when they arrive at their new country, the people are **immigrants**.

**eminent** *adjective* and **imminent** *adjective*

Someone who is **eminent** is famous for doing outstanding work in a particular area: *several eminent scientists.*

Something that's **imminent** is going to happen very soon: *With Christmas imminent, the shops are full to bursting.*

**emotional** *adjective* and **emotive** *adjective*

**Emotional** means 'connected with the emotions or feelings': *He's got severe emotional problems.* And a person who's **emotional** easily gets upset, cries about unimportant things, etc.

Something that's **emotive** makes people feel very strongly: *The hunting of whales is a very emotive issue.*

**empathy** *noun* and **sympathy** *noun*

If you feel **empathy** with someone, you understand the way they feel and think so well that it's almost as if your two minds are working as one.

If you have **sympathy** for someone you feel sorry for them and share some of their sadness or distress.



**encyclopedia, encyclopaedia** *noun*

An **encyclopedia** is a book which gives information on many subjects. **Encyclopaedia** is the traditional British spelling, but **encyclopedia** is now very common, and it's perfectly acceptable. **Encyclopedia** is the main American spelling.

**endeavour, endeavor** *verb, noun*

If you **endeavour** to do something, you try to do it: *We will endeavour to satisfy your wishes, sir.* **Endeavour** is a much more formal word than *try*.

**Endeavour** is the British spelling, **endeavor** the American.

**enforceable** *adjective*

If a law is **enforceable**, you can be made to obey it.

❶ Remember the spelling, with the **e** between the **c** and the **a**.

**enormity** *noun* and **enormousness** *noun*

The traditional meanings of **enormity** are 'a very bad or wicked act', 'a very serious mistake' and 'great wickedness': *They didn't realize the enormity of what they'd done.* But its most usual meaning in modern English is 'large and intimidating size': *They're daunted by the enormity of their problems.* Some people object to this usage, but it's very common, and can now be regarded as part of standard English. However, it's best to avoid using **enormity** to mean simply 'large size'. **Enormousness** is the word for that: *We gasped at the enormousness of their cars.*

## enquire, inquire *verb*

e

The two spellings **enquire** and **inquire** are practically interchangeable. You can use either. Some people prefer to use **enquire** for asking in a general way for information (*She enquired at the desk to see if there were any letters for her*) and **inquire** for making an official investigation (*The police are inquiring into the running of the club*) – but it's not a distinction that you need to follow. In American English **inquire** is much more common than **enquire**, and it seems to be becoming commoner in British English too.

## enrol, enroll *verb*

If you **enrol** in an organization, you become a member of it. **Enrol** is the British spelling, **enroll** the American.
❶ When you add **-ing** or **-ed** to **enrol**, you double the **l**: **enrolling, enrolled**.

## ensure see ASSURE

## enthral, enthrall *verb*

If you're **enthralled** by something, it's so wonderful that it fascinates you and you can't think of anything else: *He held all the children enthralled with his stories of life at sea.* **Enthral** is the British spelling, **enthrall** the American.
❶ When you add **-ing** or **-ed** to **enthral**, you double the **l**: **enthralling, enthralled**.

**entrust, intrust** *verb*

If you **entrust** something to someone, you give it to them, on the understanding that they'll look after it carefully: *We entrusted the map to David, and he lost it.* You can use the spelling **intrust** too, but it's not so common.



**envelop** *verb* and **envelope** *noun*

If something is **enveloped** 🔊 /in-**vel**-əpt/ in something it's completely covered, so that you can't see it: *The hills were enveloped in mist.*

An **envelope** is what you put a letter in. There are two pronunciations of the word, 🔊 /**en**-və-lohp/ and /**on**-və-lohp/. Both are acceptable in standard English, but /**en**-və-lohp/ is commoner.

**equal** *verb*

When one thing **equals** another, they're the same in quantity or quality.

❶ When you add -**ing** or -**ed** to **equal** you double the **l** in British English (**equalling**, **equalled**), but not in American English (**equaling**, **equaled**).

**equally** *adverb*

⚠ Don't use *as* after **equally** – sentences like *Mark is equally as clever as Kate* aren't acceptable in standard English. There are plenty of acceptable alternatives, such as ✔ *Mark is just as clever as Kate* and ✔ *Mark and Kate are equally clever.*

**equip** *verb*

When you **equip** someone or something, you supply them with what's needed: *The gym is fully equipped with weights, exercise bikes, a rowing machine, etc.*

❶ When you add **-ing** and **-ed** to **equip**, you double the **p: equipping, equipped.**

**equivalent** *adjective, noun*

**Equivalent** means 'equal in value or amount'. When it's an adjective, you use **to** with it: *A hundred metres is equivalent to about a hundred and ten yards.* When it's a noun, you use **of** with it: *A hundred metres is the equivalent of about a hundred and ten yards.*

**escalate** *verb*

Something that **escalates** goes up and up, often rapidly: *The cost of buying a house has escalated in recent years.* For some reason the word has become unpopular. Some people think it's used too often. It's really a perfectly good word, but because of its bad reputation, it's best to use it sparingly.

**Eskimo** see RACES AND PEOPLES

**especial, especially** see SPECIAL

**esthetic** see AESTHETIC

**etc.** *abbreviation*

You use **etc.** after a list of items, to show that there are more of the same type that you could have mentioned: *For details of hotels, boarding houses, camping sites, etc. contact the local tourist office.* Because people need to be able to work out what sort of things you mean by 'etc.', it's helpful to give at least two items before the **etc.** It's usual to put a comma after the word in front of **etc.**

**Etc.** tells you that the list of items isn't complete, so there's no need to use another expression with it that says the same thing, like *including, such as* or *for example.*

**even** *adverb*

Compare these two sentences: *I haven't even met Matthew* and *I haven't met even Matthew.* The first one emphasizes the fact that I haven't *met* Matthew (let alone spoken to him or made friends with him). The second one suggests that of all the people I might meet, *Matthew* is the most likely, but I haven't met him.

When you speak, you can make clear what you mean by the way you emphasize the words. That means that you don't have to change the position of **even**. You can put it in its most natural position, which is before the verb: *I haven't even* met *Matthew* or *I haven't even met* Matthew. But when you write, you can't do that, so you have to put **even** in front of the word it refers to – *met* or *Matthew.*

e

**ever** *adverb*

Compare these two sentences: *Who ever told you that?* and *Whoever told you that was lying.* The first is a question, and the word **ever** gives extra force to the question word *who.* The second is a statement. Other ways of expressing the same meaning would be *Anyone who told you that was lying* and *No matter who told you that, they were lying.*

In standard English, **ever** is written as a separate word in the first type of sentence, but it's joined on to the *wh*-word in front of the second type. The same goes for other *wh*-words, such as *what, when, where, which* and also *how.*

**everyone** *pronoun* and **every one** *pronoun*

**Everyone** means 'every person, all the people': *I've asked everyone I know to come.* **Every one** means 'every single thing or person': *I bought a kilo of apples, and every one was rotten.*

*Everyone has their own views about this.* You use a singular verb (here, *has*) after **everyone**, but in modern English it's increasingly common to follow this with a plural pronoun (here, *their*). This is because people don't like to leave out women by using *he*, and it's clumsy to keep repeating *he or she*. *They* is a sensible alternative, and it's gradually becoming accepted as part of standard English.

**evoke** *verb* and **invoke** *verb*

If something **evokes** a feeling or memory, it reminds you of something in the past, or it gives you similar feelings to ones you had in the past: *The film evoked memories of childhood holidays by the sea.*

If you **invoke** a law or regulation, you use it or bring it into operation: *The government invoked the little-known Street Offences Act to control the riots.* To **invoke** someone's help is to ask for it.

**exceed** see ACCEDE

**excel** *verb*

If you **excel** at something, you're very good at it: *Roland's always excelled at maths.*

❶ Remember the spelling, with an **x** and a **c**. When you add **-ing** and **-ed** to **excel**, you double the **l**: **excelling**, **excelled**.

**except** *preposition*

**Except** is the usual preposition to use when you mean 'but not': *Everyone was there except Steve.* You can also use **except for**, especially at the start of a sentence: *Except for Steve, everyone was there.* **With the exception of** is a formal alternative: *Everyone was there, with the exception of Steve.* **Excepting** is mainly used with **not** in front, to mean 'including': *Everyone was there, not excepting Steve* (= Steve was there). This too is fairly formal.

To find out more about **except**, look at the entry for ACCEPT.



**exceptional** *adjective* and
**exceptionable** *adjective*

**Exceptional** means 'different from (and better than) most others': *She's a swimmer of exceptional talent.* Don't get it mixed up with **exceptionable**, which is a formal word meaning 'that people could reasonably object to'. It's usually used in the negative form **unexceptionable**, meaning 'satisfactory': *She's not an outstanding student, but her grades are unexceptionable.*

**exchangeable** *adjective*

Something that's **exchangeable** can be exchanged for something else.

❶ Remember the spelling, with the **e** between the **g** and the **a**.

**exclamation mark**

An exclamation mark is a vertical line with a dot under it (!). It's used at the end of sentences that express very strong feelings of anger (*Shut up, you idiot!*), surprise (*What an amazing sight!*) or dismay (*Oh no!*). It's also used after strong commands (*Put that down!*) and warnings (*Look out!*), and after interjections (*Oi!*), and you can use it to emphasize an amusing or striking remark (*My knickers fell down!*).

You use an exclamation mark rather than a question mark after exclamations in the form of a question (*Haven't you grown!*).

e

⚠ In serious writing, you shouldn't use several exclamation marks together (*Damn!!!*) or a combination of exclamation mark and question mark (*He said what?!*).

## executioner *noun* and executor *noun*

An **executioner** is someone who executes criminals, for example by chopping their heads off.

An **executor** is someone who makes sure that the instructions in a dead person's will are properly carried out.

## exercise *noun, verb* and exorcise *verb*

**Exercise** is physical activity that you do in order to keep fit, such as walking, jogging or lifting weights. And an **exercise** is a task you do in order to improve your skill: *Have you done this week's French exercise yet?* You can also use **exercise** as a verb: *She exercises in the gym every other evening.*

**Exorcise** means 'to drive an evil spirit out of a person or place by performing a religious ceremony'.

## exhausting *adjective* and exhaustive *adjective*

Something that's **exhausting** makes you really tired: *an exhausting five-mile run.*

Something, such as a list, that's **exhaustive** is complete, with absolutely nothing left out: *We were treated to an exhaustive description of the football match.*

**exhibit** *noun, verb* and **exhibition** *noun*

An **exhibit** is something that's **exhibited** – that's to say, 'put on show to the public': *Every exhibit in the museum is carefully catalogued.* Americans also use **exhibit** to mean 'a display of paintings, sculpture, etc. to the public'. British people only use **exhibition** with this meaning: *The new exhibition will open at the National Gallery next week.*



**exorcise** see EXERCISE

**expel** *verb*

**Expel** means 'to force to leave'. If you're expelled from school, you're thrown out of it.

❶ When you add **-ing** and **-ed** to **expel**, you double the **l**: **expelling, expelled**.

**explicit** see IMPLICIT

**extol** *verb*

**Extol** is a very formal word for 'to praise'. People sometimes use it ironically in an informal context: *She's always extolling the virtues of some new diet or another.*

❶ When you add **-ing** and **-ed** to **extol**, you double the **l**: **extolling, extolled**.

**eyrie** *noun*

An **eyrie** is an eagle's nest. It's also a high place where someone lives or works. 🔊 It's pronounced /**eer**-i/, rhyming with *weary*, or /**ire**-i/, rhyming with *wiry*.

# Ff

**facility** *noun* and **faculty** *noun*

**Facilities** are the equipment, buildings and other things you need for doing something: *The sports facilities at this school are excellent – they even have their own squash courts.*

**Facility** is also a formal word for the ability to do something difficult skilfully and effortlessly: *At the age of eight, her facility as a violinist astonished everyone.* ⚠ Don't get it mixed up with **faculty**, another rather formal word, which means simply 'the ability to do a particular thing': *He has a faculty for expressing himself clearly.*

Your **faculties** are also your mental and physical abilities. In a British university, a **faculty** is a group of departments covering a particular area of knowledge. And in America, the **faculty** are the teachers in a university or college.

**faint** *adjective, verb, noun* and **feint** *adjective, noun*

The adjective **faint** has several meanings, including 'giddy', 'too dim to see or hear properly' and (of paper) 'with barely visible lines to help you write straight'. In this last meaning, it's usually spelt **feint** on the cover of writing pads.

**Faint** is also a verb, meaning 'to become unconscious', and a noun, meaning 'a sudden loss of consciousness'. **Feint** can also be a noun, meaning 'a pretended attack'.

**fair** *adjective, adverb* and **fairly** *adverb*

**Fair** is the adjective (*a fair tackle, fair hair, a fair number*) and **fairly** is the adverb that usually goes with it (*Was the election conducted fairly?*). But with the verbs *to* *fight* and *to play*, you can use **fair** as an adverb: *He doesn't fight fair.*

**Fairly** also means 'to some extent, quite': *It was fairly easy.*

**farther, farthest** *adjective, adverb* and
**further, furthest** *adjective, adverb*

When you're talking about the actual distance of something, in metres, miles, etc., you can use either **farther/farthest** or **further/furthest**, although **further/furthest** is commoner: *The shop you want is about 500 metres farther/further down the road. We had a competition to see who could throw an egg the farthest/furthest.*

But when you're talking about time, or abstract distance, **further/furthest** is the one to use: *These gates are closed until further notice. I shall take this matter further with the head teacher.* And only **further** can be used as an adjective meaning 'additional': *If you need any further help, let me know.*

**fascination** *noun*

If something has a **fascination** for you, you're fascinated by it – that is, you're extremely interested in it: *Old steam engines have a fascination for him.* Don't get it round the wrong way – it's not standard English to say ⚠ *He has a fascination for old steam engines.*

❶ Remember the spelling, with an **sc**.

**favour, favor** *noun, verb*

A **favour** is something kind or helpful that someone does for you. **Favour** is also a verb, meaning 'to give your support to one person or thing in preference to another'. **Favour** is the British spelling, **favor** the American.

**feasible** *adjective*

**Feasible** is a rather formal word meaning 'that can be done': *Do you think it'd be feasible to finish the project within three months?* (= could it be finished in that time?).

⚠ It's sometimes used to mean simply 'likely' or 'possible' (as in *'Do you think it will rain today?' 'It's feasible.'*), but this hasn't become generally accepted in standard English, so it's best to avoid it in writing.

❗ Remember the spelling: -**ible** not -**able**.

**February** *noun*

The traditional 'correct' pronunciation is 🔊 /**feb**-roo-ə-ri/, but not many people actually say this in ordinary speech. The usual pronunciations are /**feb**-rə-ri/ and /**feb**-yə-ri/, and they're perfectly acceptable in standard English.

**fed up** *adjective*

**Fed up** is an informal expression meaning 'discontented' or 'bored'. The standard preposition used with it is ✔ **with**: *I'm fed up with this music – can't we have something different.* **With** is sometimes replaced with ⚠ **of** (probably copied from ⚠ **bored of**), but this is not acceptable in standard English, and shouldn't be used in written work.

**feint** see FAINT

**feminine forms**

English has special words for referring to women with particular roles or jobs. For instance, an *actress* is a woman who acts, and a *policewoman* is a woman who is a member of the police force.

It's becoming less common to use these words, because it's widely felt that using a separate word for women suggests that they are not the equivalent of men in the same roles or jobs. Most women who belong to the police force would probably rather be called a *police officer*, which doesn't mention what sex they are, and many women who act prefer to be called an *actor* rather than an *actress*.



There isn't an equal amount of objection to all these words for women. For example, probably not many female cabin staff would mind being called a *stewardess*, but at the other extreme, a female poet would probably be insulted if you called her a *poetess*. You need to check each of these words separately.

To find out about the use of *lady* and *woman* in front of other nouns (as in *lady doctor*), look at the entry for LADY.

To find out more about using pronouns for males and females, look at the entry for SEXIST LANGUAGE.

**few** *adjective, pronoun* and **less** *adjective, pronoun*

**Few** means 'not many': *Few people would disagree with that.*

The main problem with it comes when you use the **-er** form, **fewer**, meaning 'not so many'. Traditionally, this is the right adjective to use with plural nouns: *I've been told to eat fewer potatoes.* But it's very common in modern English to use **less** instead: ⚠ *I've been told to eat less potatoes.*

This use of **less** isn't yet generally accepted as part of standard English, so it's best to avoid it in writing, and stick to **fewer**. Keep **less** for use with singular nouns, when it means 'not so much': ✔ *I've been told to eat less bread.*

The same goes for the **-est** form, **fewest**: ✔ *Smith holds the record for the fewest goals conceded in a season.*

Keep **fewest** for the meaning 'smallest number of', and use **least** to mean 'smallest amount of': ✔ *He has the least conceit of anyone I know.*

## fibre, fiber *noun*

A **fibre** is a thread of plant or animal tissue, or one of the threads in a piece of cloth.

**Fibre** is the British spelling, **fiber** the American.

## fictional *adjective* and fictitious *adjective*

A **fictional** character or event is one that occurs in a story but doesn't really exist: *Hercule Poirot, the fictional detective.*

Something that's **fictitious** is invented, possibly with the intention of deceiving people, rather than being real: *He'd given the police a fictitious name.*

## fidget *verb*

To **fidget** is to move around in a nervous, twitchy way.

❗ When you add -**ing** and -**ed** to **fidget**, you don't double the **t**: **fidgeting**, **fidgeted**.

## first *adverb* and firstly *adverb*

There used to be a big argument over whether it was all right to use **firstly**, **secondly**, etc. when giving lists of things (*My favourite films of all time are, firstly,* Close Encounters of the Third Kind, *secondly,* Jaws, *thirdly ...*), or whether you should use **first**, **second**, etc. Some people even thought you should start with **first** and then go on to **secondly**, **thirdly**, etc.

In present-day English all these are regarded as perfectly standard usage, so you can choose whichever you prefer. It's best, though, to avoid starting with **firstly** and then going on to **second**, **third**, etc., as this sounds rather odd.

**first name** see CHRISTIAN NAME

**fit** *verb*

If something **fits**, it's the right size or shape to go somewhere, and if you **fit** something you fix it in place.

In British English, the past tense and past participle are always **fitted**, but American English also uses **fit** to mean 'was the right size': *His new jacket fit him badly, so he took it to be altered.*

❶ When you add -**ing** and -**ed** to **fit**, you double the **t**: **fitting, fitted**.

**flair** *noun* and **flare** *noun, verb*

**Flair** is a particular talent or ability: *She has a flair for languages* (= She's good at learning foreign languages). A **flare** is a bright light used as a signal, and also a gradual widening, such as is found in a skirt or at the bottom of trouser legs: *I didn't think flares would ever come back.* And **flare** is also used as a verb: *Fighting has flared up* (= got much more intense or fierce) *again.*

**flammable** see INFLAMMABLE

**flannel** *verb*

If you **flannel** someone, you try to deceive them with flattery.

❶ When you add -**ing** and -**ed** to **flannel**, you double the **l** in British English (**flannelling, flannelled**) but not in American English (**flanneling, flanneled**).

**flare** see FLAIR

f

**flaunt** *verb* and **flout** *verb*

If you **flaunt** something, you show it off proudly in a way that annoys people: *Don't you think wearing diamonds with jeans is rather flaunting your wealth?*

If you **flout** a rule, an instruction, etc., you deliberately and openly disobey it: *He enjoyed flouting convention by wearing a baseball cap with his dark suit.*

Remember, don't confuse **flaunting** 'showing off' with **flouting** 'disobeying'.

**flautist, flutist** *noun*

Both words mean 'someone who plays the flute'. British people use **flautist**, Americans **flutist**.

**flavour, flavor** *noun*

The **flavour** of something is its taste. British people use the spelling **flavour**, Americans **flavor**.

**fledgling, fledgeling** *noun*

A **fledgling** is a young bird. **Fledgling** is the main spelling, but in British English you can also use **fledgeling**.

**flee** *verb*, **fly** *verb, noun* and **flow** *verb*

To **flee** is to run away from a place, usually to escape from danger: *The inhabitants of the city were forced to flee from the advancing army.*

**Fly** can be used with this meaning too, but it's a rather literary usage. It's best to keep **fly** to its more usual meaning, 'to move through the air'.

The past tense and past participle of **flee** is **fled**: *They fled in panic when they heard the gunfire.* The past tense of **fly** is **flew** and its past participle is **flown**. (Don't confuse this with the verb **to flow**, meaning 'to move in a stream'. Its past form is **flowed**: *Blood flowed from his wound.*)

The sort of insect that flies is a **fly**. The sort of insect that jumps is a ✔ **flea** (not a ⚠ *flee*).

**floor** *noun*

When British people talk about the *first floor* of a building, they mean the level at the top of the first flight of stairs. But to Americans, the *first floor* is the level you walk into off the street (what British people call the *ground floor*), and the level at the top of the first flight of stairs is the *second floor*. The same difference applies all the way up a building – the British *tenth floor*, for instance, is the American *eleventh floor*.

**flounder** *verb* and **founder** *verb*

If you're **floundering**, you're struggling awkwardly: *The swimmer was floundering, clearly out of his depth.*

A ship that **founders** has filled with water and is sinking.

Those are the literal meanings of the two words. But they can also be used metaphorically. If you say that someone is **floundering** through a speech, you mean that they're giving a speech very awkwardly or badly. And if you say that a company or a plan has **foundered**, you mean that it's collapsed or failed.

**flutist** see FLAUTIST

**fly** see FLEE

**focus** *noun, verb*

**Focus** is a word that refers to the point where beams of light meet. Its usual plural is **focuses**, but in scientific writing **foci** 🔊 /**foh**-sy/ is used too.

To **focus** a camera, a telescope, etc. is to adjust it so that it gives a sharp picture.

❶ When you add **-ing** and **-ed** to **focus** you can either use a single **s** (**focusing, focused**) or double it to **ss** (**focussing, focussed**).

## foetus, fetus *noun*

A **foetus** 🔊 /**fee**-təs/ is an unborn baby, still in its mother's womb.

f

**Foetus** is the standard spelling in British English, but **fetus** is becoming increasingly common, and can be used instead. **Fetus** is the standard American spelling.

## foot *noun*

The usual plural of **foot** is **feet** (*Hasn't he got big feet!*). But when **foot** is used as a measurement word, its plural can be **feet** or **foot**. When it follows a number and a hyphen and it comes in front of a noun, use **foot**: *an eight-foot giant*. When it comes in front of a number standing for inches, use **foot**: *five foot six*. But when the word inches appears, use **feet**: *five feet six inches*. Otherwise you can use either **feet** or **foot**: *That tree must be about fifty feet/foot high*.

## forbid *verb*

To **forbid** something is to say that it mustn't be done. The past tense of **forbid** is **forbade** 🔊 /fə-**bad** or fə-**bayd**/ or **forbad** 🔊 /fə-**bad**/. You can use either.

The present participle is **forbidding** and the past participle is **forbidden**.

You **forbid** someone **to** do something: ✔ *I forbid you to leave*. It's not acceptable in standard English to say ⚠ *forbid someone from* doing something.

## forceps *noun*

A **forceps** is a tool like tweezers, used by doctors for holding things. Remember that it's a singular noun, so you use **a** in front of it and a singular verb after it.

The plural of **forceps** is **forceps**: *two forceps*.

## forecast *verb*

To **forecast** something is to say in advance that it's going to happen.

The usual past tense and past participle is **forecast** (*Everyone had forecast a victory, but in fact we lost*), but you can also use **forecasted**.

## forever, for ever *adverb*

It's traditional in standard British English to make a difference between **for ever**, meaning 'for all future time' (*I wish I could stay here for ever*), and **forever**, meaning 'continually' (*She's forever complaining*). But it's now quite common, and perfectly acceptable, to use **forever** for both, as American English does.

## forgivable *adjective*

Something that's **forgivable** can be forgiven: *His reluctance was forgivable in the circumstances.*

❗ Remember the spelling – no **e** after the **v**.

## forgo, forego *verb*

If you **forgo** something, you willingly go without it: *They were asked if they'd be prepared to forgo a wage rise for one year*. **Forgo** is the main spelling, but you can also use **forego**.

There used to be another verb **forego** 'to go in front', but this now survives only in the adjective **foregoing**, meaning 'previously mentioned', and in the expression **foregone conclusion**, meaning 'a predictable result'.

f

**former** *adjective, pronoun* and
**latter** *adjective, pronoun*

**Former** refers to the first two things you've previously mentioned: *Of hares and rabbits, the former* (= hares) *have the longer ears.*

**Latter** refers to the second of two things you've previously mentioned: *We tried the apple crumble and the tiramisu, the latter* (= tiramisu) *being an Italian pudding made with cream and sponge cake.*

When you've mentioned more than two things, use **first** for the first and **last** for the last: *Of coffee, tea and cocoa, I prefer the first* (= coffee).

All these usages are very formal. They're suitable for serious writing, but not for more informal writing or speech. There, it's better to repeat the noun you're referring to: *Of coffee, tea and cocoa, I prefer coffee.*

**formidable** *adjective*

Something that's **formidable** is very difficult to overcome: *We face some formidable problems.*

The traditional standard pronunciation of the word is 🔊 /**for**-mi-də-bəl/, but /fə-**mid**-ə-bəl/ is also very common, and most people find it perfectly acceptable.

**fortuitous** *adjective* and **fortunate** *adjective*

Something that's **fortuitous** happens by accident: *It was quite fortuitous that I met him yesterday – we hadn't planned it at all.*

Don't confuse it with **fortunate**, which means 'lucky': *It was quite fortunate that I met him yesterday, because I'd been wanting to speak to him for some time.*

**Fortuitous** is a very formal word, so it's best to avoid it in ordinary speech and writing, especially as people get it confused with **fortunate**. Use some other way of expressing what you mean, such as *by chance.*

**forty** *noun, adjective*

❶ **Forty** is the way you spell 40. Don't forget, no **u** – just **forty**.

**forward** *adjective, adverb* and **forwards** *adverb*

In American English you only use **forward** as an adverb. But in British English there's a choice – you can use either **forward** or **forwards**.

**Forwards** can be used when you're talking about movement ahead or to the front: *She took off the handbrake and the car began to roll forwards down the hill.* You can use **forward** in this way too.

For other meanings, though, you can only use **forward** – for example, 'ahead in time' (*We've moved the meeting forward to next week*) and 'so as to make progress' (*We haven't got much further forward with our project*).

The adjective is always **forward**: *He made a clear forward movement with his right foot.*

**founder** see FLOUNDER

**free** *adjective, adverb* and **freely** *adverb*

The adverb **free** means 'without having to pay' (*Anyone arriving after 4 p.m. was let in free*) and 'without being restricted' (*She lets her children run free and do anything they like*).

Otherwise **free** is only an adjective, and you have to use **freely** as the adverb (*I freely admit I was wrong. She spends her money very freely*).

**friend** *noun*

Someone you like and who likes you (and isn't a member of your family) you'd probably call your **friend**.
❶ Remember the spelling: -**ie**-, not -**ei**-.

**frolic** *verb*

Someone who **frolics** plays and jumps about happily.
❶ When you add -**ing** and -**ed** to **frolic**, you put a **k** after the **c**: **frolicking**, **frolicked**.

**fuel** *verb*

If you **fuel** something, such as an argument, you keep it going, or even make it worse: *His outspoken comments fuelled the controversy.*
❶ When you add -**ing** and -**ed** to **fuel**, you double the **l** in British English (**fuelling**, **fuelled**) but not in American English (**fueling**, **fueled**).

**-ful** *suffix*

You put -**ful** on the end of nouns to give the idea of 'as much as a container will hold'. For instance, a *bucketful* of sand is as much sand as a bucket will hold, and a *spoonful* of salt is as much salt as a spoon will hold.

The usual way of making these words plural is by putting an **s** on the end: *two spoonfuls of salt.* But you can also put the **s** in the middle, before the **f**: *two spoonsful of salt.*

**fulfil, fulfill** *verb*

When you **fulfil** a promise, you do what you promised to do. **Fulfil** is the British spelling, **fulfill** the American.
❶ When you add -**ing** and -**ed** to **fulfil**, you double the **l**: **fulfilling**, **fulfilled**.

**full stop**

A full stop (.) marks the end of a sentence which is an ordinary statement, rather than a question or an exclamation. A new sentence which comes after it has to start with a capital letter.

Full stops can also be used at the end of abbreviations. For example, *p.* is an abbreviation of page, and *perh.* is an abbreviation of perhaps. However, it's becoming less common to use full stops like this. In particular, they're not used in acronyms (words made from the first letters of other words, like *NATO*), and they're not usually used in abbreviations consisting of the first letters of several words (like *BBC* and *TUC*). Many British people don't now use full stops in titles (like *Mr* and *Dr*). On the other hand it's usual to use a full stop with the abbreviations *etc.*, *e.g.* and *i.e.*

You also use full stops in decimal numbers (*17.25*), in amounts of money (*£2.55*) and, in Britain, between hours and minutes (*3.15 p.m.*) (Americans use a colon – *3:15 p.m.*).

In American English, the full stop is often called a period.

## funnel *verb*

When things **funnel** into place, they come in from a wide area through a narrow space: *Crowds funnelled into the little football ground.*

❶ When you add -**ing** and -**ed** to **funnel**, you double the **l** in British English (**funnelling**, **funnelled**) but not in American English (**funneling**, **funneled**).

## further, furthest see FARTHER

## fused participle

Should you say *She was annoyed at my leaving* or *She was annoyed at me leaving*? Traditionally, it's standard to use a possessive form (here, *my*) in sentences like this, but it's becoming increasingly common to use a non-possessive form (here, *me*), and it's perfectly acceptable to do so.

In the case of pronouns, use either the possessive or the non-possessive, but remember that the possessive can sound rather stiff and formal. In the case of names and other nouns, the possessive (*She was annoyed at John's leaving*) tends to sound uncomfortably formal, and it's better to use the non-possessive (*She was annoyed at John leaving*).

# Gg

**gallop** *verb*

A horse that's **galloping** is going at its fastest possible pace.

❶ When you add -**ing** and -**ed** to **gallop**, you *don't* double the **p**: **galloping**, **galloped**.

**gambol** *verb* and **gamble** *verb*

When lambs **gambol**, they skip and jump about playfully.

Don't confuse **gambol** with **gamble**, which means 'to bet'.

❶ When you add -**ing** and -**ed** to **gambol**, you double the **l** in British English (**gambolling**, **gambolled**) but not in American English (**gamboling**, **gamboled**).

**gaol** see JAIL

**garage** *noun*

A **garage** is a building where you keep a car, or where you take a car to be repaired

🔊 There are lots of different ways of pronouncing the word. The three commonest in Britain are /**ga**-rahzh/, /**ga**-rahj/ and /**ga**-rij/. All of them are perfectly acceptable in standard English. The main American pronunciation is /gə-**rahzh**/.

**gas** *noun, verb*

If you **gas** someone, you kill them by making them breathe poisonous gas.

❶ When you add -**ing** and -**ed** to **gas**, you double the **s**: **gassing, gassed**. (The plural of the noun **gas**, on the other hand, is **gases**, with a single **s**.)

## gauge *noun, verb*

A **gauge** 🔊 /gayj/ is an instrument for measuring things – for example, a rain gauge measures how much rain has fallen. You can also use **gauge** as a verb: *Try to gauge her reaction* (= to judge how she reacts).



⚠ Don't get **gauge** mixed up with **gouge** 🔊 /gowj/, which means 'to scoop out forcefully'.

❶ Remember the spelling: -**au**-, not -**ua**-.

## get *verb*

**Get** is a very common verb. It does all sorts of useful jobs. It means 'to obtain': *Get me some milk when you go to the shops.* It means 'to become': *She's getting old.* It means 'to come or arrive': *We hope to get home by midnight.* It means 'to cause to go': *I can't get this key into the lock.* It's used to make verbs passive: *Keep your head down or you might get hit.*

**Get** has a rather bad reputation, because some writers on grammar in the past have said that it's not good English. But it's perfectly standard in spoken English, and there's no reason at all to avoid it there. In formal written English it's best not to use **get** to make the passive, but the other uses of **get** are completely acceptable.

The present participle of **get** is **getting**. In British English its past tense and past participle is **got**. American English uses **got** too, but it also has another past participle, **gotten**, which it uses as an alternative to **got**: *We should have gotten his approval before we went ahead.* **Have got** for 'have' or 'possess' (as in *I've got two brothers*) and **have got to** for 'must' are also disapproved of by some people, but again they're a perfectly normal usage, and there's no good reason to avoid them unless you're trying to sound very formal.

In American English, **have got** for 'have' is rare. An American would usually say *I have*, or in the negative *I don't have*, and in questions *Do you have?* This use of *do* with *have* is becoming quite common in British English.

**gild** see GUILD

**gipsy** see GYPSY

**glamour, glamor** *noun*

**Glamour** is an exciting or fascinating quality that someone or something has, usually because they're beautiful or attractive.

❶ **Glamour** is the only spelling in British English and the main spelling in American English, but Americans also use **glamor**. The adjective **glamorous** is spelt without a **u** before the **r** in both British and American English.

**good** *adjective* and **well** *adjective, adverb*

In standard English, **good** is only an adjective: *She's a good swimmer*. The adverb that goes with it is **well**: *She swims well*.

**Well** can be an adjective too, but only with the meanings 'healthy' (*You don't look well*) and 'satisfactory' (*All is well*).

**gorilla** *noun* and **guerrilla** *noun*

A **gorilla** is a large African ape. A **guerrilla** is a soldier who's not part of a regular army, but attacks the enemy as part of a small group.

The two words are normally pronounced in the same way – /gə-**ril**-ə/ – but some people pronounce **guerrilla** /ge-**ril**-ə/, to make it clear that they're not saying **gorilla**.
**Guerrilla** can also be spelt **guerilla**, with one **r**.

## gossip *verb*

Someone who **gossips** talks about other people's private affairs and spreads rumours.
When you add -**ing** and -**ed** to **gossip**, you *don't* double the **p**: **gossiping, gossiped**.

g

## graceful *adjective* and gracious *adjective*

Someone who's **graceful** is very smooth and elegant in movement or shape: *a graceful ballet dancer*.

Someone who's **gracious** is very polite and kind, especially to inferiors, or behaves honourably: *He was gracious enough to admit that he'd been wrong. Gracious living* is the sort of elegant lifestyle that rich people have.

## graffiti *noun*

**Graffiti** are words, designs, etc. painted or sprayed on walls, the sides of trains and other public places.

In standard English **graffiti** is a plural noun, so it needs a plural verb after it: *The graffiti aren't going to be easy to clean off.*
Don't forget the spelling – two **f**s and one **t**.

## grammar *noun*

The **grammar** of a language is the way in which its words are put together to form meaningful clauses and sentences.
Remember the spelling – **-ar** at the end, not *-er*, and two **m**s.

**grey, gray** *adjective*

**Grey** is the colour of ashes and dark clouds. In British English the word's spelt **grey**. In American English it's usually spelt **gray**, though **grey** is also used.

**grief** *noun*

**Grief** is a feeling of great sadness: *They were overcome with grief at the death of their young daughter.*

❶ Remember the spelling: **-ie-**, not **-ei-**. The same applies to the verb **grieve**, meaning 'to be or make someone very sad'; to the noun **grievance**, meaning 'something you want to complain about'; and to the adjective **grievous** meaning 'very severe or bad': *a grievous error*. And remember, too, that it's not ⚠ *grievious* /**gree**-vi-əs/ but ✔ /**grievous** 🔊 /**gree**-vəs/.

**grill** *noun, verb* and **grille** *noun*

A **grill** is a heated piece of metal that's used for cooking food. You can also use **grill** as a verb: *It's healthier to grill meat than to fry it.* It's mainly a British usage – Americans use the verb *to broil* instead.

A **grill** can also be a framework of bars used as a screen, but the more usual spelling for this is **grille**.

**guerrilla** see GORILLA

**guild** *noun* and **gild** *noun, verb*

A **guild** is a sort of association or club for people of a similar type or occupation. The word's sometimes spelt **gild**, but **guild** is by far the main spelling.

To **gild** something is to cover it with a thin layer of gold.

## gypsy, gipsy *noun*

**Gypsies** are a travelling people who don't live in one place for very long. **Gypsy** is the main spelling, but **gipsy** is also widely used, especially in British English.

g

# Hh

**habitual** *adjective*
If something that you do is **habitual**, you behave that way all the time: *He apologized with his habitual politeness.*

In standard English you put **a** before it, not **an**: *a habitual criminal.*

**haemorrhage, hemorrhage** *noun*

**Haemorrhage** is the word doctors use for 'bleeding'.

**Haemorrhage** is the British spelling, **hemorrhage** the American.

❶ Remember the two **rs** and the **h**.

**half** *adjective, noun*

You can say either *half the people* or *half of the people.* Both are acceptable in standard English.

Whether you use a singular verb or a plural verb afterwards depends on the noun. If it's plural, use a plural verb: *Half the people want to go home.* But if it's singular, use a singular verb: *Half of the room was in darkness.*

You can say either *a mile and a half, a kilo and a half, a billion and a half,* etc. or *one and a half miles, one and a half kilos, one and a half million,* etc. Both are acceptable. *Half a dozen* and *a half dozen* are both acceptable too. ⚠ Don't get the two types mixed up, though. *A half a dozen* isn't standard English.

Phrases containing measurements like *one and a half miles* and *one and a half kilos* take a singular verb, even though the noun is plural: *One and a half miles isn't a very long way to run.*

**hallo** see HELLO

**handicap** *verb*

Something that **handicaps** you makes it more difficult for you to do what you're trying to do: *The England team were handicapped by having their goalkeeper sent off in the second half.*

❶ When you add -**ing** and -**ed** to **handicap**, you double the **p**: **handicapping**, **handicapped**.

**hang** *verb*

The usual past tense and past participle of **hang** is **hung**: *She hung her coat on the hook.*

But when **hang** means 'to execute a criminal by hanging him or her from a rope', it's traditional to use **hanged** as the past tense and past participle: *He was hanged for murder.*

**harass** *verb*

To **harass** someone is to keep annoying them or troubling them: *With all these jobs to finish in just a few hours, it's no wonder I'm feeling harassed.*

🔊 The standard British pronunciation of the word is /**ha**-ris/. In American English, the main pronunciation is /hə-**ras**/. This is now very common in British English too, but some people still find it annoying, so it can't yet be counted as part of standard British English.

❶ Remember the spelling: only one **r**.

**harbour, harbor** *noun, verb*

A **harbour** is an area of water where ships dock. **Harbour** can be a verb too, meaning 'to give shelter to': *They suspect she's been harbouring fugitives in her house.*

**Harbour** is the British spelling, **harbor** the American.

**hardly** *adverb*

It's wrong in standard English to use **not** with **hardly**: ✔ *I'd hardly got in when there was a knock on the door* is acceptable, but ⚠ *I hadn't hardly got in when there was a knock at the door* isn't.

**have** *verb*

*If I'd seen it coming, I'd have got out of the way.* In sentences like this, be careful not to put an extra **have** in after the *if I'd*: ⚠ *If I'd have seen it coming, I'd have got out of the way* isn't acceptable in standard English.

Sentences like ⚠ *I'd have loved to have done that* aren't standard English either. Write either ✔ *I'd love to have done that* or *I'd have loved to do that.*

In writing, take care to follow *could*, *might* and *would* with **have**, not *of*. When we speak, *could have*, *might have* and *would have* often sound just as if they might be ⚠ *could of*, *might of* and *would of*, but ✔ *could have*, *might have* and *would have* are the only acceptable written forms in standard English.

To find out about **have got**, see GET.

**heave** *verb*

The usual past tense and past participle of **heave** is **heaved**: *He heaved a brick through the window.*

But there are two special uses of **heave** where its past form is **hove**. Sailors use **heave to** to mean 'to bring a ship to a standstill', and in this usage, the past form is **hove to**: *The aircraft carrier was hove to in the bay.*

And when you say someone or something *hove into sight* or *into view*, you mean that they came into view. Remember, this **hove** is a past form, not the present tense, so don't make a new past form ⚠ *hoved* out of it: *Gary hoved into view around the corner* isn't acceptable in standard English.

h

**height** *noun*

The **height** of something is how high it is. 🔊 **Height** is pronounced /hyt/ in standard English, not ⚠ /hytth/.

❶ Remember the spelling: -**ei**-, not -**ie**-.

**hello, hallo, hullo** *interjection, noun*

Of these three spellings, **hello** is the commonest in British English, and **hallo** is also quite widely used. They're all pronounced the same way: 🔊 /hə-**loh**/.

❶ When **hello** and the others are used as nouns, their plural ends in -**os**.

**help** *verb*

When you put another verb after **help**, you can either put in a **to** or leave it out. Both *She helped (me) to bath the cat* and *She helped (me) bath the cat* are acceptable.

**hereditary** *adjective* and **heredity** *noun*

Something that's **hereditary** is passed down from one generation to the next. A title, such as 'Lord', can be hereditary, and so can brown eyes.

In standard English, you put **a** before **hereditary**, not **an**: *a hereditary peerage.*

Don't get **hereditary** mixed up with the noun **heredity**, which means the way particular bodily or mental characteristics are passed down from one generation to the next.

**heroic** *adjective*

If you do something **heroic**, you're very brave: *How heroic of him to go into that burning building to save a child.*

In standard English, you put **a** before **heroic**, not **an**: *a heroic effort.*

**heroin** *noun* and **heroine** *noun*

**Heroin** is an illegal drug that people take to make them feel good but that they can get addicted to.

A **heroine** is a very brave woman, or the main female character in a book, play, etc. The male form of the word is **hero**.

**historic** *adjective* and **historical** *adjective*

Something that's **historic** is so important or remarkable that it'll be remembered for a long time in history: *Neil Armstrong's historic first step on the Moon.*

**Historical** means 'connected with history, as a subject' (*historical research*), or 'having really existed in the past' (*Is Robin Hood a historical character or just a legend?*), or 'dealing with things that happened in the past' (*I like historical novels*).

In standard English, you put **a** before **historic** and **historical**, not **an**: *a historic victory.*

**hoard** *noun, verb* and **horde** *noun*

A **hoard** is a large store of something which you keep for future use: *Deep beneath the mountain was the dragon's hoard of gold.* You can also use **hoard** as a verb: *He'd been hoarding away tins of soup in case there was a food shortage.*

A **horde** is an overlarge group of people: *Hordes of people crowd on to the beach each morning.*

**holey** *adjective*, **holy** *adjective* and **wholly** *adverb*

Something that's **holey** is full of holes: *You're not going to wear those holey old socks, are you?*

Something that's **holy** is connected with a religion: *the Holy Bible.*

**Wholly** means 'completely': *I wasn't wholly convinced.* 🔊 In careful speech it's pronounced /**hole**-li/, but in ordinary conversation people often say /**hoh**-li/ (the same as **holey** and **holy**), and this is perfectly acceptable.

## home in *verb*

The verb **home in** means 'to approach closer and closer to a target'. It's usually used with **on**: *The missile homed in on the enemy bomber.* It can also be used metaphorically: *Critics often homed in on her weight.*



*Home* sounds quite like *hone*, which means 'to sharpen a blade', and *hone* is sometimes used instead of *home*, especially in American English: ⚠ *Right from page 1 he hones in on the main problems.* This is not considered acceptable in standard English, though, and you should avoid it in written work.

## honorary *adjective* and honourable *adjective*

If your job or position is **honorary**, you don't get paid for it: *the honorary secretary of the golf club.* If you have an **honorary** degree, you were given it as an honour, not because you passed an exam.

Someone who's **honourable** behaves in a way that's honest and decent. **Honourable** is the British spelling, but in American English the word is spelt **honorable**.

## honour, honor *noun, verb*

**Honour** is the respect in which you're held by other people, or keeping to the very highest standards of behaviour. It's also an award given to someone for their achievements. **Honour** can be a verb too: *He's going to Buckingham Palace today to be honoured by the queen* (= she's giving him an award, such as a knighthood).

**Honour** is the British spelling, **honor** the American.

**hopefully** *adverb*

**Hopefully** can mean 'in a hopeful way': *When he smelt freshly baked bread, he poked his head round the door hopefully.*

It can also mean 'I hope that': *Hopefully we won't have to wait so long next time.* This is a perfectly reasonable thing for it to mean, but it's a usage that annoys some people. Many other English adverbs behave like this, so there's no logical reason not to use it, but as not everyone likes it, it's best to avoid it in serious writing.

Just occasionally it may not be clear which meaning of **hopefully** you intend. For instance, does *We'll arrive hopefully on Tuesday* mean that we'll arrive full of hope, or that I hope we'll arrive then? In cases like this, it's best to rewrite the sentence another way.

To find out more, look at the entry for SENTENCE ADVERBS.

**horde** see HOARD

**hotel** *noun*

In standard English, you put **a** before **hotel**, not **an**.

**how** *adverb*

The main meaning of **how** is 'in what way': *Can you tell me how this switch works?*

It's also used to mean 'that': *She told me how she'd had to wait ages for a bus.* But this is informal, and it's best to use *that* instead in serious writing.

⚠ **As how** (as in *He said as how he'd be late*) isn't part of standard English. Use *that* instead.

**however** *adverb*

There's a difference between *How ever did you manage it?* and *However you do it, just get it finished quickly.* The first is a question, and the word **ever** gives extra force to the **how**. This sort of **how ever** is spelt as two words. The second is a statement, and **however** means 'in whichever way'. This **however** is spelt as one word.

There's another, more formal, use of **however**, to mean 'in spite of this': *It was snowing hard. However, we decided to start out.* It's very close in meaning to *but*, so it's best not to use **however** and *but* together in the same sentence, like this: ⚠ *It was getting very late, but we decided however that we'd better wait for Richard.* Either use *but* on its own (✔ *but we decided that we'd better wait for Richard*) or use **however** on its own (✔ *However, we decided that we'd better wait for Richard*).

h

## humour, humor *noun, verb*

**Humour** is the quality of being amusing. **Humour** is also a verb, meaning 'to keep a person contented by doing what they want'.

**Humour** is the British spelling, **humor** the American. But ❗ **humorous**, meaning 'funny', and **humorist**, meaning 'a humorous writer or performer', are spelt the same way in British and American English.

## hyphen

A hyphen is a short line (-) which comes between parts of a word.

It has two uses. It joins separate words to make a single word, and it separates the parts of a word when you have to split it at the end of a line.

***The joining hyphen*** A word made of two other words is called a compound word. When you write it you can join the two words together or keep them separate, or you can put a hyphen between them.

There's no fixed set of rules in English that says which of these three ways you should use to write a particular compound word. You need to look each one up in a dictionary.

There are some points to remember about the joining hyphen, though.

When groups of two or more words come before a noun, you should put in a hyphen. For example, there's no hyphen between *big* and *game* in *They were hunting for big game,* but there is in *They were big-game hunters* (the hyphen shows that they were hunters of big game, not big hunters of game).

An exception to this is that you don't put a hyphen after adverbs ending in *-ly*: *a beautifully painted picture.*



When a compound made up of a verb and an adverb is used as a noun or an adjective it can have a hyphen in it: *Our car had a break-down. We sent for a break-down truck.* But when it's used as a verb, it must be kept as two separate words: *Our car broke down.*

Compounds with *year* and *old* have hyphens: *my nine-year-old daughter, a group of twelve-year-olds.*

Expressions for telling the time, like *half past one* and *a quarter to four,* don't have hyphens.

***The separating hyphen*** If there's not room to put the whole of a word at the end of one line, break it into two parts, and put a hyphen on the end of the first part.

Don't split a word with only one syllable: *hal-ves* isn't acceptable. And don't split off a single letter at the beginning of a word (*a-brupt*) or one or two letters at the end of a word (*refug-ee*).

A hyphen is shorter than a DASH, and it goes between parts of a word. A dash goes between parts of a sentence.

## hysterical *adjective*

Someone who's **hysterical** loses control and starts crying, screaming, etc.

In standard English you put **a**, not **an** before **hysterical**: *a hysterical outburst.*

# Ii

**I, me** *pronoun*

**I** and **me** are the words you use to refer to yourself. Before a verb, you use **I**: *I don't eat meat.* In other places you use **me**: *Don't bother me now. Give it to me.* This sounds quite simple, but there are three problem areas.

First, *you and I, Sally and I, my brother and sister and I,* etc. Before a verb, *you and I* and the rest are fine: *You and I would never do anything so stupid.* But a lot of people also use them after prepositions, like *between, for* and *with*, and after verbs: ▲ *Between you and I, I didn't believe him. He gave my brother and sister and I five pounds each.* This isn't acceptable in standard English. You should use *you and me, Sally and me, my brother and sister and me,* etc. after prepositions and verbs: ✔ *Between you and me, I didn't believe him. He gave my brother and sister and me five pounds each.*

Second, *it's me.* If someone says to you 'Who's that?', the natural thing to reply is *It's me.* In fact, the traditionally 'correct' way of saying it is *It's I,* but this now sounds so ridiculously pompous that hardly anyone says it any more. ✔ *It's me,* and the past form *it was me,* are perfectly acceptable in modern standard English.

Third, what do you say when someone asks you 'Who did that?' One possible answer is *I did.* But a more informal way of saying the same thing would be ✔ *Me.* Some people object to this use of **me** and say it's ungrammatical, but it's actually perfectly normal and acceptable in spoken standard English.

**-ible** see -ABLE

**identical** *adjective*

If you say that two things or people are **identical**, you mean that they're the same or exactly alike.

You can also say that one thing or person is **identical to** another, meaning that they're alike or the same: *Look at those glasses – they're practically identical to the ones we've got.*

But if you say that one thing or person is **identical with** another, you can only mean that they're the same: *The symptoms are identical with those of measles.*

**idle** *adjective* and **idol** *noun*

**Idle** is a formal word for 'lazy': *an idle boy.* It can also mean 'unused' (*The machines are lying idle*) and 'having no particular purpose' (*idle curiosity*).

**Idol** is a disapproving word for a statue or picture of a god. It also means 'someone you think is especially wonderful': *Elvis! He's my idol!*

**i.e.** see E.G.

**-ie-** and **-ei-**

❶ It's often difficult to remember whether a particular word's spelt with an **ie** or an **ei**. But there are some simple rules that cover most of the problems.

If the word's pronounced with an /ee/ sound you spell it with an **ie**, unless a **c** comes in front, in which case you spell it with an **ei**:

/ee/ without a **c**: *believe, fiend, grieve, shield, siege, thief*

/ee/ after a **c**: *ceiling, deceit, receive*

There are a few exceptions to this rule. The main ones are *caffeine, codeine, protein* and *seize,* which are pronounced with an /ee/ but spelt with an **ei**.

If the word's pronounced with an /ay/ sound you spell it with an **ei**: *freight, sleigh, veil, weigh.*

If the word's pronounced with an /I/ sound you spell it with an **ei**: *either, height, kaleidoscope.*

There's no rule about how you spell other sounds. You just have to learn each word separately:

/e/ sound: *friend, heifer, leisure*
/i/ sound: *forfeit*
/eer/ sound: *fierce, frontier, weir, weird*
/air/ sound: *heir, their*
/ew/ sound: *lieu, view*



## ilk *noun*

**Ilk** means 'the same type': *His circle of friends consisted of drifters, drug addicts and others of that ilk.*

It's not necessary, therefore, to use words like *same* and *similar* with it: expressions like ⚠ *of the same ilk* aren't generally accepted in standard English.

Some people object to using possessive adjectives with it too, like *his* and *their* – *Jane Smith, Sandra Beckett and others of their ilk.* But this is now widely enough accepted to be regarded as part of standard English.

## illegible see ELIGIBLE

## illicit *adjective* and elicit *verb*

Something that's **illicit** is against the law: *the trade in illicit drugs.*

If you **elicit** a reply, some information, etc., you manage to get someone to give it to you: *My knock at the door elicited no response from inside.*

These are both pronounced 🔊 /i-**liss**-it/, and are formal words, particularly **elicit**.

**illusion** see DELUSION

**immigrant** see EMIGRANT

**imminent** see EMINENT

**imperil** *verb*

If you **imperil** something or someone, you put them in danger: *A moment of carelessness on the part of the pilot could imperil the passengers' lives.*

❶ When you add -**ing** and -**ed** to **imperil**, you double the **l** in British English (**imperilling, imperilled**), but not in American English (**imperiling, imperiled**).



**implicit** *adjective* and **explicit** *adjective*

If something's **implicit** you don't actually say it, but people can tell from what you say that it's what you mean: *Implicit in her comments was a strong criticism of the company's action.*

Something that's **explicit** is said openly, clearly and definitely, without any possibility of doubt: *The report is quite explicit about the need to remove some of the senior members of the staff.*

**imply** *verb* and **infer** *verb*

If you **imply** something you suggest it, even though you don't actually say it: *'I've never seen you buy anyone a drink.' 'Are you implying I'm stingy?'*

If you **infer** something, you work it out from what someone says or does, even though they don't actually say it: *From what he said I inferred that he thought I was stingy.*

❶ When you add -**ing** and -**ed** to **infer**, you double the **r**: **inferring, inferred**.

**impresario** *noun*

An **impresario** is someone who makes the arrangements for concerts, plays, etc. to be put on.

❶ Remember the spelling – only one **s**. The word has nothing to do with 'impressing' people.

**improvise** *verb*

If you **improvise** you do something on the spur of the moment, without preparing it beforehand: *I lost the notes for my speech, and had to improvise.*

❶ The word's always spelt with an ✔ **-ise** in both British and American English – never ⚠ **-ize**.



**incredible** *adjective* and
**incredulous** *adjective*

If something's **incredible**, it's so strange or unlikely that you can't believe it: *Your dog's got five legs? I find that totally incredible.*

If you're **incredulous**, you don't believe what someone says: *When I told her my dog had five legs, she looked incredulous.*

**incur** *verb*

If you **incur** something bad, you bring it on yourself: *Any person dropping litter will incur a fine of £100.* It's a formal word.

❶ When you add **-ing** and **-ed** to **incur**, you double the r: **incurring, incurred**.

**indefinite article** see ARTICLES

**index** *noun*

When **index** means 'an alphabetical list of the things in a book' its plural is **indexes**.

When **index** means 'the number of times a number is multiplied by itself' its plural is **indices** 🔊 /**in**-də-seez/.

When **index** means 'a number showing how an amount has changed from a previous level' (*the cost-of-living index*) or 'a sign by which you can measure something' (*an index of public opinion*) its plural is either **indexes** or **indices.**

**Indian** see RACES AND PEOPLES

**indifferent** *adjective*

The word **indifferent** has nothing to do with being 'not different'.

It means either 'not very good' (*Your spelling's indifferent to say the least, Matthew*) or 'not caring about something or not interested in it' (*They appeared to be indifferent to all the appeals for help they'd received*).

**indirect speech** see INVERTED COMMAS

**infamous** *adjective*

**Infamous** doesn't mean 'not famous'. Quite the opposite, in fact. It means 'very well known indeed, but for something bad': *the infamous 'Yorkshire Ripper'.*

**infer** see IMPLY

**inferior** *adjective*

Someone or something **inferior** is worse, less important, of lower quality, etc. The preposition that goes with **inferior** is **to**: *In speed and range the new European plane is noticeably inferior to its American rival.*

**infinitive** see SPLIT INFINITIVES

**inflammable** *adjective*, **flammable** *adjective* and **non-flammable** *adjective*

There are two adjectives you can use in English when you want to say that something can catch fire: **inflammable** and **flammable**. They mean the same: *an inflammable/flammable substance.*

**Inflammable** is the commoner in ordinary speech and writing. But there is a problem about it. Because it begins with **in-**, it sounds as though it might mean 'not able to catch fire' (in the same way as *inactive* means 'not active' and *insane* means 'mad'). When you're telling people whether something can catch fire or not, it's important to use language that can't be misunderstood, so in official and technical writing it's common to use **flammable**, which has a much clearer meaning.

If you want to say that something can't catch fire, you can use the adjective **non-flammable**.

**inflict** see AFFLICT

**informant** *noun* and **informer** *noun*

An **informant** is someone who tells you something: *My informant tells me that you're looking for a flat to rent.* This is quite a formal word.

An **informer** is someone who tells the police about what a criminal has done or is planning to do.

**ingenious** *adjective* and **ingenuous** *adjective*

An **ingenious** /in-**jee**-nee-əs/ plan, machine, etc. is very cleverly or cunningly made or thought up: *She'd invented an ingenious little gadget for pruning tall* *plants*. The noun that comes from **ingenious** is **ingenuity** 🔊 /in-jə-**new**-ə-ti/: *the ingenuity of his scheme.*

Someone who's **ingenuous** 🔊 /in-**jen**-yoo-əs/ is very simple and natural and doesn't suspect people of being bad. The noun that comes from **ingenuous** is **ingenuousness.**

## initial *verb*

If you **initial** a document you sign your initials on it, to show that you've seen it or you agree to it.

❶ When you add -**ing** and -**ed** to **initial**, you double the **l** in British English (**initialling, initialled**) but not in American English (**initialing, initialed**).

## inoculate *verb*

When you're **inoculated**, you're given an injection to protect you against a disease.

❶ Remember the spelling – only one **n** and one **c**.

## input *verb*

**Input** is a verb used about computers. When you **input** information, you put it into a computer, for example by keyboarding it.

**Input** has two possible past forms. You can use either **input** (*Have you input the data yet?*) or **inputted**. The present participle is **inputting.**

## inquire see ENQUIRE

## inside *preposition*

**Inside** or **inside of**? In writing it's best to use only **inside**: ✔ *What's inside the box? They should be back inside half an hour.* In spoken English it's common and perfectly acceptable to use **inside of** to mean 'before the end of a particular period of time' (*They should be back inside of half an hour*), but it's best to avoid it in writing.

## install, instal *verb*

To **install** something is to fix it into its proper place, ready to be used: *They're coming to install the washing machine today.*

❶ **Install** is the main spelling, but you can also use **instal**. When you add **-ing** and **-ed** to **instal**, you double the **l**: **installing, installed.**

An **instalment** is an episode in a serial story, or a part of a repayment. ❶ **Instalment** is the British English spelling, but in American English it's spelt **installment**.

## instil, instill *verb*

If you **instil** an idea into someone, you gradually put it into their mind.

**Instil** is the British spelling, **instill** the American.

❶ When you add **-ing** and **-ed** to **instil**, you double the **l**: **instilling, instilled.**

## insure see ASSURE

## integral *adjective*

A part that's **integral** is necessary to the whole: *The night attack is an integral part of our plan – without it the whole thing would collapse.*

🔊 The standard pronunciation of **integral** is /**in**-ti-grəl/, with the main stress on the first syllable, but /in-**teg**-rəl/ is an acceptable alternative.

## inter *verb* and intern *verb*

**Inter** 🔊 /in-**ter**/ is a solemn word for 'to bury a dead body'. Don't get it mixed up with **intern**, which means 'to imprison someone for military or political reasons during wartime'.

❶ When you add **-ing** and **-ed** to **inter**, you double the **r**: **interring, interred.**

## interjections

Interjections are exclamations, like *Hey!, Ouch!* and *Hurray!*

## into *preposition* and in to

**Into** means 'so as to go inside': *I dropped it into the bucket.* Don't get it mixed up with **in to**, which means 'inside to' or 'inside in order to': *She saw them going in to breakfast together. We stayed in to watch TV.*

With words that mean 'trying to find out about something', **into** is the standard preposition to use when the word begins with *in-*: *to inquire into something, an inquest into someone's death, an investigation into something.* But with other 'finding out' words like this, it's not standard English to use **into** – so it's better to say, for example, ✔ *a report on the rail crash* and *a survey of recent trends* than ⚠ *a report into the rail crash* and *a survey into recent trends.*

## intransitive see VERBS

## intrusive r

In speech, when an /aw/ sound is followed by a vowel sound, it's quite common to put an /r/ sound in between.

This is perfectly acceptable when there's a letter **r** in the word: *the floor of the cave* /dhə flawr əv dhə kayv/. But some people think that when there isn't a letter **r**, you shouldn't put an /r/ sound – so *law and order* should be /law ənd awdə/, not /lawr ənd awdə/, and *he* *saw a ship* should be /hee saw ə ship/ not /hee sawr ə ship/. When you need to speak carefully, or on a formal occasion, it's best to avoid this /r/ sound.

**intrust** see ENTRUST

**Inuit** see RACES AND PEOPLES

**invaluable** *adjective*

If a valuable piece of advice is worth a lot, you might think an **invaluable** piece of advice is worth nothing. But it's just the opposite. It's so useful to you that you can't say how much it's worth.

**Invaluable** is usually used about things that are extremely useful, such as help, suggestions, gadgets, etc., rather than about things that are worth a lot of money.

**invent** *verb* and **discover** *verb*

You **discover** something that was there before but which nobody knew about: *Someone with a metal detector discovered some Roman coins in a field next to the school.*

You **invent** something that wasn't there before: *The Chinese invented gunpowder.* Someone who invents things is an ✔ **inventor**, not an ⚠ *inventer.*

**inverted commas**

Inverted commas, or quotation marks, as they're also called, are a pair of punctuation marks put round a word, phrase, etc. to show that it's separate in some way from the sentence it's in.

In British English, inverted commas usually consist of a single upside-down comma at the beginning and a single right-way-up comma at the end, both above the line ('*Hello*'). American English uses double commas

(“*Hello*”), and in Britain it’s quite common to use double commas in books for children and in handwriting.

There are three uses for inverted commas:

***For showing what someone has said:*** *‘I’m fed up,’ said Zoe.* This is called **direct speech**, because you show exactly what someone’s words were. If you just describe what someone said, without using their exact words, it’s called **indirect speech** or **reported speech**, and you don’t use inverted commas: *Zoe said she was fed up.*

***For titles*** Titles of short poems, short stories, articles, parts of books, radio and television programmes, etc. are put in inverted commas: *Rudyard Kipling’s ‘If’; ‘The Archers’.*

i

The titles of longer poems, novels, films, plays, etc. are usually shown in italic print or, in handwriting, by underlining: Have you read *The Lord of the Rings*?

***For odd words*** Inverted commas are used for showing that you know the word you’re using doesn’t quite fit into its context – for example, if it’s not really a true description (*With ‘friends’ like that, who needs enemies?*), or if it’s a slang word (*He’s got a really ‘wicked’ stereo system*).

***Inverted commas and other punctuation*** In American English, when there’s a punctuation mark after the word or phrase in inverted commas, it’s usual to put it in front of the closing inverted commas: *“I’m fed up,” said Zoe.* British English does this for direct speech when quoting what someone says in full, but for showing titles and single words, and for quoting small or incomplete chunks of what someone says, it usually puts the closing inverted comma first: *That was Rudyard Kipling’s ‘If’, read by Bruce Ransome.*

Sometimes you may need to use a pair of inverted commas inside another pair. In that case, begin with the sort you usually use (say, the single inverted commas), and change to the other sort for the inside pair. *'With "friends" like that, who needs enemies?' she said.*

## inverted word order

In English, the subject of a sentence usually comes before the verb: *I can speak French.* There are some circumstances, though, where the word order is changed round (inverted) and the verb comes before its subject.

i

***In questions:*** *Can you speak French?*

***After the words 'so', 'nor' and 'neither':*** *She can speak French, and so can I. She can't speak French, and neither can I.*

***After a negative phrase:*** *Never in my life have I seen such a careless piece of work.*

***In saying who the speaker of a sentence was:*** *'I'm tired,' said the old man.* (Only do this with nouns and names. If you do it with pronouns, it sounds like the style of old poems and fairy stories: *'Bring me my sword,' said he.*)

***After words like 'hardly' and 'scarcely':*** *Scarcely had I sat down when the phone rang.* (This is a slightly formal way of putting it. It's more usual to say *I'd scarcely sat down when the phone rang.*)

***In conditional clauses, that express the idea 'if':*** *Had I known it was you, I'd have opened the door.* (This is a formal way of putting it. It's more usual to say *If I'd known it was you, I'd have opened the door.*)

***To put more emphasis on the subject:*** *Out of the chasm rose a thick black column of smoke* draws attention to the column of smoke more dramatically than *A thick black column of smoke rose out of the chasm.*

**invoke** see EVOKE

**irregardless** *adverb*

▲ **Irregardless of** is not acceptable in standard English. In writing you can use instead *irrespective of, regardless of* or *without regard to*, as in *Anyone can join, irrespective of age.* All three are quite formal expressions, and in ordinary speech and informal writing it would be more natural to say *Anyone can join, no matter what age they are.*

i

**is, is**

Sometimes when we end a clause with **is**, we begin the next clause by repeating **is**: ▲ *The trouble is, is that we haven't got enough plates.* The same can happen with the past tense **was**.

This is all right in casual speech, but it's not part of standard English, so in careful speech and writing, don't repeat the **is**.

**its** *adjective* and **it's**

**Its** means 'of it, belonging to it': *The dog had hurt its foot. Venice is famous for its canals.*

Don't get it mixed up with **it's**, which is the standard way of writing our usual pronunciation of **it is** and **it has**, with **it** and **is** or **has** run together as /its/: *It's hot today. It's got very cold suddenly.* In formal writing, it's best to use **it is** and **it has**.

**-ize, -ise** *suffix*

You put **-ize** on to the end of adjectives and nouns to make verbs. For example, if you *modernize* something, you make it more *modern*, and if a bone *fossilizes*, it turns into a *fossil*.

It's easy to make new verbs like this. For example, *hospitalize*, meaning 'to take into hospital', and *comprehensivize*, meaning 'to turn into a comprehensive school', were both created in the 20th century.

Some people don't like these new **-ize** verbs, but they're perfectly correctly formed, and quite acceptable in standard English. It's best not to use too many in a short space, though.

**-ize** is the only way the suffix is spelt in American English, and it's common spelling in British English too. British English also commonly uses the spelling **-ise**. You can use either, but once you've chosen the one you want, it's best to stick to it, and not keep changing from one to the other.

There are just a few verbs that only end in **-ise**. You can never spell them **-ize**, even in American English. It's best to learn them by heart. The main ones are:

| | | |
|---|---|---|
| advertise | despise | revise |
| advise | devise | supervise |
| apprise | disguise | surmise |
| chastise | excise | surprise |
| circumcise | exercise | televise |
| comprise | improvise | |
| compromise | incise | |

See also ANALYSE.

# Jj

## **jail, gaol** *noun, verb*

In American English, **jail** is the only spelling that's used. In British English you can also use the spelling **gaol**, but it's becoming rare, and **jail** is now the main British spelling. **Gaol** is pronounced in exactly the same way as **jail**. Don't confuse it with *goal*, which is what you score in football.

Someone who's in charge of the prisoners in a **jail** is a **jailer**. You can also spell the word **gaoler** or **jailor**, but not *gaolor*.

**Jew** see RACES AND PEOPLES

## **jewellery, jewelry** *noun*

**Jewellery** is a collective word for jewels that you wear. **Jewellery** is the British spelling, **jewelry** the American.

British English uses two **l**s for the adjective **jewelled** 'covered with jewels' and the noun **jeweller** 'a person who makes or sells jewellery', American English one **l**: **jeweled, jeweler**.

## **judgement, judgment** *noun*

**Judgement** is the ability to judge wisely. It's also a decision made by a law court.

You can spell the word either **judgement** or **judgment**. **Judgement** is probably commoner in British English, but American English uses mainly **judgment**.

**judicial** *adjective* and **judicious** *adjective*

**Judicial** means 'connected with judges and law courts' – for example, the *British judicial system* is the British system of law courts and trials.

Something that's done in a **judicious** way is done sensibly and carefully: *With a bit of judicious pruning this bush could be made to look quite nice.*

# Kk

**kerb** see CURB

**kerosene** see PARAFFIN

**kidnap** *verb*

To **kidnap** someone is to capture them and demand money for their release.

❶ When you add **-ing** and **-ed** to **kidnap**, you double the **p** in British English (**kidnapping**, **kidnapped**), but in American English you can also use a single **p** (**kidnaping**, **kidnaped**).

**kilometre, kilometer** *noun*

A **kilometre** is a thousand metres, or about 0.62 of a mile.

The standard British pronunciation of the word is 🔊 /**kil**-ə-mee-tə/, but /ki-**lom**-i-tə/ is also quite common, and in America this is the main pronunciation.

❶ **Kilometre** is the British spelling, **kilometer** the American.

**kind** *noun* and **sort** *noun*

When we talk, it's quite common to say things like *I don't like these kind of sausages* and *You shouldn't say those sort of things*. It's perfectly acceptable in speech to use the plural *these* and *those* with the singular **kind** and **sort**, but ⚠ in writing you should avoid them. Use ✔ *this kind of sausage* or *sausages of this kind* if you're referring to just one kind or sort, and *these kinds of sausage, these kinds of sausages* or *sausages of these kinds* if you're referring to more than one kind or sort.

⚠ It's best not to use expressions like *What kind of a gun is this?* and *That's a strange sort of beard* in writing. In speech, **kind of a** and **sort of a** are acceptable, but in writing you should use ✔ **kind of** and **sort of**: *What kind of gun is this? That's a strange sort of beard.*

## kneel *verb*

To **kneel** is to be on your knees: *She was kneeling at the side of the bed.*

The usual past form of the verb is **knelt**, but you can also use **kneeled**.

## knit *verb*

The verb **to knit** has two past forms, and which one you use depends on what you mean by **knit**.

If you mean 'to make something by joining wool together with long needles', the past form is **knitted**: *I've knitted you a scarf.*

But if you use **knit** in a more abstract way, to mean 'to bring together', the past form can also be **knit**. And if you use the past form as an adjective with this meaning, it's always **knit**: *a loose-knit association of clubs.*

## knowledgeable, knowledgable *adjective*

Someone who's **knowledgeable** knows a lot: *Ask John. He's a knowledgeable sort of guy.*

❶ The main spelling of the word is **knowledgeable**, with an **e** between the **g** and the **a**, but you can also use **knowledgable**.

# Ll

## label *verb*

To **label** something is to put a label on it, or to put it into a particular category: *All through my time at school I'd been labelled a troublemaker.*

❶ When you add -**ing** and -**ed** to **label**, you double the **l** in British English (**labelling, labelled**), but in American English you usually don't (**labeling, labeled**).

## laboratory *noun*

A **laboratory** is a place where scientific research is done.

🔊 In British English **laboratory** is pronounced /lə-**bor**-ə-tri/, and in American English it's pronounced /**lab**-rə-tri/ (rather like *lavatory*).

## labour, labor *noun, verb*

**Labour** is a rather formal word for 'work'.

❶ **Labour** is the British spelling, **labor** the American. But the related adjective **laborious** 'needing a lot of hard work' is spelt the same, without a **u**, in British and American English.

## lackadaisical *adjective*

**Lackadaisical** 🔊 /lak-ə-**day**-zi-kəl/ means 'careless' or 'unenthusiastic': *Your lackadaisical attitude to work will just not do, Roger.*

⚠ It has no connection with the word *lax*, so don't pronounce it /laks-ə-**day**-zi-kəl/.

**lady** *noun* and **woman** *noun*

The ordinary word for a grown-up female person is **woman**: *It was so dark I couldn't tell whether it was a man or a woman.*

But there are times when it's usual to use **lady** instead: When you're talking about a woman in her presence, it's rude to call her a 'woman': *This lady wants to know whether we have the shoes in size 4.*

It's generally thought to be rather rude to call an old female person an 'old woman'. It's politer to say 'old lady'.

When you're talking to a group of women, it's usual to address them as 'Ladies' (if there are men there as well, say 'Ladies and gentlemen').

Some people use **lady** much more generally, because they think it's more polite: *The lady in the flat upstairs died last week.* This can sound as if you're trying too hard to be polite, though. Unless the woman you're talking about is present, it's better and more straightforward to say **woman**.

It used to be thought polite to use **lady** in front of the title of a job to show when you were talking about a woman: *a lady doctor, a lady teacher.* ⚠ This is no longer standard usage. If you need to refer to the fact that the person is female, ✔ use **woman** or **female**: *a woman doctor, a female teacher.*

**lama** see LLAMA

**lamentable** *adjective*

Something that's **lamentable** is terribly bad or unsatisfactory: *England's lamentable performance last night means they're out of the World Cup.*

🔈 In British English the word's pronounced /**lam**-ən-tə-bəl/, but Americans often say /lə-**ment**-ə-bəl/.

## language change

English is changing all the time. That's the way languages work. As long as people speak and write a language, small grammatical alterations will develop, new words will be introduced and old ones forgotten, slight changes will take place in the way words are pronounced, and so on. If these small differences catch on among enough people, they become established as new features of the language.

In English, for example, *cross* used to rhyme with *sauce*. This pronunciation survived into the middle of the 20th century, but now hardly anyone uses it. It's become established that *cross* rhymes with *moss*. Before the late 18th century, sentences like *The castle is being built* weren't possible. You had to say *The castle is building*, or *The castle is a-building*.

This process of change doesn't stop until people stop using the language. That's what happened to the classical Latin of ancient Rome.

It's part of human nature that many people don't like change, and try to resist it. For instance, new styles of building often annoy people. It's the same with language. If people notice a change taking place, they're likely to object to it – not necessarily because it's a change for the worse, but simply because it's different.

Therefore because standard English depends on people's view of what is acceptable, it tends to lag behind the changes that are actually happening in English. A change that's happening now might not become fully accepted as part of standard English for ten, twenty, thirty or more years. For instance, *contact* has been used as a verb with the meaning 'to get in touch with' (as in *I'll contact you if I have any news*) since the 1920s. As recently as the 1950s and 1960s some people continued to object to it strongly, but now it's a perfectly normal part of standard English. The word *tourism* goes back to the early 19th century, but as late as the mid 20th century some people still disliked it. In 1949 someone wrote to the *Radio Times*: 'Surely the BBC, of all bodies, should make a stand against the inclusion in our language of such a misbegotten, ill-conceived monstrosity of a word.' Nowadays, no one can see what all the fuss was about.

In many of the entries in this book, you'll see that a particular usage is still disliked by some people. This means that it hasn't yet become completely standard. The entry will say whether the usage is widely enough accepted that it can reasonably be considered as standard (for example *It's me*), or whether it's still better to avoid it, especially in writing (for example *looking out the window*).

1 **last** *adjective, pronoun*

**Last** has three meanings that are quite close together: 'final', 'previous' and 'most recent'. It's important not to use **last** in a way that doesn't make it clear which of these meanings you intend. For instance, if you say *The last time I saw him he didn't look very well*, you could simply mean 'the most recent time', but if he's since died, you could mean 'the final time'. And does *In the last chapter the detective caught up with the murderer* mean 'in the previous chapter' or 'in the final chapter'? Usually the context shows you what's meant, but if it doesn't, write the sentence in a different way.

With **last but one** you can say either *the last programme but one* or *the last but one programme*, but it's best to write *the last programme but one*.

To see how **last** is used for the last thing in a list of three or more, look at the entry for FORMER.

**latter** see FORMER

## lay *verb* and lie *verb*

Because the meanings of **to lay** and **to lie** are so similar, and the past tense of **to lie** with this meaning is **lay**, people often get the two verbs mixed up. In particular, they often use **to lay** when they mean **to lie**, saying ⚠ *I think I'll go and lay down for a while* instead of ✔ *lie down for a while.*

The way to remember the difference between the two is that **to lay** has to have an object after it. You always **lay** 'something': *Lay the books down carefully over there. Lay the potatoes on top of the meat.* The past form is **laid**: *She laid the baby on the bed.*

**To lie**, on the other hand, doesn't have an object after it. You simply **lie** somewhere: *You can't just lie in bed all day.* Its past tense is **lay**: *She lay on the sofa thinking.* Its past participle is **lain**: *The wreck has lain at the bottom of the sea for nearly two hundred years.* To find out about the difference between this and the other verb **to lie**, look at the entry for LIE.

## lead *noun, verb*

There are two words **lead** in English, and they're not pronounced the same.

**Lead** 🔊 /leed/ is mainly a verb. It means 'to take someone to a place' or 'to be in front'. Its past form is **led**, pronounced 🔊 /led/: *She led me to a room at the back of the house.* It can also be a noun – people who are *in the lead* are ahead of other people, and you take a dog for a walk on a **lead**.

**Lead** 🔊 /led/ is a noun. It means a kind of soft heavy metal, and also the black material inside pencils. Something described as **leaden** 🔊 /**led**-ən/ is dull, depressing or dark: *leaden skies.*

## leading question *noun*

When a judge tells off a lawyer for asking a **leading question** in court, he or she means that the lawyer has phrased the question in such a way that it suggests what the answer should be. For example, if a lawyer asks a witness 'Did you then see the accused pick up an axe and hit the victim?' this would be a **leading question**, because it suggests the whole scenario of picking up an axe and hitting the victim, which hadn't been mentioned before. What the lawyer should have asked is 'What did you see then?'

**Leading question** is sometimes used to mean ⚠ 'a question that is difficult or embarrassing to answer', but this use hasn't yet become accepted in standard English, so it's best to avoid it.

1

## lean *verb*

To **lean** is to bend your body downwards, or to slope: *She was leaning down to pick up a book.* There are two past forms of **lean** – **leaned** and **leant** 🔊 /lent/. In British English you can use either, although many people who use the spelling **leaned** pronounce it /lent/ rather than /leend/. American English uses **leaned**.

## leap *verb*

When you **leap**, you make a big jump: *Watch him leap into the air when you drop that big book behind him.* There are two past forms of **leap** – **leaped** and **leapt** 🔊 /lept/. You can use either, although many people who use the spelling **leaped** pronounce it /lept/ rather than /leept/.

## leap-frog *verb*

When you **leap-frog**, you make progress by sudden jumps, getting ahead of someone who was in front of you as if you had jumped over them in a game of leap-frog.

● When you add -**ing** and -**ed** to **leap-frog**, you double the **g** in both British and American English: **leap-frogging, leap-frogged**.

**learn** *verb*

When you **learn** something, you get knowledge or information about it: *The best way to learn a foreign language is to go and live in the place.* ▲ It's not acceptable in standard English to use learn to mean 'to teach' – don't write *He learned me everything I know.*

There are two past forms of **learn** – **learned** and **learnt** ◙ /lernt/. In British English you can use either, although many people who use the spelling **learned** pronounce it /lernt/ rather than /lernd/. American English uses mainly **learned**.

When **learned** is used as an adjective, meaning 'knowing lots of things' (*a very learned man*), it's pronounced ◙ /**lern**-id/.

**least** *adjective, pronoun, adverb*

When you're comparing three or more things or people, use ✔ **least**, not ▲ *less*: *I don't know who was least surprised, Jackie, Allan or me.* Keep *less* for two things or people.

In standard English, use **least** to mean ✔ 'smallest amount of', not ▲ 'smallest number of'. To find out more about this use of **least**, look at the entry for FEW.

**lend** *verb*

Don't get **lend**, which means 'to give for a short time', mixed up with **borrow**, which means 'to take for a short time'. To find out more about the use of **lend** and **borrow**, look at the entry for BORROW.

To find out about the difference between **lend** and **loan**, look at the entry for LOAN.

## **less** *adjective, pronoun, adverb* and
## **lesser** *adjective, pronoun, adverb*

In standard English, use **less** to mean 'a smaller amount of, not so much': *I've got less meat than you.* When you mean 'a smaller number of, not so many', use **fewer**: *I've got fewer chips than you.* To find out more about this use of **less** and **fewer**, look at the entry for FEW.

When you're comparing two things or people, use **less**: *Of Shula and Jane, Jane is less intelligent.* When there are more than two, use **least**: *Of Shula, Jane and Kim, Kim is least intelligent* (or *Kim is the least intelligent*).



**Lesser** means 'less large, important or serious'. It's less widely used than **less**. It's mainly used in the names of animals, plants and places (*the lesser celandine, Lesser Slave Lake*) and in certain fixed phrases (*to a lesser extent, the lesser of two evils*). It can also mean 'of less worth, not so admirable': *A lesser man would have given up at that point.*

As an adjective, **lesser** has to come before a noun: you can't say ⚠ *Their wealth is lesser than it used to be.* As an adverb it means 'less', and it's usually joined with a hyphen to the adjective it describes: *one of our lesser-known actors.*

## **lest** *conjunction*

**Lest** means 'in case something happens' or 'so that something should not happen': *Wear a disguise lest they see you.*

It's a very formal word, and rather old-fashioned, and there are particular rules about how to use it. You either have to put *should* in front of the verb (*Take an umbrella lest it should rain*), or you have to put the verb in the subjunctive, which means that it has no **-s** on the end in the third person present singular (*Take an umbrella lest it rain*).

## let *verb*

*Let me go! Let them stay if they want to.* As you can see, the pronouns after **let** in these sentences are in the object form – *me* and *them.* This is the standard form, even where there are two or more nouns or pronouns: *Why don't you let Sacha and me do the washing-up?* It's common to hear people use the subject form instead, especially when the last pronoun comes before a verb (*Why don't you let Sacha and I do the washing-up?*). ⚠ This is all right when you're speaking, but keep to the object form in serious writing.

When **let us** means 'allow us', you have to say it and write it out in full: *Let us out! We can't breathe in here.* But when you use it to make a suggestion, it's usual to shorten it to **let's**: *Let's have another one.* It would be very formal to use **let us** in sentences like this.



The standard negative form of **let's** is **let's not**: *Let's not argue about it.* In British English you can also use **don't let's**, and Americans can say **let's don't**, but ⚠ these are both quite informal, and not suitable for serious writing.

## level *verb*

If something has been **levelled**, it's even and smooth: *the beautifully levelled gravel of the pathway.*

❶ When you add **-ing** and **-ed** to **level** you double the last **l** in British English (**levelling, levelled**), but not in American English (**leveling, leveled**).

## liable *adjective* and likely *adjective*

**Liable to** and **likely to** both refer to probability. But there is a difference between them.

In standard English, **liable to** refers to permanent characteristics of things (*Wasps are liable to sting you*), but **likely** can also be used for one-off probabilities (*If you hit him, he's likely to hit you back*). It's quite common to use **liable** in the second sense (⚠ *If you hit him, he's liable to hit you back*), but this hasn't become established in standard English, so it's best to avoid it in serious writing. If you do use it like this, it's only appropriate for bad or undesirable things: *Do you think it's liable to rain tomorrow?* For good things, use **likely**: *Do you think it's likely to be sunny tomorrow?*

## liar *noun*

A **liar** is someone who tells lies.

❗ Remember the spelling: -**ar**, not -**er**.

## libel *noun, verb* and slander *noun, verb*

**Libel** and **slander** both involve making false statements about someone which damage their reputation. The difference between them is that in **libel**, the statements are made in some permanent form, usually printed in a book, newspaper, magazine, etc., but **slander** is spoken. ❗ When you add -**ing** or -**ed** to the verb **to libel**, you double the second **l** in British English (**libelling, libelled**), but not in American English (**libeling, libeled**).

## liberalism *noun* and liberality *noun*

**Liberalism**, with a capital **L**, is the policies and principles of a political party called 'the Liberal party'. With a small **l**, **liberalism** is the quality of being broad-minded, not prejudiced.

**Liberality** is generosity: *She dispensed gifts with great liberality.*

Both **liberalism** and **liberality** are very formal words, best kept for serious writing.

**licence** *noun* and **license** *noun, verb*

A **licence** is an official document that allows you to do something, for instance to own a television or run a pub. In British English the spelling is always **licence** (*a gun licence*), but American English uses **license** (*a gun license*).

To **license** something is to give official permission for it by issuing a licence: *How many licensed firearms are there in this city?* The verb is spelt **license** in both British and American English.

❶ Remember – in Britain, **c** for the noun and **s** for the verb; in America, **s** for the noun and the verb.

**lichen** *noun*

**Lichen** is a sort of flat plant that grows on walls, rocks, tree-trunks, etc.

Plant experts tend to say the word as /**ly**-kən/, but there is another pronunciation, /**lich**-ən/, and this is perfectly acceptable in standard English.

**lie** *verb*

To **lie** is to be in a flat or resting position. The verb doesn't take an object after it: *She was lying on the bed.* Its past tense is **lay** and its past participle is **lain**. To find out about the differences between **to lie** and **to lay**, look at the entry for LAY.

To **lie** is also to say things that aren't true: *She said she'd been in all night, but I could tell she was lying.* When **lie** means this, its past form is **lied**.

**lieutenant** *noun*

A **lieutenant** is an officer in the army or navy. In British English the word's pronounced /lef-**ten**-ənt/, but Americans say /loo-**ten**-ənt/.

## **lifelong** *adjective* and **livelong** *adjective*

**Lifelong** means 'lasting all your life': *He was a lifelong Arsenal supporter*. The word's pronounced 🔊 /**lyf**-long/.

**Livelong** means 'entire': *the livelong day*. It's a very old-fashioned word, mainly used in poetry. It's pronounced 🔊 /**liv**-long/.

## **light** *verb*

To **light** something is to start it burning or to provide it with light: *Light the fire*.

**Light** has two past forms – **lit** and **lighted**. **Lit** is much commoner in British English, espeically for the past tense: *She lit the firework*. But when the past participle acts as an adjective, use **lighted**: *It's dangerous to throw a lighted firework*.



In American English, **lighted** is more widely used.

## **lightning** *noun*

**Lightning** is a bright flash of electricity in the sky.

❗ Remember the spelling – don't get it mixed up with *lightening*, which is the *-ing* form of the verb *to lighten*: *We ought to be lightening the load they're bearing*.

## **like** *preposition, conjunction, adverb*

**Like** means 'in the same way as'. In standard English, it's used before nouns: *She crept up on him stealthily, like a cat*. It's also quite commonly used before verbs: ⚠ *You played brilliantly, like you always do. You look like you need a drink*. But this is not accepted in standard English. In writing, you should use *as* or *as if* before a verb: ✔ *You played brilliantly, as you always do. You look as if you need a drink*.

In some dialects, **like** is used as a practically meaningless filling-up word in sentences: *I told him,* *like, that I couldn't make it.* ⚠ Don't use **like** in this way in writing.

**likely** see LIABLE

**lingerie** *noun*

**Lingerie** means 'women's underwear and nightclothes'. It comes from French. The preferable way of pronouncing it is /**lan**-zh-ri/, which is closest to the French original. Many people say /**lon**-zhə-ri / or /**lon**-jə-ri/. Both of these pronunciations are acceptable, but it's best to avoid /**lon**-jə–ray/.

**liqueur** *noun* and **liquor** *noun*

A **liqueur** /lik-**yoor**/ is a strong sweet alcoholic drink, usually flavoured with fruit, herbs, etc. People generally drink it after dinner.

In Britain, **liquor** /**lik**-ə/ is an informal word for alcoholic drink in general – if someone 'can't hold their liquor', they easily get drunk. In America it's the standard word for alcoholic drink: *He went to the liquor store.*

**literally** *adverb*

**Literally** means 'really, actually'. You use it when you say something surprising or make a big claim, which people otherwise might not believe: *There were literally hundreds of people there.*

Since we often exaggerate, **literally** tends to get tagged on to things that aren't quite true. And in particular, people use it with metaphors: *It was so cold out there, I was literally freezing.* Obviously I wasn't 'really' freezing, or I'd have turned into a lump of ice.

## **litre, liter** *noun*

A **litre** is a measure of the amount of space taken up by a liquid. It's equal to about 1.75 pints. **Litre** is the British spelling, **liter** the American.

## **livelong** see LIFELONG

## **llama** *noun* and **lama** *noun*

A **llama** /**lah**-mə/ is a large animal with brownish-white fur that lives in South America.

A **lama** is a Buddhist priest in Tibet.

## **loan** *noun*, *verb*

**Loan** is mainly a noun. It means 'something that's lent': *She asked for a loan of £100.*

1 It can also be used as a verb: *Could you loan me £100?* Some people dislike this usage, and think you should only use **lend** as a verb, but **loan** is now well established in standard English, and there are no good reasons for avoiding it.

In American English you're more likely to find **loaned** used than **lent**, the past form of **lend**.

## **loath** *adjective* and **loathe** *verb*

If you're **loath** /lohth/, rhyming with *both*, to do something, you're very unwilling to do it: *I was loath to admit I'd made a mistake.*

If you **loathe** /lohdh/, rhyming with *clothe*, someone or something, you think they're awful and you dislike them very much: *I loathe getting up before daylight.*

## longevity *noun*

**Longevity** is a formal word for 'long life': *Lord Meldrum was remarkable for his longevity* (= he lived a long time).
🔊 The **g** is pronounced like a **j**: /lon-**jev**-ə-ti/.

## longitude *noun*

The **longitude** of a place is how far it is east or west of the Greenwich meridian (an imaginary north-south line which goes through Greenwich, to the east of London). So the longitude of Helsinki, for instance, is 25 degrees east.

🔊 **Longitude** is usually pronounced /**long**-gi/tyood/ or /**lonj**-i-tyood/. It's not acceptable in standard English to say ⚠ /**long**-di-tyood/ or /**long**-ti-tyood/.

1

## loose *adjective, verb and* lose *verb*

**Loose** 🔊 /looss/ is mainly an adjective. It's the opposite of *tight* or *fixed*: *Some of the fastenings have come loose.* It can also be used as a verb, meaning 'to set free' or 'to undo or untie'.

**Lose** 🔊 /looz/ is a verb. It means 'to be without something you once had': *Don't lose those keys.*

## lot *noun*

The use of **lots** to mean 'a large amount' (*We've got lots of time*) and 'very much' (*I feel lots better this morning*) is standard in spoken English, but it's best to avoid it in serious writing.

On the other hand, **a lot** (*There are a lot of people here. He's looking a lot older*) is perfectly acceptable in writing. In very formal writing, though, it's more usual to use alternatives like 'a large number', 'a great deal' and 'much'.

## **loud** *adverb* and **loudly** *adverb*

Both **loud** and **loudly** can be used to mean 'noisily': *Am I playing too loud/loudly?* But when you mean 'insistently', use **loudly**: *If you protest loudly enough, they might reconsider their decision.*

## **lovable, loveable** *adjective*

A **lovable** person is easy to love. **Lovable** is the main spelling, but you can also use **loveable**.

## **lustre, luster** *noun*

**Lustre** is a shiny surface that something has: *The silver gleamed with a brilliant lustre in the candlelight.* **Lustre** is the British spelling. American English uses mainly the spelling **luster**.

## **luxuriant** *adjective* and **luxurious** *adjective*

Plants that grow very vigorously, so that there are a lot of them, can be described as **luxuriant**: *the luxuriant growth of the tropical rain forest.* You can also use **luxuriant** to describe thick long hair, or a very long bushy beard or moustache.

Something that's **luxurious** is very comfortable and usually expensive: *He always stays at the most luxurious hotel in town.*

## **-ly** *suffix*

You add **-ly** to an adjective to make an adverb. It usually means 'in a particular way'. For example, *bravely* means 'in a brave way': *She acted bravely.*

Sometimes it means 'from a particular point of view'. For example, *musically* can mean 'from a musical point of view, as far as music is concerned': *I'm afraid I'm very ignorant musically.*

Some of these adverbs can start a sentence: *Apparently he's left* (= It appears that he's left). They're a perfectly normal part of standard English, but there are just a few of them, especially *hopefully*, which annoy some people, and it's best to avoid these, or at least use them sparingly, in serious writing. (To find out more about this, look at the entries for HOPEFULLY, REGRETFUL and SENTENCE ADVERBS.)

❶ When an adjective ends in -**ical**, you only need to add -**ly** to it to make an adverb: *musical, musically*. But for adjectives ending in -**ic**, you have to add -**ally**: *fantastic, fantastically*. The only exception to this is *public*, which adds -**ly**: *publicly*.

# Mm

**macho** *adjective*

**Macho** means 'showing off your masculine strength'.

🔊 Its first syllable is pronounced to rhyme with *match*.

**Machismo** is 'the quality of being macho'. It's pronounced 🔊 /mə-**chiz**-moh/.

**mainly** *adverb*

In writing, try to put **mainly** as near as possible to what it refers to. *I do my shopping mainly on Fridays* means that Fridays are the days when I do most of my shopping. *I mainly do my shopping on Fridays* means that shopping is the main thing I do on Fridays.

When you speak you can make clear what you mean by the way you stress the words, so the placement of **mainly** is not so important.

**majority** *noun*

The **majority** is most people or things. The word can be used with either a singular or a plural verb: *Some people are happy with the rule, but the majority wants* or *want it changed*. Both *wants* and *want* are acceptable here. However, *wants* does sound rather stiff and formal. Most people would prefer *want*. And when **majority** is followed by a plural noun (as in *a majority of people*), it's much better to use a plural verb: *The majority of people want a change*.

**The majority of** can simply be a long-winded way of saying 'most'. ⚠ Don't overdo it.

**man** *noun*

The main meaning of **man** is 'adult male person'. ⚠ It's best not to use it to mean 'human beings in general' (as in *Man is polluting the planet*) or, in the plural, to mean 'people' (as in *All men are equal*). Expressions like this make it seem as though women aren't included, even though they are. (See also MANKIND.)

There's the same problem with many of the compound words that contain the word **man**. If there's an established alternative to the 'man' word, it's preferable to use it – for example, *firefighter* for *fireman*, and *synthetic* for *man-made*. You can find out more about this under FEMININE FORMS and SEXIST LANGUAGE.

**manageable** *adjective*

If something's **manageable** you're able to deal with it or control it: *We've got a few problems, but they're manageable.*

❗ Remember the spelling – there's an **e** between the **g** and the **a**.

**mankind** *noun*

The main meaning of **mankind** is 'human beings in general': *Perhaps one day mankind will establish colonies on Mars.*

The trouble with this is that it uses 'man' to refer to both men and women. There are various alternatives you can use to avoid this, including *humankind*, *humanity*, *the human race*, *the human species* and *human beings*. Which one to choose depends on the context, but *human beings* is the most straightforward, and it's usually appropriate in most ordinary non-technical writing. Often, you can use simply *people*.

**Mankind** can also mean 'men in general', but because of the possibility of confusion with the meaning 'human beings in general' it's best to avoid this.

You can find out more about this under FEMININE FORMS, MAN and SEXIST LANGUAGE.

## manoeuvre, maneuver *noun, verb*

A **manoeuvre** 🔊 /mə-**noo**-və/ is a planned action, or a clever or skilful action, and **to manoeuvre** is to do such an action: *She managed to manoeuvre the car into the narrow space.*

**Manoeuvre** is the British spelling, **maneuver** the American.

## marshal *verb*

m

When you **marshal** people or things you bring them together and arrange them in an effective way: *Before you begin to write your report, marshal all your facts.*

❗ When you add **-ing** or **-ed** to **marshal**, you double the **l** in British English (**marshalling, marshalled**) but not in American English (**marshaling, marshaled**).

## marvel *verb*

If something is completely astonishing or wonderful, you may well **marvel** at it: *I couldn't but marvel at the skill with which they wove the intricate patterns.*

❗ When you add **-ing** or **-ed** to **marvel**, you double the **l** in British English (**marvelling, marvelled**) but not in American English (**marveling, marveled**).

The adjective **marvellous** is spelt with two **lls** in British English, but in American English it's spelt **marvelous**.

## masterful *adjective* and **masterly** *adjective*

Someone who's **masterful** likes to command other people and tell them what to do.

Something that's **masterly** is very skilfully done: *She gave a masterly summary of the very complicated arguments.*

**Masterful** is often used to mean 'very skilfully done' but it's useful to keep to the main meaning, and avoid confusion between the two words.

## may *verb* and might *verb*

You use **may** and **might** to say what will possibly happen: *I may go tomorrow. I might go tomorrow.*

Those two sentences mean more or less the same. But the less certain you are about something, the more likely you are to use **might** rather than **may**: *Well, I suppose I might go, but I'm not very keen.*

**May** and **might** are used about the present and the future: *She may/might not want to.* But when you talk about the past, you use **might**: *He said she might not want to.*

**May have** and **might have** mean different things. **May have** means that a possibility still exists – *She may have been badly hurt* means that you don't yet know whether she has been hurt or not. **Might have** means that something was a possibility, but it isn't any longer – *She might have been badly hurt* means that she could have been hurt, but she wasn't.

**May have** is now quite commonly used in place of **might have**, especially in speech, but it's not accepted as part of standard English; in writing, stick to **might have** for things that are no longer possible.

To find out about the difference between **may** and **can**, look at the entry for CAN.

## maybe *adverb* and may be

**Maybe** means 'perhaps': *Maybe we should go by train rather than drive.*

Don't get it mixed up with **may be**, which is a verb: *I may be wrong.*

**me** see I

## **meagre, meager** *adjective*

If something's **meagre**, there isn't enough of it: *I don't know how they manage to exist on that meagre salary.*

**Meagre** is the British spelling, **meager** the American.

## **means** *noun*

When **means** refers to 'a way' or 'a method', it's usually treated as a singular noun: *We must find a means of reducing our costs.* But it can also be treated as a plural noun: *There are various means by which we can go about getting what we want.*

When **means** refers to 'the amount of money you have', it's treated as a plural noun: *Our slender means aren't enough to allow us to take a holiday each year.*

## **media** *noun*

Television, radio and newspapers are known collectively as the **media**. This can have either a plural verb after it (*The media only report the bad news*) or a singular verb (*The media only reports the bad news*). Some people don't like the use of a singular verb, but it's now widely established in standard English.

Remember, though that it's always a collective noun. ⚠ You can't say *a media* to refer to one of the parts of the media, and there's no plural form *medias*.

To find out more about **media**, look at the entry for MEDIUM.

## Mediterranean *noun, adjective*

The **Mediterranean** is a sea between southern Europe and North Africa.

❶ Remember the spelling – one **t**, two **rs** and **ean** at the end.

## medium *noun*

The noun **medium** has two main meanings. First, it means 'what's used to express thoughts or ideas': *Television is a vital medium of communication. Marble is a favourite medium for sculptors to work in.* In this meaning, its plural can be either **mediums** or **media**.

Second, it means 'someone who says they can communicate with people who are dead'. In this meaning, its plural is **mediums**.

## meet with *verb*

If you **meet with** an accident, you have an accident. If you **meet with** success, you succeed.

If you **meet with** someone, you have a prearranged meeting with them, usually in order to discuss something with them. This meaning of **meet with** originated in American English, and there are some people who dislike its use in British English. But it's quite useful to be able to make a difference between '**meet** someone' (by accident) and '**meet with** someone' (intentionally), and there's really no good reason not to use **meet with**.

## metal *noun* and mettle *noun*

**Metal** is a general word for substances such as iron, steel, gold, silver, brass, lead, etc.

**Mettle** is an old-fashioned word for 'strength of character' or 'courage': *This new challenge will test their mettle.*

**meter** *noun* and **metre** *noun*

A **meter** is a device which measures something. For example, an electricity meter measures how much electricity you use in your home.

A **metre** is a measure of length. It's equal to about three feet and three inches. **Metre** is also the rhythm of poetry. **Metre** is the British spelling – in American English the word's spelt **meter**.

**mettle** see METAL

**might** see COULD, MAY

**migraine** *noun*

A **migraine** is a type of very bad headache. 🔊 You can pronounce the first syllable of the word to rhyme with either *me* or *my*.

m

**mileage, milage** *noun*

**Mileage** is the number of miles travelled: *This old car's got a lot of mileage on the clock.* It can also refer to the advantages of long use: *He's got a lot of mileage out of that joke over the years.*

**Mileage** is the main spelling, but you can also use **milage**.

**millennium** *noun*

A **millennium** is a thousand years, or the end of a thousand-year period – for example, the year 2000 was a millennium. The plural is either **millenniums** or **millennia**.

❗ Remember the spelling – two **l**s and two **n**s.

**miner** *noun* and **minor** *adjective, noun*

A **miner** is someone who works in a mine – a *coal miner,* for instance.

**Minor** is a legal word for someone who hasn't reached the age when the law can apply to them: *Alcoholic drinks may not be sold to minors.*

**Minor** is also an adjective, meaning 'not of great importance or seriousness': *a minor operation.*

**minority** *noun*

A **minority** is a small number of people or things within a group, less than half. The word can be used with either a singular or a plural verb: *Most people support the proposals, but a sizeable minority is* or *are against it.* Both *is* and *are* are acceptable. However, *is* sounds rather stiff and formal. Most people would prefer *are.*

A **minority** is also a group of people who are different from most others in race, religion, language, interests, etc.

m

**minuscule** *adjective*

Something that's **minuscule** is very tiny: *The difference between the two photos is minuscule.*

❶ Remember the spelling. There's a ✔ **u** between the **n** and the **s** – as in *minus* – ⚠ not an *i.*

**mischievous** *adjective*

Someone who's **mischievous** is naughty or causes trouble.

Remember it's ✔ **mischievous** 🔊 /**miss**-chi-vəs/, not ⚠ *mischievious* /miss-**chee**-vi-əs/. There's no such word as *mischievious* in standard English.

## misspell *verb*

If you **misspell** a word, you spell it wrongly.

The past form of **misspell** is **misspelt** or **misspelled**. **Misspelt** is the main British form. Americans usually use **misspelled**.

❶ Remember the spelling – **ss**. Don't ✔ **misspell** it ⚠ *mispell.*

## mistakable, mistakeable *adjective*

If something is **mistakable**, you may think it's different from what it really is: *In the dim light, the coat hanging on the door was easily mistakable for a human figure.*

The main spelling is **mistakable**, but you can also use **mistakeable**.

## mitre, miter *noun*



A **mitre** is the pointed hat worn by bishops.

**Mitre** is the British spelling and **miter** the American spelling.

## model *verb*

If you **model** something, you make a model of it, or you base it on something else: *Their laws are modelled on the British legal system.*

❶ When you add **-ing** and **-ed** to **model**, you double the **l** in British English (**modelling**, **modelled**), but in American English you usually don't (**modeling**, **modeled**).

## mollusc, mollusk *noun*

A **mollusc** is a sort of animal that has a soft wet body with no bones. Molluscs usually have a shell. Snails, oysters, mussels and clams are all **molluscs**.

**Mollusc** is the British spelling, **mollusk** the American.

**moment** *noun*

The expression *at this moment in time* means 'now'. It has become a cliché, and many people find it long-winded, pretentious and annoying. It's certainly much simpler and more straightforward to say *now* or *at the moment.*

**momentarily** *adverb*

**Momentarily** means 'just for a moment': *I was momentarily confused by what she said.* In American English, it can also mean 'at any moment' or 'straightaway'.

🔊 The usual British pronunciation of **momentarily** is /**moh**-mən-trə-li/. Americans pronounce it /moh-mən-**te**-rə-li/, and this way of saying it is coming into British English too.

m

**moral** *noun*, **morale** *noun* and **morals** *noun*

The **moral** 🔊 /**mor**-əl/ of a story is the lesson in good or sensible behaviour which it teaches: *And the moral of that tale is, never put urgent things off till the next day.*

The **morale** 🔊 /mə-**rahl**/ of a person or group is their confidence and enthusiasm: *The team's morale was high after its victory.*

**Morals** 🔊 /**mor**-əlz/ are right or acceptable behaviour.

**more** *adverb* and **most** *adverb*

**More** is used when you're comparing two things: *I think windsurfing's more exciting than sailing.* **Most** is used when you're comparing more than two things: *What's the most delicious meal you've ever had?*

It's quite common in ordinary speech to use **most** to compare two things when there's no *than* afterwards: ⚠ *Out of history and geography, which do you think's the most interesting?* But this is not regarded as acceptable in standard English, so you should avoid it in writing, and use **more** instead.

**More** can also be a determiner and a pronoun. When you use it in the expression *more than one*, it's standard to use a singular verb after it: *More than one person has expressed surprise at the announcement.*

## Moslem see MUSLIM

## most see MORE

## mould, mold *noun, verb*

A **mould** is a shaped container which substances are put into so that they can take the shape of the container. **Mould** is also a furry growth of fungus on the surface of something. To **mould** something is to shape it.

**Mould** is the British spelling and **mold** the American.



## moult, molt *verb*

When an animal **moults**, some of its hairs fall out. When a bird **moults**, some of its feathers fall out.

**Moult** is the British spelling and **molt** the American.

## moustache, mustache *noun*

A **moustache** is hair growing on the upper lip.

**Moustache** is the British spelling, **mustache** the American.

## movable, moveable *adjective*

Something that's **movable** can be moved: *These movable screens can be used to close off part of the room.*

**Movable** is the main spelling, but you can also use **moveable**.

**mow** *verb*

To **mow** grass is to cut it.

**Mow** has two past participles – **mowed** and **mown**. **Mowed** is mainly used as an active verb (*Have you mowed the lawn yet?*) and **mown** as an adjective (*the smell of newly mown grass*).

**Ms**

**Ms** is put before the name of a woman, as *Mr* is before the name of a man: *Ms Stella Pertwee*. Unlike *Mrs* and *Miss*, it doesn't show whether the woman is married.

🔊 **Ms** is pronounced /miz/, or sometimes /məz/.

**much** see VERY

**Muslim, Moslem** *adjective, noun*

A **Muslim** is a follower of the Islamic religion. **Muslim** is the usual spelling. **Moslem** is an acceptable alternative, but it's now rather old-fashioned.

m

**mutual** *adjective*

**Mutual** has two meanings. First, it describes feelings which each of two people has for the other or things which two people do to each other – if you say that *Gary and Nigel have a mutual dislike*, you mean that Gary dislikes Nigel and Nigel dislikes Gary.

Second, it describes a friend or acquaintance that two people have in common – if you say *A mutual friend told me that Gary's getting married*, you're referring to someone who's a friend of yours and a friend of Gary.

**Mutual** is also sometimes used to refer to other things that two people share or have in common: ⚠ *Our two nations have a mutual determination to outlaw these evil practices*. But this use isn't generally accepted as part of standard English, so in writing it's best to use **mutual** 'shared' only about friends.

# Nn

**naive, naïve** *adjective*

Someone who's **naive** behaves as if they were very young and inexperienced, and therefore does and says silly things.

The spelling **naïve**, with two dots over the **i**, is rather old-fashioned. Most people nowadays use the spelling **naive**.

The quality of being naive is **naivety** or **naïvety**. Some English people use the French word **naïveté** instead.

**names** see CHRISTIAN NAME

**nationalize** *verb* and **naturalize** *verb*

If a government **nationalizes** a company or industry, it takes over the ownership of it, so that it belongs to the country as a whole.

Someone who's a **naturalized** citizen of a country wasn't born there, but the government of the country has officially allowed them to become a citizen of it.

**native** *noun*

A **native** of a place is a person who was born there: *I'm a native of Brighton.*

⚠ It's rude in modern English to refer to people who live in non-Western countries, in places like Africa and Asia, as 'natives'.

**Native American** see RACES AND PEOPLES

## nature *noun*

If you find yourself using expressions like *of this nature*, stop and think whether you really need to. They sound wordy and there's usually a shorter and simpler way of putting what you want to say. For instance, *problems of this nature* could be *problems like this* or *such problems*, and *matters of a confidential nature* could be *confidential matters*. See also CHARACTER.

## naught *noun* and nought *noun*

**Naught** is an old word for 'nothing'. In stories about knights and battles, someone might say 'There is naught to fear'.

**Nought** means '0' or 'zero': *Two plus nought equals two*. It's always spelt with an **o** in British English, but American English usually uses **naught** with an **a**.

## need *verb*

n

When you put another verb after **need**, you can do it in two ways. You can either put **to** in front of the other verb: *I need to have this mended*, or you can just use the other verb on its own: *I need never work again*.

If you do it the first way, **need** behaves like an ordinary verb. But if you do it the second way, you don't add **-s** to it in the third person singular form: **he need**, **she need**. You only use this second method in negative sentences and in questions where **need** comes before its subject: *She need never work again. Need he take his shoes off?*

## negatives

We use negative sentences to deny that something is true. The usual way to express the negative in English is to add the word *not*. For example, if someone said 'That's a true story', you could deny it by saying 'It's not true'.

There are other negative words, mostly beginning with an **n** – for instance *no, nobody, neither*: *There's no point in worrying. Nobody can hear us.* See also DOUBLE NEGATIVES.

**negligent** *adjective* and **negligible** *adjective*

People who are **negligent** don't do the things they're supposed to do, and don't take care to do things properly.

An amount that's **negligible** is so small that it's not worth considering: *The difference between the two pictures is negligible.*

**neighbour, neighbor** *noun*

Your **neighbours** are the people who live near you.

**Neighbour** is the British spelling, **neighbor** the American.

**neither** *adjective, pronoun, adverb, conjunction*



Do you use a singular or a plural verb after **neither**?

When **neither** is the subject of a clause, the answer is easy – use a singular verb: *Both colleges are good, but neither offers the sort of course I want.*

When **neither** is followed by **nor**, it can make the choice more difficult. When a singular noun comes second, use a singular verb: *Neither Annie nor Warren wants to come.* When a plural noun comes second, use a plural verb: *Neither Chris nor his friends are interested.*

The main British pronunciation of **neither** is /**ny**-dhə/, but some people say /**nee**-dhə/. In America, it's the other way round – /**nee**-dhər/ is the main pronunciation, and /**ny**-dhər/ is rare.

**never** *adverb*

The main meaning of **never** is 'not at any time': *I've never been to America.* But it's also quite common to use it to mean 'not': *I never thought he'd really do it* (= I didn't think he would). This is perfectly normal standard English when you speak, but when you write it's best to stick to **not** in this sort of sentence.

⚠ **I never** meaning 'I didn't' (*'You promised you'd help.' 'No I never.'*) is not part of standard English.

**nice** *adjective*

If you like something, you can call it **nice**. **Nice** is a general word to describe anything that's pleasant or good: *That's a nice jacket you're wearing.*

But when you're producing written work, remember that there are other words for things you like. Don't just keep using **nice** for everything. Try and think of more specific words. For example, if something tastes nice, you can call it *tasty* or *delicious*; and if something looks nice, you can call it *attractive* or *beautiful*. Instead of saying 'It's nice that I've got the day off today', you could say 'I'm pleased I've got the day off today'.



**nicety** *noun*

**Niceties** are fine details or subtle points: *He wasn't interested in all the niceties of the game – he just wanted to see his side win.* They have nothing to do with being nice. The word to use for 'being nice' is **niceness**.

**nondefining relative clause, nonrestrictive relative clause** see CLAUSES

**none** *pronoun*

**None** means 'not one' or 'not any'. When it refers to a single thing you use a singular verb with it: *I'd have liked some more ice cream, but none was left.*

When it refers to several things or people, you can use either a singular or a plural verb: *They were very expensive – none was/were under £50. None of the children wants/want to go.* Both the singular verb and the plural verb are perfectly acceptable in standard English. The singular verb is traditionally regarded as the 'correct' one to use, but it usually sounds very stilted and awkward. Most people use the plural verb when they're talking, and it sounds more natural to use it in writing too. It's also a useful way to avoid having to choose between *his, her* or *his or her*: *None of the staff have had their wages yet.*

**non-flammable** see INFLAMMABLE

**nonplus** *verb*

To **nonplus** someone is to puzzle them completely: *I was nonplussed by her unhelpful attitude.*

❶ When you add **-ing** and **-ed** to **nonplus**, you double the **s**: **nonplussing**, **nonplussed**.



**no one** *pronoun*

**No one** means 'no person'. ❶ **No one** is the most usual spelling, but you can also use **no-one**.

It can be tricky to choose the right pronoun after **no one**: *No one's handed in ... work yet.* Unless you know that all the people involved are either male or female you can't use *his* or *her*, and *his or her* is very long-winded. It sounds more natural when you talk to use *their*, and this is perfectly acceptable in ordinary written English too. In very formal writing it's better to use *his or her*.

**nor** *conjunction*

**Nor** means much the same as *or*, but you use it in negative sentences. You have to use it after *neither*: *It was neither cheap nor good value.* After other negative words, like *not* and *never*, it depends whether they come after an auxiliary verb or not. If they do, you use *or*: *They won't come this week, or next week.* If they don't, you can choose between *or* or **nor**: *She never spoke or/nor looked in my direction.*

When **nor** means 'also not', you can use it interchangeably with *neither*: *'I don't eat meat.' 'Nor/Neither do I.'*

**not** *adverb*

You need to be careful where you put **not** when you use it with words like *all* and *everyone*. For instance, if you say *Not all his later novels are worth reading*, you mean that some of them are, even if most of them aren't. But if you say *All his later novels aren't worth reading*, you mean that none of them are.

In speech and ordinary writing it's perfectly normal and standard to shorten **not** to **-n't** after certain verbs: *aren't, can't, couldn't, daren't, didn't, don't, hadn't, haven't, isn't, mightn't, mustn't, needn't, oughtn't, shan't, shouldn't, usedn't, wasn't, weren't, won't, wouldn't.* Only use the full form with **not** in very formal or official writing.

❗ Remember, the apostrophe goes ✔ between the **n** and the **t**, ⚠ not before the **n**.

**nothing** *noun*

You always use a singular verb after **nothing but**, even if it goes with a plural noun: *Nothing but a few broken bottles was left.*

**noticeable** *adjective*

Something that's **noticeable** is easily seen or noticed: *The changes haven't had any noticeable effect yet.*

❗ Remember the spelling – there's an **e** between the **c** and the **a**.

## not only ... but also

When you're writing, make sure that the part of a sentence that follows **not only** matches the part that follows **but also** grammatically.

For example, *They've stolen not only the video but also some of my wife's jewellery.* In this sentence, *the video* and *my wife's jewellery* match grammatically, because they're both objects of the verb *stolen.*

When you're speaking, it would be quite usual to say *They've not only stolen the video but also some of my wife's jewellery,* ⚠ but it's best to avoid this in writing.

## nought see NAUGHT

## nouns

Nouns name things. **Common nouns** name things, places or people in general (*measles, orangeade, gentleness, bedroom, child*). **Proper nouns** name particular things, places or people (*France, Stephanie*).

Nouns can be the subject of a verb (*Stephanie is beautiful*), or the object of a verb (*I love Stephanie*), or the complement of a verb (*She is Stephanie*) (look at the entry on VERBS to see what a complement is).

Many nouns can be used in front of other nouns, like adjectives: *an orangeade bottle.*

## nuclear *adjective*

**Nuclear** refers to the energy that's produced when the nuclei of atoms are split.

🔊 The standard British pronunciation of the word is /**new**-kli-ə/. It's not regarded as correct to pronounce it ⚠ /**new**-kyə-lə/.

## number *noun*

**A number of** means 'several', and you use a plural verb after it: *Quite a number of people have asked me where they can buy these shirts*. This applies when it's introduced by *there* too: *There are a number of reasons why she had to refuse.*

**The number of** means 'the total of when added up', and you use a singular verb after it: *The number of accidents on this stretch of road has gone up in recent years.*

## number agreement see SINGULARS AND PLURALS

## numbers

It's usual to write small numbers as words (*five people*) and large numbers as figures (*379 people*). There's no general rule, though, about what counts as a small number. Some people write anything below 100 in words, but others use words only for numbers below 20, 13 or even 10. Choose what you want to do, and stick to it.

Don't put words and figures together in the same sentence. If one number is in figures they should both be: ✔ *from 5 to 379*, not ⚠ *from five to 379*.

Numbers, including dates, at the beginning of a sentence should be written as words: *A hundred and fifty children were there*. If the number's very long and would take up a lot of space in words, try to rewrite the sentence so that it doesn't come at the beginning: *They sold 3724 copies of the book* (rather than *Three thousand seven hundred and twenty-four copies of the book were sold*).

To find out about the word *billion*, look at the entry for BILLION. To find out about punctuation in long numbers, look at the entry for COMMA.

# Oo

## **object** *see* NOUNS

## **oblivious** *adjective*

If you're **oblivious of** or **to** something, you're not aware of it: *She ran back into the building, oblivious of/to the danger she was in.*

## **obsolescent** *adjective* and **obsolete** *adjective*

Something that's **obsolescent** is going out of date: *This obsolescent missile system is going to be scrapped next year.*

Something that's **obsolete** is already out of date: *Our factories are still using machinery that was obsolete many years ago.*

## **obverse** *noun*

**Obverse** is a technical term used by coin collectors to mean 'the side of a coin that has the head on it'.

It's also a more general word, which describes what happens if you turn a situation round the other way: *The more you learn, the more you realize you don't know – and of course the obverse is true too* (= if you're ignorant, you don't realize how little you know).

## **occasion** *noun*

An **occasion** is the time when something happens. It's also an opportunity.

❶ Remember the spelling – two **c**s, an **a** and one **s**.

## occur *verb*

**Occur** is a more formal way of saying 'happen': *Eruptions occur about twice a year on average.*

❶ When you add **-ing** and **-ed** to **occur**, you double the **r**: **occurring, occurred**. The noun that comes from **occur** is **occurrence**, with two **rs**.

## odour, odor *noun*

An **odour** is a smell – usually a bad one.

❶ **Odour** is the British spelling, **odor** the American. But the adjective **odorous** 'having a scent' is spelt without a **u** before the **r** in both British and American English.

## of *preposition*

When we talk, we usually say *could have* as /kuud əv/, *may have* as /may əv/, etc. This /əv/ sounds like *of*, but don't write ⚠ *could of, may of*, etc. – they're not acceptable in standard English.

*A friend of Roger* or *a friend of Roger's*? You can either use the apostrophe **s** or leave it out when you're talking about people (like *Roger*), but when you're referring to things or organizations, don't use an apostrophe **s**: ✔ *a supporter of the club* (not ⚠ *the club's*).

❶ If you have trouble deciding whether to write **of** or **off**, think of the way you'd say the word. If it ends with a /v/ sound, spell it **of**: /ə lot əv ingk/ *a lot of ink*. If it ends in a /f/ sound, spell it **off**: /get of dhə bus/ *Get off the bus*.

## of course

⚠ Don't get into the habit of using **of course** simply as a way of reinforcing what you say, or trying to make something sound obviously true when it may not be.

For example, if you say *There are of course two atoms of hydrogen in a molecule of water*, you avoid appearing to say something obvious to people who already know it, but you also risk suggesting that people who don't know it are stupid. You can usually do without **of course** in cases like this.

If you say things like *Of course everyone thinks they're rubbish,* you risk dishonestly suggesting that something is common knowledge when it's only your opinion and may not be true.

## off *adverb, preposition*

With 'taking' verbs, it's standard to use *from,* not **off**: *I got this cold from* (not **off**) *Christine. They took all his money from* (not **off**) *him.* It's quite common to use **off** in some varieties of spoken English, but in written English, use *from.*

**Off of** is common in spoken English too (⚠ *Keep your feet off of the chair*), and it's normal in American English, but the standard British usage is simply **off** (✔ *Keep your feet off the chair*), and it's best to stick to this in writing.

## offence, offense *noun*

An **offence** is an illegal act, and **offence** is a feeling of resentment.

❶ **Offence** is the British spelling, and **offense** the American. But remember that **offensive** is the same in British and American English.

## often *adverb*

🔊 **Often** is traditionally pronounced /**off**-ən/, without a /t/, but the pronunciation /**off**-tən/ is becoming increasingly common. Both are perfectly acceptable in standard English.

**older** see ELDER

**omit** *verb*

If you **omit** something or someone, you leave them out: *McGregor was surprisingly omitted from the Scottish team.*

❶ When you add -**ing** and -**ed** to **omit**, you double the **t**: **omitting, omitted**. And don't forget, there's only one **m**.

**one** *pronoun*

Do you use a singular verb or a plural verb after **one of**? It depends on the meaning of the sentence. In *One of our teachers has resigned*, it's just 'one' of the teachers that has done the action, so the verb is singular. But in *I'm not one of those who are always complaining*, 'those' is plural, so the verb is plural too.

In formal writing and speech, **one** is used to mean 'any person': *One shouldn't make assumptions without checking the facts.* ⚠ Avoid using **one** too often in a sentence, as this tends to sound rather silly, as in: *One should try to keep oneself busy, and use one's time as profitably as one can.* As an alternative you can use *you* (*You should try to keep yourself busy, and use your time as profitably as you can*), although this isn't appropriate for very formal writing. In American English, you can follow the first **one** with *he, him, his,* etc.: *One should try to keep himself busy, and use his time as profitably as he can.* But as it's become less acceptable to use *he* as a general pronoun (see the entry for SEXIST LANGUAGE), *they* is tending to replace it: *The truth often poses a threat to power, and one often has to fight power at great risk to themselves* (from the 1991 film *JFK*).

⚠ Avoid using **one** instead of *I* (*One couldn't believe one's ears*), as it sounds as if you think you're more important than you really are.

To find out about **one another** and **each other** look at the entry for EACH OTHER.

**only** *adverb*

You need to be careful where you put **only** in a sentence, because it can change the meaning of what you say.

The usual place to put it is before the verb: *I've only dusted the table.* This could mean 'I've dusted the table but I haven't done anything else to it, such as polish it' or 'I've dusted the table but not the chairs, the television, etc.' When you speak you can make it obvious which you mean by putting the emphasis on *dusted* or *table.* And when you write, the context will usually show what you mean. But if there's any possibility that people might misunderstand, put **only** before the word it refers to: *I've only dusted the table or I've dusted only the table.*

**onto, on to** *preposition*

In standard English you used to have to write **onto** as two words: *He collapsed on to the bed.* But it's very common to write it as one word, and although some newspapers, book publishers, etc. continue to use **on to**, **onto** is now widely accepted as being part of standard English: *He collapsed onto the bed.*

But remember, when **on to** means 'onwards to', you must write it as two words: *I'll pass the message on to Sarah.* You can see the difference in these two sentences: *We drove on to the next town* and *We drove onto the grass verge by mistake.*

**or** *conjunction*

To find out about the use of **or** for joining unlike things, look at the entry for AND.

See also AND/OR.

**oral** see AURAL

**orbit** *verb*

A satellite that **orbits** the Earth goes round it.

❶ When you add **-ing** and **-ed** to **orbit** you don't double the **t**: **orbiting, orbited**.

**orient** *noun, verb* and **orientate** *verb*

To **orient** and to **orientate** both mean 'to find or set the direction of something': *It took me a while to orient/ orientate myself when I came up out of the underground station.*

**Orient** is the word usually used in American English. British English used to use mainly **orientate**, but **orient** is now becoming commoner.

🔊 The verb **orient** is pronounced /**aw**-ri-ent/. The noun **Orient**, which refers to the countries of Asia, is pronounced /**aw**-ri-ənt/.

**orthopaedic, orthopedic** *adjective*

**Orthopaedic** refers to the medical treatment of injured or badly formed bones, joints or muscles.

**Orthopedic** is the spelling used in American English. British English uses mainly **orthopaedic**.

**ought** *verb*

The standard negative form of **ought to** is **ought not to** or **oughtn't to**: *You oughtn't to hit your little brother like that.* ⚠ *Didn't ought to* and *hadn't ought to* aren't part of standard English.

If you use **ought** in questions, do it like this: *Ought I to have told him?* ⚠ Again, *did I ought to?* and *had I ought to?* aren't standard English.

**ours** *pronoun*

Something that's **ours** belongs to us: *The hut's ours, but you can use it if you like.* Remember, it's always ✔ **ours**, never ⚠ *our's*.

**out** *preposition* and **out of** *preposition*

It's very common to use **out** as a preposition, meaning the same as **out of**: *What did you see when you looked out the window?*

In American English *out the window* is standard, but in Britain it's not widely accepted as part of standard English, so in formal writing it's best to use **out of**.

**outside** *preposition* and **outside of** *preposition*

The preposition **outside** is standard in both British and American English: *She lives just outside Norwich.*

In American English it's quite normal to use **outside of** instead: *They've bought a little place just outside of town.*

In British English, **outside of** isn't usually used when you're talking about an actual physical place or position, but it's becoming more acceptable to use it about abstract things: *She has few interests outside of her work,* or to mean 'apart from': *Outside of Graham, who do you know who can wiggle his ears?*

O

**outwit** *verb*

If you **outwit** someone, you get the better of them by being clever: *She managed to outwit her captors and escape.*

❶ When you add **-ing** and **-ed** to **outwit** you double the **t**: **outwitting, outwitted**.

**owing to** *preposition*

**Owing to** means 'because of'. You use it after a complete clause: *The train was delayed owing to leaves on the track.*

To find out about the difference in usage between **owing to** and **due to** look at the entry for DUE TO.

# Pp

**paed-, ped-** *prefix*

The prefix **paed**- is used in words that refer to children – for instance, a *paediatrician* is a doctor who treats children and their diseases.

The spelling **ped**- is used in American English. British English usually uses the spelling **paed**-, but **ped**- is becoming acceptable too.

**pair** *noun, verb* and **pare** *verb*

When **pair** means 'two people', you use a plural verb with it: *The unlikely pair have set up a business in the house opposite.*

When **a pair of** refers to two things that usually go together in a set (like *a pair of gloves*) or a single thing with two parts (like *a pair of glasses*), you use a singular verb with it: *A small pair of scissors costs about £3.*

But when **a pair of** simply refers to two people or things that just happen to be together, you use a plural verb with it: *A pair of odd-looking men were seen hanging around the school grounds.*

The verb **pair** means 'to form into a pair': *Jane and Graeme paired off for the dance.* Don't get it mixed up with **pare**, which means 'to cut a thin layer off': *Pare the apples and cut them into pieces.*

**panel** *verb*

If you **panel** a room, you cover the walls with panels: *an oak-panelled dining room.*

❶ When you add -**ing** and -**ed** to **panel**, you double the **l** in British English (**panelling**, **panelled**) but not in American English (**paneling**, **paneled**).

**panic** *verb*

If you **panic**, you're suddenly filled with fear and alarm: *Don't panic! It's not a real tiger!*

❶ When you add **-ing** and **-ed** to **panic**, you put in a **k** after the **c**: **panicking, panicked**.

**paraffin** *noun*

**Paraffin** is a kind of oil used as a fuel. In America, Australia and New Zealand it's usually called *kerosene*.

❶ Remember the spelling – one **r** and two **fs**.

**parallel** *adjective, verb*

If two lines are **parallel**, they run beside each other and never get closer together or further apart. No matter how long they are, they never meet.

**Parallel** can be a verb, meaning 'to be parallel to' or 'to be similar to': *Your experience parallels mine.*

❶ When you add **-ing** and **-ed** to it, you don't double the last **l**, in either British or American English – **paralleling, paralleled**.

Remember the spelling – one **r**, two **ls**, and then one **l**.

**paralyse, paralyze** *verb*

If someone's **paralysed**, they can't move some or all of their body.

**Paralyse** is the British English spelling, **paralyze** the American.

**parameter** *noun* and **perimeter** *noun*

In mathematics and science, a **parameter** is a quantity that stays the same in the particular case you're talking about, but can vary in other cases.

The word's used much more generally, usually in the plural, to mean 'factors that act as a limit to the things you're talking about': *The parameters within which the inspectors work need to be made clearer.* There's nothing wrong with this usage, but it has become rather overused, so remember that there are perfectly good alternatives – *limits,* for instance, or *scope.*

Don't confuse **parameter** with **perimeter**, which means 'the outer edge or boundary of something'.

## parcel *verb*

When you **parcel** something up, you make it into a parcel: *She parcelled up the old clothes to send them to the Oxfam shop.*

❶ When you add **-ing** and **-ed** to **parcel** you double the **l** in British English (**parcelling, parcelled**) but not in American English (**parceling, parceled**).

## pardon *interjection*

⚠ **Pardon** is not a well-loved word. People who use it tend to sound as though they're trying too hard not to seem rude or common.

If you're apologizing for something, such as making a rude noise by mistake, you can always say *Sorry* or *I'm sorry* or, if you're being very formal, *I beg your pardon.*

If you didn't hear what someone has said to you, you can say *Sorry?* or *Could you repeat that, please?* (*What?* and *Eh?* are all right between friends, but they're not very polite.)

## parlour, parlor *noun*

A **parlour** is a shop where you can get a particular sort of goods or services: *an ice-cream parlour.* In the past, people used to call the ground-floor front room of their house a 'parlour'.

**Parlour** is the British spelling, **parlor** the American.

## partially *adverb* and partly *adverb*

**Partially** and **partly** are very close in meaning. They both mean 'not completely' (*The painting had only been partially/partly finished*) or 'to some extent' (*The decrease in visitors had been partially/partly offset by the higher entrance fee charged*). When you could use either, it's usually better to choose **partly**, which is shorter and simpler.

There are differences between them, though. When **partly** comes before a whole clause (*Partly because I was tired, I decided not to go to the meeting*), you can't replace it with **partially**. And when you describe two things that together make up a whole, use **partly**: *The knife's handle was partly bone and partly metal.* But when you're referring to bodily conditions, it's usual to use **partially**: *facilities for the partially sighted.*

**Partially** also means 'in a biased way': *I try not to judge their work partially.*

## participles



English verbs have two forms called participles: the **present participle** and the **past participle**.

The **present participle** has **-ing** on the end: *cook, cooking.* It's used when you talk about actions which are still going on, and haven't been completed: *Don't go into the kitchen while he's cooking the dinner.* You can also use the **present participle** as an adjective: *The light of the setting sun shone through the window.*

The **past participle** of most verbs has **-ed** on the end: *cook, cooked.* But there are some that have a different sort of **past participle**, without **-ed** – for example *break, broken* and *get, got.*

The **past participle** is used with *have* to talk about the past: *Someone has broken the door down.* You can also use **past participles** as adjectives: *Rain was getting in through the broken window.*

You can find out more about **participles** in the entries for DANGLING PARTICIPLES and FUSED PARTICIPLE.

## parts of speech (word classes)

The term 'part of speech' refers to all the different types of word there are, according to the job they do in a sentence. Different experts have different opinions on how many types exist, but these are the main ones in English:

| | | | |
|---|---|---|---|
| adjective | conjunction | noun | pronoun |
| adverb | determiner | prefix | suffix |
| article | interjection | preposition | verb |

To find out more about them, look up the entry for each word.

Words sometimes change their part of speech. For instance, nouns can be used as verbs: *I should bin that letter if I were you* (= put it in the bin). Adjectives can be used as nouns: *He reads all the dailies* (= daily newspapers). Adverbs can be used as verbs: *She upped* (= got up) *and left*.

The technical name for this process is 'conversion'. Some people dislike it. They think words should stick to their original part of speech. But it's a perfectly normal part of the way English works and it's been going on for many centuries, so there's no good reason for avoiding it.



## passed *past tense* and *past participle* and
## past *adjective, noun, preposition*

**Passed** is the past form of the verb **to pass**: *She passed me in the street without saying hallo. I've passed all my exams!*

**Past** is an adjective (*I regret all my past mistakes*), a noun (*In the past people had to rely on horses for quick transport*) and a preposition (*A seagull flew past the window*).

It's easy to get them confused when they come after a verb. Remember, after the verb *to have* use **passed**: *Those days have passed now.* After the verb *to be* use **past**: *The days are long past when you could buy a paperback book for 25p.*

**passive** see CLEAR WRITING, VERBS

**past** see PASSED

**patent** *noun, adjective, verb*

🔊 There are two ways of pronouncing **patent**: /**pay**-tənt/ and /**pat**-ənt/.

In British English, /**pay**-tənt/ is the usual pronunciation, but people, such as lawyers, who use **patent** as a technical term for 'a protection given to an invention' tend to pronounce it /**pat**-ənt/.

In American English, /**pat**-ənt/ is the usual pronunciation, but when **patent** means 'obvious' (as in *patent nonsense*) it's pronounced /**pay**-tənt/.

**patrol** *verb*

People who **patrol** a place walk or travel around it to make sure everything is all right.

❗ When you add **-ing** or **-ed** to **patrol**, you double the **l**: **patrolling, patrolled.**

**pay** *verb*

The past tense and past participle of **pay** is ✔ **paid**, not ⚠ *payed*: *Have you paid for that magazine?*

## **peaceable** *adjective* and **peaceful** *adjective*

Someone who's **peaceable** doesn't quarrel, get into fights, etc.: *We are a peaceable people, who have no quarrel with our neighbours.*

**Peaceful** means 'quiet and calm' (*How peaceful it is when they turn their radio off!*) or 'not using war or physical violence' (*I hope we can reach a peaceful settlement of this dispute*).

❶ Remember the spelling of **peaceable** – there's an **e** between the **c** and the second **a**.

## **pedal** *verb*

When you **pedal** a bicycle, you operate it by turning its pedals with your feet.

❶ When you add -**ing** and -**ed** to pedal, you double the **l** in British English (**pedalling**, **pedalled**) but not in American English (**pedaling**, **pedaled**).

## **pejorative** *adjective*

**Pejorative** is a very formal word which means 'insulting': *'Skinny' is usually a pejorative term.* 🔊 Its standard pronunciation is /pə-**jor**-ə-tiv/.

❶ Remember the spelling – it's ✔ **pejorative**, not ⚠ *perjorative.*

## **pencil** *verb*

You can use **pencil** as a verb, meaning 'to write or draw with a pencil'. If you 'pencil something in', you write it, but you might change it later: *I've pencilled in Thursday for our meeting.*

❶ When you add -**ing** and -**ed** to **pencil** you double the **l** in British English (**pencilling**, **pencilled**), but not in American English (**penciling**, **penciled**).

**pendant** *noun* and **pendent** *adjective*

**Pendant** is a noun. It means 'an ornament worn round the neck on a chain'.

**Pendent** is a rare word. It's an adjective, meaning 'hanging down': *pendent branches.*

**people** see PERSON

**per cent** *adverb, noun*

In British English it's standard to write **per cent** as two words, but American English joins them together as **percent**.

It's not generally accepted in standard English to use expressions like *a per cent, half a per cent* and *a quarter of a per cent.* Say *one per cent, point five per cent* or *half of one per cent,* etc.

The verb you use after **per cent of** can be singular or plural, depending on the noun that goes with it: *Fifty per cent of my time is spent on administration. Ninety per cent of the children eat school meals.*

p

**percentage** *noun*

It's perfectly acceptable to use **percentage** to mean 'a proportion', as in ✔ *What percentage of your school budget goes on books?* But it's better not to use it on its own to mean just 'some', as in ⚠ *A percentage of our members would like to change the rule.* It's simpler to say some (or *many,* or a *few,* or whatever is most appropriate).

**perennial** see ANNUAL

**period** see FULL STOP

**permit** *verb, noun*

To **permit** 🔊 /pə-**mit**/ someone to do something is to allow them to do it: *Permit me to congratulate you on your performance.* It's a more formal word than *let* or *allow*. A **permit** 🔊 /**per**-mit/ is a document showing that you're officially allowed to do something.

❗ When you add **-ing** and **-ed** to **permit** you double the **t**: **permitting, permitted.**

**person** *noun* and **people** *noun*

The standard plural of **person** in British English is **people**: *one person, two people.* **Persons** is only used in very formal or legal contexts: *Persons convicted of this offence are liable to a fine of £500.* In American English, **persons** is more widely used as the plural.

**People** when it means 'more than one person' is plural, but **a people**, meaning 'a group of human beings who form a community or nation', is singular: *The Welsh are a musical people.*

p

**person agreement**

Verbs have to agree with the person of their subject: the first person (*I am, we have*); the second person (*you are*); and the third person (*she is, they were, the shop opens, problems arise*).

This can be tricky when there are two subjects joined by *or* or *nor*: *Neither I nor my sister want* (?)/*wants* (?) *to go.* The best way of getting round this is to rewrite the sentence so that there aren't two subjects: *I don't want to go, and nor does my sister.* But if you want to keep the two subjects, the verb should go with the second one:

*Neither I nor my sister wants to go.* This is because it's not a good idea to have a subject and a verb next to each other that don't agree.

## **personnel** *noun*

The **personnel** of a large organization, such as a business company or the army, are the people who work for it. It sounds rather pretentious to talk about the **personnel** of a small organization. 🔊 The word's pronounced /per-sə-**nel**/.

❶ Remember the spelling – two **n**s, and an **e** in the last syllable.

## **pharaoh** *noun*

The **pharaohs** 🔊 /**fair**-ohz/ were the kings of ancient Egypt.

❶ Remember the spelling: -**aoh**.

## **phenomenon** *noun*

A **phenomenon** is something that happens or exists and that you can experience with one of your senses or with your mind: *The growth in popularity of computer games in recent years has been a remarkable phenomenon.* The plural form of the word is **phenomena**: *The space telescope had observed several previously unknown phenomena.*

⚠ Remember that in standard English **phenomena** is *not* a singular noun and that you can't make a plural *phenomenas* out of it.

## **Philippines**

The **Philippines**, or the **Philippine Islands**, are a group of islands in the western Pacific Ocean.

❶ Remember the spelling – one **l** and two **p**s.

## phrases

A phrase is a group of words which go together but don't form a complete sentence. There are five sorts of phrase. They're mostly named after the main word they contain:

***Noun phrases*** The main word in a noun phrase is a noun: *a great big* ***plate*** *of chips*

***Verb phrases*** The main word in a verb phrase is a verb: *could have been* ***resting***

***Adjective phrases*** The main word in an adjective phrase is an adjective: *absolutely* ***wonderful***

***Adverb phrases*** The main word in an adverb phrase is an adverb: *quite* ***unexpectedly***

***Prepositional phrases*** A prepositional phrase contains a preposition followed by a noun or a noun phrase: ***under*** *the table*

## physician *noun* and physicist *noun*

A **physician** is a medical doctor. A **physicist** is an expert in physics.

## picket *verb*

If striking workers **picket** a place, they stand outside it and try to persuade other people not to go in.

❶ When you add -**ing** and -**ed** to **picket**, you don't double the **t**: **picketing, picketed**.

## picnic *verb*

To **picnic** is to have a picnic: *On hot summer days people love to picnic by the river.*

❶ When you add -**ing** and -**ed** to picnic, you put a **k** after the last **c**: **picnicking, picnicked**. The same happens when you add -**er**: **picnicker**.

## pilot *verb*

If you **pilot** a plane, you fly it: *She managed to pilot the plane to safety through the thunderstorm.*

❶ When you add -**ing** and -**ed** to **pilot**, you don't double the **t**: **piloting, piloted.**

## plain *noun* and plane *noun*

It's easy to confuse **plain** and **plane** since they both mean 'a flat surface'. The difference is that a **plain** is a large area of flat treeless land (*the great plains of America*), but a **plane** is a flat surface in geometry or, in a more abstract sense, a particular level (*He seems to live on a different plane to the rest of us*).

## plead *verb*

If you **plead** with someone, you beg them to do something: *He pleaded with me to take him back.*

The standard past form of **plead** is **pleaded**, but in American English, Scottish English and some other sorts of English **pled** or **plead** (pronounced /pled/) can be used as the past tense.

p

## plough, plow *noun, verb*

A **plough** is a farm implement for turning over the soil.

**Plough** is the British spelling, **plow** the American.

## plurals

The plural of most English nouns is formed by putting **s** on the end of the noun: *one orange, two oranges.*

It's not acceptable to put an apostrophe before a plural **s** ending. ✔ *Two oranges* is right, ⚠ *two orange's* is wrong. (Apostrophe **s** is only used for the possessive. To find out more about this, look at the entry for APOSTROPHE.)

❹ If the noun ends in a consonant and **y**, you change the **y** to **ie** before adding the **s**: *sty, sties*. (Exceptions to this are *lay-bys* and *standbys*, and also names: *the Ashbys*.)

Most nouns ending in **o** just add **s** for the plural: *photo, photos*. But there are some that add **es**: *hero, heroes*; *potato, potatoes*. If you're not sure whether a particular -**o** noun adds **s** or **es**, check in a dictionary.

Some nouns ending in **f** or **fe** change this to **ves** in the plural: *half, halves*; *life, lives*. Others don't: *roof, roofs*. Some do either: *hoof, hoofs, hooves*. If you're not sure whether a particular -**f(e)** noun changes to **ves** or not, check in a dictionary.

Compound nouns consisting of a noun, a preposition and another word form their plural by adding **s** to the noun in front: *lady in waiting, ladies in waiting*. Compound nouns ending in *-in-law* form their plural by adding **s** to the first noun in standard English: *fathers-in-law*. Informally, though, it's quite acceptable to add **s** to *law* instead: *father-in-laws*.

In modern English, it's usual to make the plural of compound nouns like *court martial* and *solicitor general* by adding **s** to the last word: *court martials*; *solicitor generals*. You can add **s** to the first word instead (*courts martial*; *solicitors general*), but this is a very formal way of making the plural, and it's now rather old-fashioned.

Nouns ending in -**ful** form their plural by adding **s** to the end: *two teaspoonfuls of sugar*. But you can also put the **s** before the -**ful**: *two teaspoonsful of sugar*.

When you use *man* or *woman* before a noun, to show that a person is male or female, you change them to *men* and *women* when you put the noun in the plural: *a woman chef, women chefs*.

When a plural comes after a number and immediately before another noun, it doesn't have an **s** on the end, so it's *a salmon weighing eight pounds* but *an eight-pound salmon*, and *a family with two cars* but *a two-car family*.

To find out about the plural of CRITERION and PHENOMENON, look at the entries for those words.

See also SINGULARS AND PLURALS.

**plus** *conjunction*

Some people use **plus** to mean 'and also': *I've got an awful lot of work to do, plus I've got a headache, so I don't think I'll come.*

⚠ This is all right in everyday speech, but it's not suitable for serious writing.

**pore** *verb* and **pour** *verb*

If you **pore** over a book, document, etc., you study it closely: *He's spent hours poring over that map.*

You **pour** liquid out of a container: *Can I pour you a cup of tea?*

**possessives**

The possessive forms of a language show who or what something belongs to. In English, you make the possessive form of singular nouns by adding **'s** to the end: *my sister's house.* For plural nouns ending in **s**, you put an apostrophe after the **s**: *his parents' bedroom.* To find out more about this, look at the entry for APOSTROPHE.

Another way of showing possession is to use *of*: *the hands of the clock.*

For people and animals, and for groups of people, it's usual to use apostrophe **s**: *our teacher's name*; *the hamster's cage*; *the government's decision*. For things, it's usual to use *of*: *the roof of the house.* But there are lots of fixed phrases in which you use apostrophe **s** for a thing, such as *for safety's sake* and *out of harm's way*. For places or periods of time it's perfectly acceptable to use apostrophe **s**: *Britain's landscape*; *New York's traffic*; *last year's figures*; but you can use *of* and other prepositions instead: *the landscape of Britain; the traffic in New York; the figures for last year.*

Possessive adjectives go before a noun: *my brush; their car.* Possessive pronouns come after a verb: *That brush is mine. That car is theirs.* Remember, there's no apostrophe in possessive adjectives and pronouns. It's ✔ *hers, its, theirs,* etc., not ⚠ *her's, it's* and *their's* (*it's* means 'it is' or 'it has'; see the entry for ITS).

## practicable *adjective* and practical *adjective*

If something's **practicable**, it's possible to do it: *It's simply not practicable to keep the library open each day – there isn't enough money.*

If something's **practical**, it's sensible to do it: *I don't think your suggestion that we could repair it with string is very practical.*

## practice *noun* and practise *verb*

**Practice**, with a **c**, is what you do to improve your skill at an activity: *She does an hour's piano practice every day.* It's also a doctor's or lawyer's business.

If you **practise**, with an **s**, something, you do it a lot of times so as to get good at it: *You need to practise your backhand volleys, David.*

So **practice** is the noun and **practise** is the verb. A good way to remember which is which is to think of *advice,* which is a noun, and *advise,* which is a verb, where the different pronunciations help you to tell them apart.

These are the British spellings. But American English is different. It uses **practice** for both the noun and the verb.

## practitioner *noun*

A **practitioner** is someone who does something – for example, a 'medical practitioner' is a doctor.

❶ Remember the spelling – ✔ **-titioner**, not ⚠ *-ticioner*.

## precede *verb*, proceed *verb* and procedure *noun*

If one thing **precedes** another, it comes before it: *June precedes July.*

If you **proceed**, you continue with an action: *We can't proceed with the building programme unless we can get some more money.*

❶ Remember the spelling – **precede** has **-ede** and **proceed** has **-eed**. But the noun **procedure** is different. Even though it comes from **proceed**, it only has one **e** before the **d**.

## prefer *verb*

If you **prefer** something, you like it better than others: *I prefer coffee to tea.*

**To** is the standard preposition to use with **prefer** and **preferable** (*Anything would be preferable to spending the whole afternoon with him*), not ⚠ *than*.

❶ When you add **-ing** and **-ed** to **prefer**, you double the **r**: **preferring, preferred**. But for the adjective **preferable** and the noun **preference** you don't double the **r**.

## prefixes

Prefixes are added to the beginning of other words. They don't mean anything on their own, but they change the meaning of the word they're added to. Put the prefix *un-* onto *happy* and you get the opposite, *unhappy*.

## prepositions

Prepositions link nouns and pronouns with another part of a sentence, often a verb. For example, *on* is a preposition in *Sally sat on the chair*, and *until* is a preposition in *We waited until the end.*

The usual place for a preposition is in front of a noun or pronoun: *in bed*; *below ground*; *despite my protests.* But it's quite normal for most common prepositions to be used at the end of a sentence as well: *You ought to have that cut seen to.*

Some people like to avoid putting prepositions at the end of a sentence. Instead of saying *This is the book which Baxter is best remembered for*, they say *This is the book for which Baxter is best remembered.* This is perfectly acceptable, but you don't have to do it, and if you do it in ordinary casual writing and conversation it can sound uncomfortably formal.

## prestigious *adjective*

Something that's **prestigious** makes anyone who owns it or is connected with it seem very important. For example, if you live at a **prestigious** address, people will think you must be very rich, successful, fashionable, powerful, etc.

⚠ It's a word to beware of when you come across it, because some people use it to try to make what they're talking about sound more important and glamorous than it really is.

## pretence, pretense *noun*

**Pretence** is when you're pretending: *He said his mother was a duchess, but it was all pretence – she's wasn't really.*

**Pretence** is the British spelling, **pretense** the American.

## prevent *verb*

If you **prevent** someone, you stop them doing something. The standard way to use **prevent** is with

**from**: *They tried to prevent me from seeing her.* You can also use it just with the **-ing** form of a verb, without **from**: *They tried to prevent me seeing her.* Another way of using it is with a possessive word before the **-ing** form of a verb (*They tried to prevent my seeing her*), but this is rather formal and old-fashioned (to find out more about this, look at the entry for FUSED PARTICIPLE).

## primitive *adjective*

**Primitive** describes something that's in an early stage of its development, and therefore very simple: *It's amusing now to look at pictures of those primitive aeroplanes they had in the early 1900s.*

❶ It usually suggests that what you're talking about is crude and unsophisticated, so don't use it about groups of people, especially in the modern world. A tribe and its culture might seem simple compared to Western European society, but it's probably just as sophisticated in different ways, so it's rude to call it 'primitive'.

## principal *adjective, noun* and principle *noun*

p

**Principal**'s an adjective. It means 'main': *What's the principal reason you resigned?*

**Principal**'s also a noun. It means 'the head of a college or school'. It also means 'an amount of money that's invested or lent'.

**Principle**'s only a noun. It means 'a basic truth or rule': *I understand the general principle on which an engine works, but I couldn't repair one myself.* It also means 'a rule of behaviour': *It's against my principles to eat meat.*

## prise *verb* and prize *verb, noun*

**Prise** is a verb. If you **prise** a lid off a tin or a box, you force it off using a lever.

**Prize** can be a verb too. It means 'to value something very highly': *She prizes her independence too much to want to get married.*

**Prize** is also a noun. It means 'something you're given if you win a race, a competition, etc.': *My prize for winning the competition was a holiday for two in the Caribbean.*

## proceed, procedure see PRECEDE

## programme, program *noun, verb*

In British English, **programme** is spelt differently depending on what it means.

When it means 'a show on television or radio' or 'a list of planned events', it's spelt **programme**. But when it means 'a set of coded instructions for a computer to carry out' or (as a verb) 'to give a computer instructions on how to do something', it's spelt **program**.

In American English, the spelling **program** is used for all meanings.

❶ When you add-**ing** or -**ed** to the verb **program**, you double the **m** in British English: **programming**, **programmed**. In American English it's usual to double the **m**, but you can also leave it as a single **m**.

p

## prone *adjective* and prostrate *adjective*

**Prone** and **prostrate** both mean 'lying face downwards'. They can both be used more generally for 'lying flat'. **Prostrate** can have the additional suggestion of being exhausted, or of being overcome with grief.

There's a special word you can use when you want to say 'lying face upwards' – *supine* – but it's rather rare and technical, and in ordinary writing it's best to say simply 'lying face upwards'.

## pronounceable *adjective*

If a word's **pronounceable**, you can pronounce it: *He had some strange foreign name – it was scarcely pronounceable.*

❶ Remember the spelling – there's an **e** between the **c** and the **a**.

## pronouns

Pronouns are words used to avoid repeating a noun you've already used. For example, instead of saying *I saw Sunil today. Sunil was looking better*, you can use the pronoun *he*: *I saw Sunil today. He was looking better.* Other pronouns include *it, we, they, mine, that, each, which.*

## pronunciation *noun*

**Pronunciation** is the way words are pronounced: *Don't you find French pronunciation rather difficult?*

❶ Remember the spelling – it's ✔ **pronunciation**, not ⚠ *pronounciation*. And it's pronounced 🔊 /prə-nun-see-**ay**-shən/, not ⚠ /prə-nown-see-**ay**-shən/.

p

## propel *verb*

To **propel** something is to make it go forwards: *This gun propels a shell over a distance of several miles.*

❶ When you add -**ing** or -**ed** to **propel**, you double the **l**: **propelling, propelled**.

## propellant *noun* and propellent *adjective*

A **propellant** is a substance used to propel something – for example, the fuel used to power a rocket might be called 'rocket propellant'.

**Propellent** is an adjective. It means 'having the power to propel something'. For instance, you could talk about 'the propellent force of an explosive'. But it's quite a rare word, mainly used in technical language.

**proper noun** see NOUNS

**prophecy** *noun* and **prophesy** *verb*

A **prophecy** (pronounced 🔊 /**prof**-ə-si/) is a statement about what you think is going to happen in the future: *Remember your prophecy – 'In a year's time I'll be running this company'? It didn't come true, did it?*

If you **prophesy** something (pronounced 🔊 /**prof**-i-sy/), you say that you think it'll happen in the future: *All the newspapers are prophesying a defeat for England in tomorrow's match.*

**proportion** *noun*

Using **a proportion of** to mean 'a part of' or 'some of' (as in *They stay with their father for a proportion of each school holiday*) sounds vague and a bit pretentious.

If you want to use **proportion**, it's best to put an adjective with it to show how big it is – *a small proportion, a large proportion,* etc.

Alternatively, you could use a simpler word such as *some, a part, a few* or *many.*

**prostrate** see PRONE

**protagonist** *noun*

**Protagonist** has two meanings. It can mean 'the main character in a play, film, etc.', or 'the main person in a contest': *The protagonist, played by Robert de Niro, appears in the first scene.* It can also mean 'a supporter of a particular cause': *She's one of the leading protagonists of women's rights.*

Some people object to this second use. They say that if a protagonist is *the* main person, you can't have more than one of them, and you can't be a *leading protagonist* or a *chief protagonist*. But it's now a well-established part of standard English, and there's no good reason not to use it.

## protest *noun, verb*

**Protest** can be either a noun (*Despite my protests, they chopped down the old tree*) or a verb (*I protested strongly when they said they were going to chop down the old tree*). The noun is pronounced /**proh**-test/, with the main stress on the first syllable. The verb is pronounced /prə-**test**/, with the main stress on the second syllable.

In American English you can **protest** something: *The students were protesting the war*. But in British English, you can only **protest against** something.

## provable *adjective*

If something is **provable**, it can be proved: *The accusations are not provable.*

p

Remember the spelling – there's no **e** between the **v** and the **a**.

## prove *verb*

The verb **to prove** has two past participles: **proved** and **proven**. You can use either. In British English, **proved** is commoner, especially as part of a verb: *Everyone thinks she's guilty, but no one's ever proved it.* But **proven** is becoming more widely used, and it's standard as an adjective: *He's a proven liar*.

**Proven** can be pronounced either /**proov**-ən/ or /**prohv**-ən/.

**provided** *conjunction* and
**providing** *conjunction*

**Provided** and **providing** mean 'on condition that': *You can borrow my book, provided/providing you let me have it back by Friday.* They can also be followed by **that**: *You can borrow my book, provided/providing that you let me have it back by Friday.*

The two words are equally acceptable, although in very formal writing it's probably better to use **provided**.

**publicly** *adverb*

**Publicly** means 'in public': *I can't stand him, but I'd never say so publicly.*

❶ Remember the spelling – ✔ it's **publicly**, not ⚠ *publically*.

**punctuation**

For information about punctuation marks look under the entries for

| | | | | | |
|---|---|---|---|---|---|
| ' | apostrophe | ! | exclamation mark | '' | inverted commas |
| ( ) | brackets | . | full stop | ? | question mark |
| : | colon | - | hyphen | ; | semicolon |
| , | comma | | | | |
| – | dash | | | | |

**pyjamas, pajamas** *noun*

**Pyjamas** are a jacket and trousers that you wear in bed. **Pyjamas** is the British spelling, **pajamas** the American.

p

# Qq

## quarrel *verb*

If you **quarrel** with someone, you have a strong argument or disagreement with them.

❶ When you add -**ing** and -**ed** to **quarrel**, you double the **l** in British English (**quarrelling**, **quarrelled**), but not usually in American English (**quareling**, **quareled**).

## question *noun*

Be careful how you use **no question**, meaning 'no doubt'. It's often possible to understand it in two completely opposite ways, which can be very confusing. For instance, does *There's no question that people are starting to get worried about this issue* mean that they certainly are getting worried or they certainly aren't? It's better to say clearly *There's no doubt that they are* or *There's no doubt that they're not.*

## question mark

A question mark is written at the end of questions: *How much is this jacket?*

⚠ You don't use a question mark when you refer to a question in indirect speech or reported speech (these terms are explained at INVERTED COMMAS): *He asked the shop assistant how much the jacket was.*

If you put a request in the form of a question, you should put a question mark at the end if it's fairly short: *Could you shut the door, please?* But if it's long you can use either a full stop or a question mark: *If you're going into town today, would you mind getting me another roll of wallpaper so I can finish doing the bedroom.*

In direct speech, the question mark goes inside the last inverted comma: *'Who goes there?' shouted the sentry.*

## questionnaire *noun*

A **questionnaire** is a list of questions to answer. The standard pronunciation of the word is /kwes-chə-**nair**/. There is another pronunciation, /kes-chə-**nair**/, but this is now rather old-fashioned, and many people find it odd.

## quit *verb*

If you **quit** a place, a job, etc., you leave it: *She decided to quit her job as a hairdresser and take a university course.*

**Quit** has two past forms: **quit** and **quitted**. **Quitted** is traditionally the main British form, but **quit** is becoming much commoner. Both are acceptable in standard English. **Quit** is the main American form.

## quite *adverb* and quiet *adjective*

If you say *I'm quite satisfied*, you could mean either that you're completely satisfied, or that you're fairly satisfied. When you speak, you can make clear which you mean by the way you say it. In writing, though, you can't do that, so take care how you use **quite**. If there's any possibility that you could be misunderstood, use a different word instead, such as *fairly*.

q

Don't confuse **quite** /kwyt/ with **quiet** /**kwy**-ət/, which means 'silent' or 'not noisy'.

## quotation marks see INVERTED COMMAS

# Rr

**r between vowel sounds** see INTRUSIVE R

**race** *noun*

One of the meanings of **race** is 'a large group of people who have the same ancestors and who have particular physical characteristics which make them different from other groups': *the Chinese race.*

However, **race** with this meaning has become closely linked with the words *racism* and *racist*, which refer to bad treatment of people because they belong to a different race (see RACISM).

For this reason, it's best to use another word instead of **race**. The main alternative is *people*: *the Chinese people.* In the case of Native Americans, you can use *nation: the Sioux nation.*

**races and peoples**

We have to be very careful about the words we use for different peoples. It's all too easy to give offence when we refer to racial origins.

There are a lot of slang words that people use when they want to be rude about a particular racial or national group: *Paki* for Pakistani, *Frog* for French, and so on. But it's unacceptable to insult someone because of their race or nationality, and all such words should be avoided.

The names we use for racial minority groups, particularly those who have been or are still being oppressed or persecuted, need special consideration. In many cases the old names have become linked with the idea of oppression and racial discrimination. Most of them are taken as an insult, and it's not acceptable to use them. For instance, until the 1950s, it was quite common among white people to use the word *nigger* to refer to black people (even though blacks were insulted by it). When the crime writer Agatha Christie published a book called *Ten Little Niggers* in 1939 there was no public outcry. But now, *nigger* is regarded by everyone as extremely offensive. Agatha Christie's book has been renamed *And Then There Were None*.

Because they cause such strong feelings, the names for racial minority groups and oppressed peoples tend to get changed. They're less stable than words for other racial and national groups.

The standard word for African people and people of African descent is **black**. This is both an adjective (*the black community in Britain*) and a noun (*the latest dance craze among young blacks*). The tendency is to use a small **b** for both, but some people prefer a capital **B**.

The word **black** is commonly applied to people of other dark-skinned races too, although this can give offence to Indians, Pakistanis, Bangladeshis and Chinese people.

In America, blacks are now quite commonly called **African Americans** or **Afro-Americans**. In Britain, the term **Afro-Caribbean** is often used.

Today, the word **Indian** refers mainly to the subcontinent of India, and in particular to the Republic of India. An Indian is someone who's a citizen of the Republic of India or who comes from there.

The word *Indian* is no longer much used to refer to the original peoples of North and South America. The terms *American Indian* and (mainly for South Americans) *Amerindian* are gradually going out of use too. They're being replaced in America by **Native American**. Where appropriate, you can alternatively use the name of a particular group (for instance, *Apache* or *Sioux*). It's unacceptable to refer to *Red Indians*.

The standard word for referring to people from eastern Asia is **Asian**. *Asiatic* is said to be offensive when used about people, but it's now so old-fashioned that probably very few people would realize they're supposed to be offended by it.

It's becoming less common to refer to the original peoples of northern North America and north-east Asia as *Eskimos* (the word implies 'eater of raw meat', and so is considered an insult). Those who live in northern Canada and Greenland prefer to be known as **Inuit**. The name for those who live in Alaska and Asia is **Yupik**.

The Lapps of northern Scandinavia prefer to be known by their own name for themselves, **Sami**.

Many Jewish women and girls would find it offensive to be referred to as a *Jewess*. Some people are uncomfortable about using the word *Jew* for a Jewish person. But there's no problem with the adjective **Jewish**: *Jewish people, a Jewish woman. Are you Jewish?*

## racism *noun* and racist *noun, adjective*

**Racism** is hatred or bad treatment of someone because they belong to a different race from you. A **racist** is someone who behaves in that way.



🔊 The standard pronunciations of the two words are /**rayss**-izm/ and /**rayss**-ist/. ⚠ It's not acceptable in standard English to say /**raysh**-izm/ and /**raysh**-ist/.

## racket *noun* and racquet *noun*

If you're referring to an unpleasantly loud noise, you can only use the spelling **racket**: *Tell them to turn that racket down – I can't hear myself think!* A dishonest scheme is also a **racket**.

But the thing you play tennis, squash and similar games with can be spelt either **racket** or **racquet**.

**railway** *noun* and **railroad** *noun*

The usual word in British English for the track that a train runs on is **railway**. In American English **railroad** is the main word, although **railway** is used for short tracks or ones that operate over a small area.

**raise** *verb, noun* and **rise** *verb, noun*

If you **raise** something, you lift it up: *He raised his hat.* But if something **rises**, it goes up of its own accord: *The temperature is rising.*

The past of **raise** is **raised**. The past tense of **rise** is **rose** and its past participle is **risen**.

In British English an increase in pay is a **rise**. Americans call it a **raise**.

**rancour, rancor** *noun*

**Rancour** is a long-lasting feeling of bitterness and hatred: *They accepted their defeat without rancour.*

**Rancour** is the British spelling, **rancor** the American. But the adjective **rancorous**, meaning 'filled with rancour', is spelt the same way in British and American English.

**rarely** *adverb*

It's not acceptable in standard English to say *rarely ever,* as in ⚠ *He rarely ever goes out these days.* It's usually best to say simply *never.* If you really feel you need to make **rarely** stronger, you could say *rarely if ever* or *rarely or never.*

**rateable, ratable** *adjective*

Something that's **rateable** can be rated or estimated. **Rateable** is the main spelling in British English, but American English prefers **ratable**.

**rather** *adverb*

▲ It's not acceptable in standard English to use *rather than* after *more*, as in *I'm more concerned with getting it right rather than making it look good.* Just use *than* on its own: ✔ *I'm more concerned with getting it right than making it look good.*

It's normal in speech and writing to use *I'd rather* for 'I'd prefer to': *I'd rather have coffee, please.* In formal writing use the full form *I would rather.*

**re** *preposition*

**Re** means 'about'. Even in business letters, where it was first used, it now sounds old-fashioned: *I write re your order of 27th March.* ▲ Avoid it in ordinary speaking and writing.

**reason** *noun*

There are several ways of joining **reason** onto the words that come after it.

Before a noun, use **for**: *What was the reason for her strange decision?*

Before a clause, you can use **why**: *No one seems to know the reason why he left.* Or you can leave out the *why*: *No one seems to know the reason he left.*

r

When you explain what the reason is, use **that**: ✔ *The reason I left was that I was offered a better job somewhere else.* It's not acceptable in standard English to use *because* in sentences like this – don't say ▲ *The reason I left was because I was offered a better job somewhere else.*

**rebel** *verb*

If you **rebel** against something, you refuse to obey it any longer, and you fight against it: *kids who rebel against their upbringing.*

❶ When you add **-ing** and **-ed** to **rebel**, you double the **l**: **rebelling**, **rebelled**. The noun that comes from **rebel** also has two **ls**: **rebellion**.

**rebut** *verb*

To **rebut** an accusation is to prove that it's false: *I'm confident I can rebut all the charges against me.*

❶ When you add **-ing** and **-ed** to **rebut**, you double the **t**: **rebutting**, **rebutted**. The noun that comes from **rebut** also has two **ts**: **rebuttal**.

**receive** *verb* and **receipt** *noun*

To **receive** something is to get something that's been given or sent. **Receipt** (pronounced /ri-**seet**/) is receiving: *Please acknowledge receipt of goods immediately.*

❶ Remember the spelling: it's **-ei-**, not **-ie-**.

**reconnoitre, reconnoiter** *verb*

If you **reconnoitre** /rek-a-**noy**-tə/ a place, you explore it to find out information about it: *We sent a couple of scouts on ahead to reconnoitre the ground for us.*

**Reconnoitre** is the British spelling, **reconnoiter** the American.

**recourse** *noun*, **resource** *noun* and **resort** *noun*, *verb*

If you **have recourse to** something, or you **have resort to** it, or you **resort to** it, you use it or do it because you need to, and there's often no other choice: *If your behaviour doesn't improve, I shall have to resort to severer punishment.*

If something is your only or last **recourse**, or **resource**, or **resort**, it's the only thing you can do or use in the circumstances you're in: *I hope these pills will help – they're the only recourse I have left.*

## recur *verb*

If something **recurs**, it happens again: *If the trouble recurs, come back and see me again.*
❶ When you add **-ing** and **-ed** to **recur**, you double the **r**: **recurring, recurred**. The noun that comes from **recur** also has two **rs**: **recurrence**.

## refer *verb*

To **refer to** something is to mention it: *When he said 'big red nose', we could all guess who he was referring to.*
❶ When you add **-ing** and **-ed** to **refer**, you double the **r**: **referring, referred**. But the adjective **referable** and the noun **reference** don't have a double **r**.

## reflexives

English reflexive pronouns end in *-self* in the singular (*myself, yourself, herself, himself, itself*) and *-selves* in the plural (*ourselves, yourselves, themselves*).

They're used to refer back to the subject of a sentence: *She washed herself. They can please themselves, for all I care.*



They're also used to give special emphasis to a noun or an ordinary pronoun: *The Queen herself is coming to tea. I myself have never liked opera.*

You can also use them instead of an ordinary pronoun: *Like yourselves, we feel that the school should do more to combat bullying. There were invitations for her friend and herself.* This can sound rather formal, though. In ordinary speech and writing it's better to say 'Like you' and 'for her friend and her'. And in particular, using *myself* instead of *me* often sounds pretentious. Instead of saying ⚠ *They've asked Roger and myself to help*, say ✔ *They've asked Roger and me to help.*

## refute *verb*

The traditional meaning of **refute** is 'to disprove' – if you refute someone's statement, you prove that it's not true.

It has another meaning – 'to deny': '*I absolutely refute what you've just said.*'

⚠ This second meaning is quite common, but it's not fully accepted as part of standard English. Many people dislike it.

If you use **refute** in its traditional meaning, people may mistakenly think you mean 'deny'. If you use it in its other meaning, people may object that it's not standard English. The best thing to do is use another word, such as *disprove* or *deny*, which people can't misunderstand.

## regard *noun*

Take care how you use expressions like **in regard to**, **with regard to** and **as regards**. It sounds very stiff and pompous to say, or write, *I have serious misgivings with regard to your proposals.* It's usually better to use a simpler word, such as *about* or *on.*

**With regard to** and the others are better than *about* or *on* at the beginning of sentences (*With regard to your recent letter, I should point out that* ...), but it's better still to write sentences that don't have to start with **with regard to**, etc.

If you do use them, remember it's ✔ **with regard to** and **in regard to**, not ⚠ *with regards to* or *in regards to.*

## regret *verb*

To **regret** something is to feel sorry or disappointed about it: *I regret now that I didn't buy that painting when I had the chance.*

❶ When you add -**ing** and -**ed** to **regret**, you double the t: **regretting**, **regretted**.

## regretful *adjective* and regrettable *adjective*

If you're **regretful** about something, you feel sorry or disappointed about it: *With a regretful sigh, she put the cake back in the box.* The adverb that goes with **regretful** is **regretfully**: *She sighed regretfully.*

If something's **regrettable**, it's a thing you feel sorry or disappointed about: *It's regrettable that she wasn't able to join us.* The adverb that goes with **regrettable** is **regrettably**. It means 'it's a shame that' or 'I regret that': *Regrettably she won't be able to join us.* ⚠ Don't use **regretfully** with this meaning.

## rein *noun* and reign *noun, verb*

**Reins** are what you use for controlling a horse. A king or queen's **reign** is the period during which they're on the throne. You can also use **reign** as a verb: *Queen Victoria reigned for 64 years.*

Take care not to get the two words mixed up, especially when you use **reins** as a metaphor for control – you ✔ *relinquish the reins of power*, not ⚠ *the reigns of power.*

r

## relative clause, relative pronoun

see CLAUSES

## rendezvous *noun, verb*

A **rendezvous** 🔊 /**ron**-day-voo/ is an arranged meeting with someone: *I've got a rendezvous with the Colonel at three o'clock this afternoon.* The plural form of **rendezvous** is **rendezvous**. It's spelt the same as the singular, but it's pronounced 🔊 /**ron**-day-vooz/, rhyming with *whose.*

**Rendezvous** can also be a verb: *We'll rendezvous outside the bank at twelve.* Its past form is **rendezvoused**, pronounced 🔊 /**ron**-day-vood/, and its present participle is **rendezvousing** 🔊 /**ron**-day-voo-ing/, rhyming with *mooing*.

## repairable *adjective* and reparable *adjective*

Both these adjectives mean 'able to be mended'. **Repairable** 🔊 /ri-**pair**-ə-bəl/ is used mainly about solid objects: *This watch is very badly damaged. Do you think it's repairable?* **Reparable** 🔊 /**rep**-ə-rə-bəl/ is used about abstract things, like damage and loss: *The harm it's done to her reputation is scarcely reparable.*

Both words are mainly used in questions or negative sentences, or with negative prefixes: **unrepairable**, **irreparable**.

## repel *verb*

If you **repel** an attack, you defeat it. And if something **repels** you, you feel disgusted by it.

❶ When you add -**ing** or -**ed** to **repel**, you double the **l**: **repelling**, **repelled**.

## replaceable *adjective*

If something's **replaceable**, you can get another one to take its place: *Oh dear, your beautiful Ming vase. I hope it's replaceable!*

❶ Remember the spelling – there's an **e** between the **c** and the second **a**.

## report *noun*

You write a **report on** something: *The Department of Transport has issued a report on the accident.*

It's becoming quite common to use **into** instead of **on** (⚠ *a report into the accident*), but this isn't yet part of standard English, so you should avoid it in serious writing.

## reported speech see INVERTED COMMAS

## research *noun, verb*

**Research** is work that you do to find out facts or information. It's traditionally pronounced 🔊 /ri-**serch**/, with the main stress on the second syllable. But there is another pronunciation, 🔊 /**ree**-serch/, with the main stress on the first syllable. Some people don't like this, but it's quite common and perfectly acceptable.

The verb **to research** means 'to do research': *She's researching into the history of the building trade in London.* It's much more usual to use the pronunciation 🔊 /ri-**serch**/ for the verb, and in fact many people make a difference between /**ree**-serch/ for the noun and /ri-**serch**/ for the verb.

## resource, resort see RECOURSE

## respect *noun*

The expressions **in respect of** and **with respect to** are appropriate in very formal or legal language, but in ordinary speech and writing they sound stiff: *We had some discussions with respect to the forthcoming jumble sale.* It's better to use a more straightforward word, such as *about*: *We talked about* (or *discussed*) *the forthcoming jumble sale.*

❗ Remember, its ✔ **in respect of**, not ⚠ *in respect to.*

## respective *adjective* and respectively *adverb*

**Respective** means 'of each individual person separately'. For example, *We went to our rooms* might mean that we shared several rooms between us, and that we went to them. But *We went to our respective rooms* makes it clear that each of us had a separate room to go to. ⚠ Don't use **respective** unless it's necessary, though. There's no point in saying *They returned to their respective homes.* It's obvious that they couldn't share several homes between them, so you can just say simply *They returned to their homes.*

*Tom and I had lasagna and pizza respectively* means that Tom had lasagna and I had pizza. In fact, it would be clearer to say simply *Tom had lasagna and I had pizza* – **respectively** forces people to look back over your sentence to see what you were referring to, and if it's a long sentence this can be confusing.

## restaurateur *noun*

Some one who runs a restaurant is called a **restaurateur** 🔊 /ress-tə-rə-**ter**/.

❗ Remember, there's no **n** in the word, even though it looks like *restaurant.*

## restive *adjective* and restless *adjective*

People and animals that are **restive** are jumpy and can't stop moving about, because they're anxious, bored, impatient or starting to get angry: *The crowd was getting restive, and I was afraid there might be a riot.*

People and animals that are **restless** can't stop moving about because they're anxious, nervous or ill: *His temperature was 102°, and he spent a restless night.*

## restrictive relative clause see CLAUSES

## revel *verb*

If you **revel** in something, you take a great delight in it: *She ran down the beach, revelling in the warm sunshine.*

r

❶ When you add -**ing** and -**ed** to **revel**, you double the **l** in British English (**revelling**, **revelled**) but not in American English (**reveling**, **reveled**).

## reverend *adjective* and reverent *adjective*

**Reverend** is used as the title of a clergyman: *the Reverend David Trustram.*

**Reverent** means 'showing deep religious respect': *With a reverent bow, he turned from the altar.*

## review *noun, verb* and revue *noun*

If you conduct a **review** of something, you examine it to see how well it's working. A **review** can also be a description of a book, play, film, etc. and a judgement about how good it is.

A **revue** is an entertainment consisting of a number of different items.

## rid *verb*

If you **rid** a place of something, you free it from something bad: *We're determined to rid the country of this terrible disease.*

The usual past form of **rid** is **rid**: *The Pied Piper rid Hamelin of rats.* There's also **ridded**, but that's rather old-fashioned.

r

❶ When you add -**ing** to **rid**, you double the **d**: **ridding**.

## right *adverb* and rightly *adverb*

**Right** and **rightly** both mean 'correctly' or 'properly'. The main difference between them is that **right** can only come after verbs (*Did I do that right?*). but **rightly** usually comes before the verb (*She rightly decided to turn down the offer*).

If you want to put **rightly** after the verb, it usually goes between commas in writing: *She decided, quite rightly,* *to turn down the offer*. The exception is after *remember*: you can say either *If I remember right* or *If I remember rightly*.

**rigour, rigor** *noun*

When **rigour** means 'harshness' or 'severe conditions' it's spelt **rigour** in British English and **rigor** in American English: *I don't know if we can withstand the rigours of another winter in Alaska.*

There's also a medical word **rigor** which means 'stiffness in the body'. This is always spelt **rigor**.

❶ The adjective **rigorous** is spelt without a **u** before the **r** in both British and American English.

**ring** *verb*

There are two verbs **ring**, and they have different past forms.

When **ring** means 'to make a sound like a bell', its past tense is **rang** and its past participle is **rung**: *Somebody must have rung the doorbell.*

But when it means 'to make a circle round', its past form is **ringed**: *You'll see I've ringed all the important names.*

**riot** *verb*

When people **riot**, they behave wildly and violently in a group.

❶ When you add **-ing** and **-ed** to **riot**, you don't double the **t**: **rioting**, **rioted**.

**rival** *verb*

If someone **rivals** another person, they're almost as good as that person: *I can't rival my mother when it comes to baking cakes.*

❶ When you add **-ing** and **-ed** to **rival** you double the **l** in British English (**rivalling, rivalled**) but not in American English (**rivaling, rivaled**).

## rivet *verb*

When you fix something in place with a rivet, you **rivet** it.

❶ When you add **-ing** and **-ed** to **rivet**, you don't double the **t**: **riveting, riveted**.

## rob *verb* and steal *verb*

You **rob** people and places: *I've been robbed! Somebody's robbed the flat while we've been out.*

You **steal** things: *Who's stolen my pen?*

## role *noun* and roll *noun*

An actor's **role** is the part that they have in a play or film. A **role** is also the function that a person or thing has: *the role of the computer in industry.*

A **roll** is something rolled up: *a roll of paper*. It can also be a small individually baked portion of bread.

## roof *noun*



The plural of **roof** is **roofs**. ⚠ People often say **rooves**, but it's not standard, so in writing use **roofs**.

## round see AROUND

## rumour, rumor *noun*

A **rumour** is information that spreads to a lot of people but may not be true. **Rumour** is the British English spelling, **rumor** the American.

# Ss

## sabre, saber *noun*

A **sabre** is the heavy sword with a curved blade which gives the *sabre-toothed tiger* its name. **Sabre** is the British English spelling, **saber** the American.

## same *adjective, pronoun, adverb*

The standard conjuction to use after the adjective **same** is **as**: *He told the same jokes as he told last year.* You could also use **that**, although it's not so common: *He told the same jokes that he told last year.*

When **same** is a pronoun, you can only use **as** after it: *I'd like the same as she had.*

The same applies when you use **same** as an adverb: *She always dresses the same as you.* ⚠ But this use of **same** isn't suitable for writing, where it's better to say ✔ *She always dresses in the same way as you.*

## satire *noun* and satyr *noun*

**Satire** 🔊 /**sat**-ire/ is when you use humour or exaggeration to make fun of a person, especially in order to expose their shortcomings: *Government ministers are often a target of satire.*

In Greek myths, a **satyr** 🔊 /**sat**-er/ is a woodland god with a man's body and a goat's ears, legs and tail.

## sauté *verb*

To **sauté** something is to fry it quickly in hot shallow fat. The present participle of **sauté** is **sautéing**, and its past form is either **sautéd** or **sautéed**.

## saviour, savior *noun*

If someone saves you, they're your **saviour**. **Saviour** is the British English spelling, **savior** the American.

## savour, savor *noun*

**Savour** is a rather formal word for the smell or taste of something. It's spelt **savour** in British English and **savor** in American.

In the same way **savoury**, which means 'tasty but not sweet', is spelt **savoury** in British English and **savory** in American.

## saw *verb*

To **saw** something is to cut it with a saw. The usual past participle of **saw** is **sawed**: *She'd sawed through the table leg by mistake.* There is another past participle, **sawn**, but this is mainly used as an adjective: *a sawn-off shotgun.* And in American English, it's **sawed** that's used as the adjective: *a sawed-off shotgun.*

## sceptic, skeptic *noun*

A 🔊 **sceptic** /**skep**-tik/ is someone who's inclined not to believe what they're told. **Sceptic** is the British English spelling, **skeptic** the American English. (Don't mix up **sceptic** with *septic* 🔊 /**sep**-tik/, which means 'infected with harmful bacteria'.)



The related adjective is spelt **sceptical** 🔊 /**skep**-ti-kəl/ in British English and **skeptical** in American English.

## sceptre, scepter *noun*

A **sceptre** 🔊 /**sep**-ter/ is a decorated metal stick which is used as a symbol of authority. The British English spelling is **sceptre**, the American **scepter**.

**schedule** *noun*

A **schedule** is a programme or timetable of planned events: *According to her schedule, the princess should be arriving at the hospital at 3.30.*

The standard British pronunciation of **schedule** is /**shed**-yool/. In American English it's pronounced /**sked**-yool/, and this pronunciation is sometimes used in Britain too.

**schism** *noun*

**Schism** is a very formal word meaning 'the splitting of a group into two opposing sections because they disagree about something important': *The Church of England is threatened with schism over the question of women priests.*

People who use it at all often, such as clergymen, tend to use the traditional pronunciation /sizm/. But the more modern pronunciation /skizm/ is perfectly acceptable in standard English.

**scone** *noun*

A **scone** is a sort of small flat soft cake. There are two pronunciations of **scone** – /skon/ (rhyming with *Ron*) and /skohn/ (rhyming with *bone*). They're equally acceptable in standard English.

S

**Scotch** *adjective*, **Scots** *adjective* and **Scottish** *adjective*

There's a tradition that **Scots** and **Scottish** are the adjectives you should use when talking about things and people from Scotland. Scottish people are supposed to object to **Scotch**.

In practice, **Scots** is quite rare. **Scotch** is perfectly acceptable in standard general English, and in certain fixed expressions, like *Scotch egg*, *Scotch mist* and *Scotch* *whisky*, it's the only adjective you can use. But the prejudice against it means that **Scottish** is more common, and **Scottish** has the advantage that it isn't objected to by anyone.

## sculptor *noun* and sculpture *noun, verb*

A **sculptor** is an artist who makes shapes by carving wood or stone or casting metal. **Sculpture** is what a sculptor makes.

You can also use **sculpture** as a verb to describe what a sculptor does, although a more usual word for this is **sculpt**: *The figure had been sculpted out of white marble.*

## seasonal *adjective* and seasonable *adjective*

Something that's **seasonal** varies according to the different seasons or happens only at particular times of the year: *Fruit picking is seasonal work.*

Something that's **seasonable** is suitable to the time of year: *Snow in June? That's not very seasonable, is it?*

## seeing *conjunction*

When **seeing** is used as a conjunction, it means 'because'. It's usually followed by **that**: *Seeing that you're going that way, could you give me a lift?* But you can also use it on its own: *Seeing you're paying, I'll have another one.*

S

⚠ It's not acceptable, though, in standard English to say *seeing as* or *seeing as how*.

## seize *verb*

To **seize** something is to take hold of it suddenly or with great force: *The tiger seized the little boy and ran off with him.*

❶ Remember the spelling – **seize**. It doesn't follow the usual rule about **i** before **e** except after **c**.

**-self** see REFLEXIVES

## semicolon

A semicolon is a comma with a dot above it (;). Its main job is joining parts of a sentence together.

Take these two sentences: *It was late. We were getting tired.* If you write them like that, as two separate sentences, the effect is rather abrupt. Using a semicolon, you can join them into one sentence: *It was late; we were getting tired.* To make the link even smoother, you can use a comma and put *and* before the second part: *It was late, and we were getting tired.*

You can also use a semicolon before words and phrases such as *however, nevertheless, therefore, consequently, all the same* and *for example*: *It was late; nevertheless, no one wanted to go to bed.*

The other job the semicolon does is listing things. If you have a list of things which have commas in them, you use semicolons to separate the things: *The main ingredients are four eggs, well beaten; 50 ml of cream, preferably double; mixed currants, raisins and sultanas; and 150g of plain flour.*

## sensual *adjective* and sensuous *adjective*

**Sensual** and **sensuous** both have to do with what we feel and experience through our five senses.

**Sensual** is usually a rather negative word. It's mainly used to talk in a disapproving way about the enjoyment of sex, eating and drinking.

**Sensuous** is a more positive word. It's used to talk about the pleasure you get from movement, touching, sounds, colours and so on.

## sentence adverbs

Usually, adverbs add to the meaning of verbs, adjectives and other adverbs. But there are some that can add to the meaning of whole sentences. Here are some examples: *Unfortunately, no one was at home. Predictably, Sam ate most of the cake. Musically, the piece isn't of much interest. Frankly, I couldn't care less.*

⚠ There are a few adverbs like this which some people object to. The most disliked is *hopefully* (to find out more about this, look at the entry for HOPEFULLY). The other main disliked ones are *thankfully, mercifully* and *truthfully*. There's no good reason for objecting to them. They're a perfectly normal part of English. But since they cause such strong feelings of dislike in some people, it's best not to use them in serious writing, or to use them sparingly.

You need to be careful, too, that if you do use one, it can't be mistaken for an ordinary adverb. For example, does *We'll arrive hopefully on Tuesday* mean that we'll arrive full of hope on Tuesday, or that we hope we'll arrive on Tuesday? In cases like this it's best to rewrite the sentence in another way, to make clear what you mean.

To find out about the standard English use of *regrettably* and *regretfully*, look at the entry for REGRETFUL.

S

## separate *adjective, verb*

Things that are **separate** 🔊 /**sep**-rit/ are on their own, not joined to anything else. If you **separate** /**sep**-ə-rayt/ things, you make them separate.

❗ Remember the spelling – it's ✔ **separate**, not ⚠ *seperate*.

## sepulchre, sepulcher *noun*

A **sepulchre** 🔊 /**sep**-əl-ker/ is a tomb. **Sepulchre** is the British spelling, **sepulcher** the American.

## serf *noun* and surf *noun*

In the past, a **serf** was a farm labourer who worked for a landowner.

**Surf** is waves breaking on a shore.

## serial see CEREAL

## serviceable *adjective*

If something's **serviceable** it can be used: *This old sewing machine's got a few dents and scratches, but it's still perfectly serviceable.*

❶ Remember the spelling – there's an **e** between the **c** and the **a**.

## sew *verb* and sow *verb*

You **sew** 🔊 /soh/ cloth with a needle and thread: *Could you sew up this hole in my shirt, please?* The past tense of **sew** is **sewed**, and its past participle is either **sewn** or **sewed**.

You **sow** seeds in the ground. The past tense of **sow** is **sowed**, and its past participle is either **sown** or **sowed**.

S

## sewage *noun* and sewerage *noun*

**Sewage** 🔊 /**soo**-ij/ is human waste that is carried away in large drains, called *sewers*. **Sewerage** 🔊 /**soo**-er-ij/ is the system of sewers that do this.

## sexist language

English has pronouns for male people and animals (*he, him, his*) and for female people and animals (*she, her, hers*). These are fine when you're talking about males and females. But there are times when you don't want to say, or don't know, whether a person is male or female.

In the past, it was usual to use male pronouns in cases like this: *If anyone finds my glasses, could he let me know?* But many people no longer find this acceptable, because it ignores women.

There are various things you can do instead. You can use *he or she*, or *she or he*: *If anyone finds my glasses, could he or she let me know?* But this can get very awkward if you have to repeat it several times in a short space.

You can use *she* instead of *he*, either some of the time or all of the time: *If anyone finds my glasses, could she let me know?* This is especially appropriate if most of the people referred to are likely to be female, but otherwise it can be distracting, and anyway it's just as sexist as using *he*.

You can use *they*: *If anyone finds my glasses, could they let me know?* Some people object to using *they* for a single person, but it's a neat solution to the problem, and it's gradually becoming accepted in standard English. It's all right to use it in all but the most formal writing.

Another solution which is sometimes possible is to use a plural instead of a singular, since the plural doesn't show the sex of the people involved. Instead of saying *Any member wishing to reserve a seat should make his/his or her/their booking as soon as possible*, you can say *Members wishing to reserve a seat should make their bookings as soon as possible.*

Alternatively, you can use a passive construction instead of an active construction, which makes it possible to avoid mentioning the person or people doing the action: *Bookings should be made as soon as possible* (it's best not to use the passive too often, though – look at the entry for CLEAR WRITING).

To find out more about sexism in language, look at the entries for FEMININE FORMS, MAN and MANKIND.

## **shall** *verb* and **will** *verb*

**Shall** and **will** are used to form the future tense of verbs: *They will leave tomorrow.*

**Will** is much commoner than **shall**. American English almost always uses **will**, and **shall** is becoming rarer in British English. However, some British speakers do keep up the old difference between **shall** and **will**: **shall** is used after *I* and *we* (*I shall leave tomorrow*) and **will** is used in all other cases (*They will leave tomorrow*).

**Will** is perfectly acceptable in standard English after *I* and *we*, and **shall** now tends to sound rather old-fashioned. But **shall** is still quite commonly used when you want to make a suggestion or ask a question: *Shall I turn the light on?* means 'Do you want me to turn the light on?', not 'Am I going to turn the light on?'

## **sheath** *noun* and **sheathe** *verb*

A **sheath** /sheeth/ is a close-fitting protective cover for something sharp.

To **sheathe** /sheedh/ something is to put it in a sheath: *He sheathed his sword.*



## **shine** *verb*

If you talk about the sun **shining**, or **shining** a torch somewhere, you use **shone** /shon/ as the past form of the verb: *The sun shone brightly. I shone a light in his face.*

But if you talk about **shining** your shoes, meaning 'polishing' them, you use **shined** as the past form of the verb: *A boy on the street corner shined my shoes for me.*

**ship** see BOAT

**shoot** *noun* and **chute** *noun*

A sloping channel which things (such as rubbish) or people can slide down is called a **chute** 🔊 /shoot/ or a **shoot**. In British English it's more usual to use the spelling **chute**.

A bud or small new twig growing from a plant is called a **shoot**. It can't be spelt any other way.

**should** *verb* and **would** *verb*

**Should** is mainly used to mean 'ought to': *You should write and thank her for the present.*

**Would** is used in conditional sentences (*I think he would come if you offered him more money*) and in reporting what someone has said when they've used the word *will* (*He said he would do it tomorrow*). In the past, **would** was replaced by **should** after *I* and *we* (*I said I should do it tomorrow*), but this now sounds very old-fashioned. It's much better to use **would**.

It's still quite common and normal to use **should** after *I* in expressions like *I should think*, when you're saying what your opinion is: *I shouldn't think she's back yet. I shouldn't have thought you'll need an umbrella.* (Remember, it's ✔ *I should have*, not ⚠ *I should of.*)

S

**shovel** *verb*

If you **shovel** something, you move it with a shovel or spade, or in a quick careless way: *She shovelled the books into her bag and ran off.*

❶ When you add **-ing** and **-ed** to **shovel** you double the **l** in British English (**shovelling, shovelled**), but not in American English (**shoveling, shoveled**).

## shrink *verb*

To **shrink** is to get smaller: *When Alice drank the magic potion, she began to shrink.*

The standard past tense of **shrink** is **shrank**, although **shrunk** can also be used, especially in American English: *Honey, I shrunk the kids!*

The past participle is **shrunk**: *I'm afraid your underpants have shrunk in the washing machine.* When you use it as an adjective, it becomes **shrunken**: *He had a fine collection of shrunken heads.*

## shrivel *verb*

Something that **shrivels** becomes dry and wrinkled: *There'd been no rain for weeks, and the fruit was beginning to shrivel up on the trees.*

❶ When you add -**ing** and -**ed** to **shrivel** you double the **l** in British English (**shrivelling**, **shrivelled**), but not in American English (**shriveling**, **shriveled**).

## sight *noun* and site *noun*

**Sight** is the ability to see (*She lost her sight when she was only a child*) or something that you see (*His face wasn't a pretty sight after the fight*).

A **site** is a place where something happens or is built: *This was the site of a great battle hundreds of years ago.*

S

## signal *verb*

When you **signal**, you make a signal, or send a signal to someone.

❶ When you add -**ing** or -**ed** to **signal** you double the **l** in British English (**signalling**, **signalled**), but not in American English (**signaling**, **signaled**).

**since** see AGO

**sing** *verb*

The past tense of **sing** is **sang**: *They sang a selection of Christmas carols.*

Its past participle is **sung**: *I haven't sung this song since I was a child.*

**singe** *verb*

To **singe** something is to damage it slightly by burning: *I'm afraid your hat got a bit singed when I dropped it in the fire.*

❶ When you add -**ing** to **singe**, you don't leave off the **e**: **singeing**.

## singulars and plurals

In grammar, the word **singular** refers to one single person or thing. In English, nouns and pronouns can be singular: *man* and *she* are singular. Verbs can be singular too: in *she goes, goes* is singular.

The word **plural** refers to two or more people or things. In English, nouns and pronouns can be plural: *men* and *they* are plural. Verbs can be plural too: in *they go, go* is plural.

A singular noun goes with a singular verb: *A mouse scuttles across the floor.* A plural noun goes with a plural verb: *Two mice scuttle across the floor.*

That's simple enough so far, but there are a few complications.

***Groups*** Singular nouns referring to a group of people or animals can go with a plural verb: *The committee have accepted my recommendation.*

***With 'and'*** Nouns joined by *and* usually count as plural, so they go with a plural verb: *Coffee and tea are 75p a cup*. But sometimes, the nouns joined by *and* can be thought of as a single thing, which means that you can use a singular verb with them: *Law and order has broken down in the city.*

If nouns are joined by other words or phrases, such as *with, as well as* or *in addition to*, they go with a singular verb: *A lot of money, as well as a lot of people's time, has gone into this project.*

***Measurements*** or quantities with a number in front are usually thought of as a single unit, in which case they go with a singular verb: *Five pounds is far too expensive. Fifty years is a long time.*

***Pronouns*** The pronouns *anybody, anyone, everybody, everyone, nobody, no one, somebody, someone, either, neither* and *each* always go with a singular verb: *Each of us was given a present.*

The pronouns *all, half, none* and *some* can go with a singular or plural verb, depending on their context: *All of the ice cream has melted. All of my friends are coming.*

***Nouns with -s*** Some English nouns that have an **s** on the end look as though they're plural, but in fact take a singular verb. They include *news* (*The news is good, I'm glad to say*), the names of various diseases (*measles, mumps, shingles*), the names of some sports and games (*billiards, darts, draughts*) and the names of some mainly scientific subjects ending in *-ics* (*ballistics, economics, physics*).

There are problems about using the right verb with some English nouns that were originally Latin plural nouns. Look at the entries for DATA, MEDIA and STRATA.

S

Often, another noun comes between the subject of a sentence and its verb. If this noun is plural when the subject is singular, it can be tempting to make the verb plural: ⚠ *The number of checks on inmates are being reduced.* This is wrong. It's the number that has been reduced, not the checks or the inmates, so the verb must be singular: ✔ *The number of checks on inmates is being reduced.* (See further the entry on NUMBER.)

In the same way, if a singular noun comes between a plural subject and the verb, the verb must still be plural.

You'll find more on plurals at the entry for PLURALS.

## sink *verb*

To **sink** is to go below the surface: *The ship was holed and sinking fast.*

The standard past tense of **sink** is **sank**, but **sunk** is also acceptable.

Its past participle is **sunk**: *All the sediment has sunk to the bottom.* When you use it as an adjective, it becomes **sunken**: *a sunken Spanish galleon.*

## site see SIGHT

## situation *noun*

S

It's become a habit in modern English to use **situation**, meaning 'a state of affairs', where it's not needed. For instance, it's long-winded to say ⚠ *We're now in a war situation* when you could simply say ✔ *We're now at war.* Instead of saying *In an interview situation, some people get quite nervous,* why not just say *In interviews* or *When being interviewed, some people get quite nervous?*

A lot of people find this use of **situation** annoying, and it's bad style to use it repeatedly.

**sizeable, sizable** *adjective*

Something that's **sizeable** is quite large: *We were left with sizeable debts.* **Sizeable** is the main spelling, but you can also spell it **sizable**.

**skeptic** see SCEPTIC

**ski** *verb*

If you **ski**, you travel on skis.

The third person present singular of the verb is **skis**: *Geoffrey always skis at Davos at this time of year.*

Its present participle is **skiing**. And its past form can be either **ski'd** or **skied** 🔊 /skeed/.

**skilful, skillful** *adjective*

Someone who is **skilful** has a lot of skill: *You need to be quite skilful to do the crosswords in that paper.*

**Skilful** is the British spelling, **skillful** the American.

**slander** see LIBEL

**sleight** *noun*

If someone does something by 'sleight of hand', they do it very cleverly and in a way that you don't notice: *By some sleight of hand he'd been able to slip a couple of extra items onto the bill.* 🔊 **Sleight** is pronounced the same way as *slight*.

❗ Remember its spelling – it's **ei**, not **ie**.

**slow** *adverb* and **slowly** *adverb*

After a verb, you can use either **slow** or **slowly**: *Drive slower here. Drive more slowly here.* Both are perfectly acceptable in standard English, although in formal writing it's better to use **slowly**.

Before a verb you can only use **slowly**: *Slowly she raised her eyes to meet his.*

## smell *verb*

The verb **smell** has two past forms, **smelt** and **smelled**. In British English you can use either, although **smelt** is more usual. In American English **smelled** is much commoner than **smelt**.

## smoky, smokey *adjective*

Something that's **smoky** is filled with smoke or gives off a lot of smoke: *a smoky room.*

The standard spelling is **smoky**, but you can also use **smokey**.

## smooth *adjective, verb*

Something that's **smooth** has no bumps or rough places. You can also use **smooth** as a verb, meaning 'to make something smooth': *She smoothed his hair with her hand.*

❶ Remember the spelling of the verb – it's **smooth**, with no **e** on the end.

## smoulder, smolder *verb*

S

To **smoulder** is to burn slowly without a flame: *Parts of the old building were still smouldering, even though the fire had been put out.*

**Smoulder** is the British spelling, **smolder** the American.

## sombre, somber *adjective*

Sombre 🔊 /**som**-ber/ means 'gloomily dark': *They were dressed in sombre browns and greys.*

**Sombre** is the British spelling, **somber** the American.

**some** *adjective*

When you use **some** before numbers it suggests an approximate figure, not a precise one, so don't use it with accurate measures. *We live some twenty minutes from the station* is all right, but not ⚠ *We live some nineteen and three quarter minutes from the station.*

**sometime** *adverb, adjective,* **some time**

When **sometime** is an adverb, meaning 'at some unspecified time', it can also be spelt as two words, **some time**: *You must come and have lunch with us sometime/some time.*

But when **sometime** is an adjective, meaning 'former', it can only be spelt as one word: *my sometime colleague.*

And when **some time** means 'quite a long time', it can only be spelt as two words: *I'm just going out. I may be some time.*

**sooner** *adverb*

*No sooner had I sat down than the doorbell rang.* In sentences like this, use **than** after **sooner**, not **when**.

**sort** see KIND

**sow** see SEW

S

**special** *adjective,* **specially** *adverb,* **especial** *adjective* and **especially** *adverb*

When **special** means 'particularly good or close', you can use **especial** as a stronger way of saying the same thing: *a special/an especial friend of mine.*

But when it means 'for a particular purpose', you can't use **especial** instead: *They'd laid on a special train to bring the supporters to the match.*

**Especially** and **specially** can be used instead of each other, but in formal writing it's better to choose **especially**.

## speciality *noun* and specialty *noun*

Something you do most of the time or which you're very good at is your **speciality**: *She's good at all types of skiing, but slalom is her speciality.*

**Speciality** is the word mainly used for this in British English. American English uses **specialty**, and this is becoming more widely used in Britain.

## spectre, specter *noun*

A **spectre** is a ghost.

**Spectre** is the British spelling, **specter** the American.

## speed *verb*

If you **speed**, you move fast, and if you **speed** something, you make it go faster.

The verb **speed** has two past forms, **speeded** and **sped**. Most of the time you can use either, but if you follow **speed** with **up**, you have to use **speeded**: *The whole process needs to be speeded up.*

## spell *verb*

S

The verb **spell** has two past forms, **spelt** and **spelled**. In British English you can use either, although **spelt** is more usual. In American English **spelled** is much commoner than **spelt**.

## spill *verb*

The verb **spill** has two past forms, **spilt** and **spilled**. In British English you can use either, although **spilt** is more usual. In American English **spilled** is much commoner than **spilt**.

## spin *verb*

The usual past tense of the verb **spin** is **spun**, but it's also acceptable to use **span**. The only past participle is **spun**.

## spiral *verb*

To **spiral** is to move up or down while going in circles: *The dead leaves spiralled down.*

❶ When you add **-ing** or **-ed** to **spiral** you double the **l** in British English (**spiralling, spiralled**), but in American English you usually don't (**spiraling, spiraled**).

## spendour, splendor *noun*

**Splendour** is a brilliant display or appearance: *the splendour of the setting sun.*

**Splendour** is the British spelling, **splendor** the American.

## split infinitives

If you put a word in between *to* and a verb – as the voice at the beginning of *Star Trek* does when it says '**To** boldly **go** where no man has gone before' – it's called splitting the infinitive. This is one of the normal ways in which English works, and everyone does it, especially when they're speaking.

About three hundred years ago, writers on grammar invented a rule that it's wrong to split the infinitive (the actual term *split infinitive* wasn't invented until the end of the 19th century). A lot of people still believe that this rule should always be followed – so that the *Star Trek* voice, for example, should say 'Boldly to go' or 'To go boldly'. But it often results in sentences that sound awkward or unnatural. And sometimes it changes the meaning of what you're trying to say. For instance, if you write *He asked me to kindly stop making such a noise,* you're breaking the split-infinitive rule. But if you swap

S

it round and write *He asked me kindly to stop making such a noise*, it might mean something different – 'He asked me in a kind way'. And you can't put *kindly* after *stop*, because it wouldn't make sense.

Let the meaning of the sentence and its natural rhythm show you whether or not to 'split' the infinitive. *I used secretly to wish I could fly* sounds stiff, and *I used to wish secretly I could fly* puts the emphasis in the wrong place. *I used to secretly wish I could fly* is preferable to either. But *She wants to immediately leave* sounds very unnatural. The normal way to put it would be *She wants to leave immediately*. A simple 'rule' can't fit all sentences. Decide which is best for each individual one.

## spoil *verb*

If you **spoil** something, you damage it and make it useless or less good than it was: *Don't fiddle around with the flower arrangement – you'll spoil it.*

**Spoil** has two past forms, **spoilt** and **spoiled**. In British English you can use either, although **spoilt** is more usual. In American English **spoiled** is much commoner than **spoilt**.

## spring *verb*

When you **spring** you jump, or you move very quickly: *Soldiers spring to attention as she drives past.*

S

**Spring** has two past tenses: **sprang** and **sprung**. **Sprang** is commoner and more acceptable in standard English: *He sprang over the wall and ran away.*

The past participle is **sprung**.

## stalactite *noun* and stalagmite *noun*

A **stalactite** is a stony spike which hangs down like an icicle from the roof of a cave.

A **stalagmite** is a stony spike which sticks up from the floor of a cave.

Some people like to tell which is which by remembering that a **stalactite** has to hold on *tight* to stay on the roof, and a **stalagmite** *might* grow tall enough to reach the stalactite.

## standard English

Standard English is English that is considered to be acceptable by most educated speakers of the language.

There isn't a set of fixed rules about standard English. There isn't a committee which decides what's allowed and what isn't. Standard English just represents the collective view of people who use the language.

The idea of having a standard to refer to originated with written English. When we write, we know that we're putting our thoughts in a permanent form. In theory, anyone could read them. So we need to have conventions we can use that are recognized by other users of English to be appropriate to the written language.

But there's also standard spoken English. When we speak, we hesitate, repeat ourselves, say 'er' and 'um'. We adapt the way we talk so that it's suitable to the situation we're in. We use colloquial words which we wouldn't use in writing. For example, we might say *I've bust my watch*, but we'd probably write *I've broken my watch*. So the conventions for spoken English aren't so strict as they are for written English, but they still exist.

In several of the entries in this book, therefore, you'll find that although a particular usage isn't accepted in written English, it's all right to use it when you speak. For instance, few people would object if you said *I didn't use to like eggs*, but in writing, the recommended standard usage would be *I used not to like eggs*. On the other hand, there are lots of usages that aren't accepted in either written or spoken English – for example, using *what* after nouns and pronouns, as in *the girl what I saw.*

For some people standard English, or something very close to it, is the variety of English they've grown up with and use naturally. But there are lots of other varieties of English, in various parts of Britain (and elsewhere in the world).

There are times when it's appropriate to use standard English – at a job interview, for example, or in most sorts of writing. So it's useful for people whose variety of English isn't standard English to learn its conventions. But there are also times when, if you naturally speak a different variety of English, it's appropriate to use that – when you're talking to friends who also speak that variety, for instance.

Just because something isn't standard English, it doesn't mean that it isn't correct English. The *mans the dog bite* isn't correct English – it's ungrammatical and meaningless. *Ain't* isn't standard English, but it's quite normal in certain varieties of English, and if you're using one of those varieties, rather than standard English, it's correct to use it.

Standard English applies to spelling (*minuscule* is standard English, *miniscule* isn't); to words (*mischievous* is standard English, *mischievious* isn't); to the meaning of words (*to lay* 'to put down' is standard English, *to lay* 'to lie down' isn't); to grammar (*As I turned the corner, Kemal came into view at the bus stop* is standard English, *Turning the corner, Kemal came into view at the bus stop* isn't); to which words belong together (*a report on the accident* is standard English, *a report into the accident* isn't); and to punctuation (*two oranges* is standard English, *two orange's* isn't).

It applies to the pronunciation of particular words (for *longitude*, /**long**-gi-tyood/ or /**lonj**-i-tyood/ is standard English, /**long**-di-tyood/ isn't), but not to people's accents in general. There are a lot of different accents of English – in England, for instance, there are many regional accents – and you can speak standard English in any of these accents. People in Newcastle speak standard English in a different way from people in London or people in Plymouth.

There is, though, a way of speaking called Received Pronunciation (RP for short) which dictionaries use as the standard way of showing the British pronunciation of words. It's typical of the speech of educated middle-class people from south-eastern England.

There's not just one form of standard English. English is spoken in many parts of the world, and different areas have their own standards. Standard Australian English, for example, is different from standard Jamaican English. This book points out the important differences between standard British English and standard American English.

Standard English isn't fixed for ever. As time goes by it changes. For example, English-speakers used always to use *shall* instead of *will* to form the future tense after the first-person pronouns *I* and *we*. Gradually, however, this usage changed, and it's become very common to hear *I will* and *we will*. To begin with, this change was not accepted in standard English, but now it is. To find out more about this, look at the entry for LANGUAGE CHANGE.



**stationary** *adjective* and **stationery** *noun*

Something that's **stationary** is not moving: *Wait until the vehicle is stationary before you alight.*

**Stationery** is a collective word for the things you use for writing and typing, such as paper, envelopes, pens, pencils and ink.

**steal** see ROB

**stink** *verb*

Something that **stinks** smells very bad.

**Stink** has two past tenses: **stank** and **stunk**. **Stank** is commoner and more acceptable in standard English: *His breath stank of stale garlic.*

The past participle is **stunk**.

**storey** *noun* and **story** *noun*

There are two different words in English that are pronounced 🔊 /**stor**-i/.

One of them means 'a floor or level of a building'. This is spelt **storey** in British English and **story** in American English: *a three-storey building.* ❶ The plural of **storey** is **storeys**.

The other means 'an account of an event'. This is spelt **story**: *She told us the story of Red Riding Hood.* ❶ The plural of **story** is **stories**.

**straight** *adjective, noun* and **strait** *noun*

Something that's **straight** has no bends in it. And a **straight** is the straight part of a race track, just before the finishing line: *Lucky Shot overtook Clansman in the final straight.*

S

A **strait**, or **straits**, is a narrow stretch of water connecting two seas. And someone who is *in dire straits* or *in desperate straits* is in serious trouble.

**strata** *noun*

**Strata** are layers: *The members of the organization come from all strata of society.*

**Strata** is a plural noun, and it should always have plural words with it – for example, ✔ *these strata are*, not ⚠ *this strata is*.

If you want to use a singular word, you can use **stratum**, which is the singular form of **strata**, but it's a rather formal, technical word, mainly used in geology to talk about layers of rock.

## subject see NOUNS

## submit *verb*

If you **submit** to someone, you let them have authority over you.

❶ When you add **-ing** or **-ed** to **submit**, you double the **t**: **submitting, submitted**.

## subordinate clauses see CLAUSES

## subsidence *noun*

**Subsidence** is when the earth sinks, often damaging buildings, roads, etc.

🔊 **Subsidence** has two pronunciations: /səb-**side**-ənss/ and /**sub**-si-dənss/. They're equally acceptable in standard English.

## subtly *adverb*

**Subtly** means 'in a subtle way': *I think he was trying to suggest, very subtly, that I should go.* 🔊 You can pronounce it /**sut**-li/ or /**sut**-ə-li/.

❶ Remember the spelling – it's **subtly**, without an **e**.

## succour, succor *noun, verb*

**Succour** is a very formal word for 'help'.

**Succour** is the British spelling, **succor** the American.

S

## suffixes

**Suffixes** are added to the end of other words. They don't mean anything on their own, but they change the meaning or function of the word they're added to. Put the suffix *-ly* onto the adjective *happy* and you get the adverb *happily*.

## suit *noun* and suite *noun*

A **suit** /soot/ is a set of clothes, a set of cards (clubs, diamonds, hearts or spades) or a law case.

A **suite** /sweet/ is a set of rooms, a set of furniture or a set of short pieces of music.

## sulphur, sulfur *noun*

**Sulphur** is a yellow chemical.

**Sulphur** is the British spelling, **sulfur** the American. Related words are spelt with **ph** in British English and with **f** in American English – for example, British **sulphate** and American **sulfate**.

## summon *verb* and summons *noun, verb*

To **summon** someone is to order them to come or appear: *The king summoned his advisers and asked them what he should do.*

A **summons** is a command to come, especially an official order to appear in court to answer a charge: *She received a summons for speeding.* Its plural is **summonses**.

A person who is **summonsed** is given a summons.

## superior *adjective*

Something that's **superior** is better. You use **to** with **superior**, not *than*: *Our products are superior to any other manufacturer's.*

**superlatives** see ADJECTIVES

**supersede** *verb*

Something that **supersedes** something else takes its place: *CDs have superseded vinyl discs as the main medium for recorded music.*

❶ Remember the spelling – there's an **s** between the **r** and the **e**, not a **c**.

**surf** see SERF

**swap, swop** *verb*

To **swap** something is to exchange it for something else. In British English you can also use the spelling **swop**.

**swell** *verb*

To **swell** is to get bigger and bigger: *Its head swelled up, and I thought it was going to burst.*

**Swell** has two past participles – **swelled** and **swollen**. **Swollen** is mainly used when the swelling is a bad thing: *Heavy rains had swollen the river, and there was a danger that it might overflow.* Otherwise, **swelled** is more usual: *News that a member of the Royal Family would be appearing had swelled the crowd.*

S

**swim** *verb*

The past tense of **swim** is **swam**: *Who first swam the English Channel?*

Its past participle is **swum**: *I haven't swum in the sea for years.*

**swingeing** *adjective*

Something that's **swingeing** 🔊 /**swin**-jing/ is very harsh or severe: *Swingeing cuts in spending are expected in this year's budget.*

❶ Remember the **e** between the **g** and the **i**, which is there to make the spelling different from *swinging* 🔊 /**swing**-ing/.

**swivel** *verb*

When something **swivels**, it turns round on a fixed point: *At the sound of her voice he swivelled round.*

❶ When you add -**ing** and -**ed** to **swivel** you double the **l** in British English (**swivelling, swivelled**), but not usually in American English (**swiveling, swiveled**).

**swop** see SWAP

**symbol** see CYMBAL

**sympathy** see EMPATHY

S

# Tt

**talisman** *noun*

A **talisman** is a magic object supposed to bring good luck or protect you from harm.

The plural of **talisman** is ✔ **talismans**, not ⚠ *talismen.*

**target** *verb*

To **target** something is to aim to hit it or achieve it as your target: *Tomorrow's bombing raids will target enemy air bases.*

❗ When you add -**ing** or -**ed** to **target**, you don't double the **t**: **targeting**, **targeted**.

**taxi** *verb*

When a plane **taxis**, it goes along the ground before taking off or after landing.

The present participle of **taxi** is **taxiing** or **taxying.** Its past form is **taxied.**

**team** *noun, verb* and **teem** *verb*

A **team** is a group of people who play or work together. You can also use **team** as a verb, meaning 'to join together as a team': *We teamed up to play in the golf tournament.*

To **teem** is to rain very hard: *It was really teeming outside.* It also means 'to be full of something': *Her brain was teeming with ideas.*

**tenterhooks** *noun*

If you're **on tenterhooks**, you're in a state of great suspense or tension, especially because you're waiting to hear the outcome of something (tenterhooks was originally the name of hooks used for attaching cloth to a frame, so that it could be stretched).

Remember, it's ✔ **tenterhooks**, not ⚠ *tenderhooks*.

## thankfully *adverb*

**Thankfully** can mean 'in a pleased or grateful way': *Relieved that her guests had at last gone, she thankfully locked the door and went to bed.*

It can also mean 'I am thankful or grateful that': *Thankfully all my guests have at last gone, so I can go to bed.* ⚠ This is a perfectly reasonable thing for it to mean, but it's a usage which annoys some people. It's in line with the way many other English adverbs behave, so there's no logical reason not to use it like this, but as not everyone likes it, it's best to avoid it in serious writing.

## thank you

**Thank you** is the standard way of thanking someone in formal English. It's usual to write it as two words rather than as one, although when you use it as a noun or an adjective it should be hyphenated: *I'd like to say a big thank-you to everyone who wrote to me. He received hundreds of thank-you letters.*

When you speak, it's quite normal to use other expressions, such as *thanks,* but in writing – for example, if you're writing a letter to thank someone for something – it's better to use **thank you**.

t

## that *conjunction*

*I think that I saw him over there.* In spoken English it's perfectly normal to leave out the conjunction **that**: *I think I saw him over there.* In fact it sounds rather unnatural to include the **that**.

In formal writing, it's better to include the **that**. ⚠ But don't put two **that**s together: *I've been told that that* *painting is for sale* is awkward – change it to, for example, *That painting is for sale, I've been told.*

## **that** *pronoun* and **which** *pronoun*

*Martian spaceships which have ion drive can travel at half the speed of light.*

That sentence can mean two different things. Either 'All Martian spaceships have ion drive and they can all travel at half the speed of light', or 'Martian spaceships with ion drive can travel at half the speed of light (but the ones that haven't got it can't)'.

When you talk, you can make it clear which one you mean by the way you say it. For the first meaning, you'd leave a short pause before *which* and after *drive*. For the second meaning, you wouldn't.

You can't do that when you write, so you have to use another method. You can put a comma before *which* and after *drive* (*Martian spaceships, which have ion drive, can travel at half the speed of light*) to show you intend the first meaning.

Another thing you can do is use *that* instead of *which* to show the second meaning: *Martian spaceships that have ion drive can travel at half the speed of light.*

Remember, **which** can be used with both these sorts of meaning, but **that** can only be used with the second sort. To find out more on this subject, look at the entry for CLAUSES.

## **the**

**The** is the English definite article. 🔊 In standard English it's pronounced /dhə/ in front of consonants (*the bed* /dhə bed/ and /dhee/ in front of vowels (*the onion* /dhee-un-yən/). People also usually pronounce it /dhee/ when they're not sure which word they're going to say next.

Some people get into the habit of giving an unnatural emphasis to **the** and pronouncing it /dhee/ wherever it comes, especially when they're speaking in public. This sounds awkward, and it's best to avoid it.

**theatre, theater** *noun*

A **theatre** is a place where plays are performed. **Theatre** is the British spelling. American English usually uses the spelling **theater**, but it does also use **theatre**.

**their** *adjective* and **there** *adverb*

Remember the difference between **their** and **there**, which are both pronounced /dhair/, rhyming with *fair*.

**Their** means 'belonging to them': *Their house burnt down.*

**There** means 'in that place': *Who's that man over there?*

And it's ✔ **there is**, not ⚠ *their is*: *There's a fly in my soup.*

**theirs** *pronoun*

**Theirs** means 'the one or ones belonging to them': *I think this car must be theirs.*

❗ Remember the spelling – it's ✔ **theirs**, not ⚠ *their's*.

t

**there** see THEIR

**though** *conjunction, adverb* and
**although** *conjunction*

When they come at the beginning of a clause or sentence, **though** and **although** mean exactly the same, and you can use either: *Though/Although she was feeling very tired, she kept going.* The only difference between them is that **although** is a bit more formal than **though**.

But in the middle of a sentence or at the end, you can only use **though**: *It was fun while it lasted. I wouldn't want to do it again, though.*

**threshold** *noun*

The **threshold** of a building is a strip of stone or wood at the bottom of a doorway, which you cross when you go in.

❶ Remember the spelling – although **threshold**'s often pronounced 🔊 /**thresh**-holed/, there's only one **h** between the **s** and the **o**.

**throes** *noun* and **throws** *verb*

If you're in the **throes** of something, you're doing it with difficulty: *It's a bad time to ask us – we're in the throes of moving.*

**Throws** is part of the verb *to throw*: *A difficult question throws him into confusion.*

**through** *preposition*

In American English, **through** is used to mean 'from one to another, including the last one' – so *Monday through Friday* means 'Monday, Tuesday, Wednesday, Thursday and Friday', and *page one through ten* means 'pages one and ten and all the pages in between'.

It's sometimes used in this way in Britain, but it hasn't become established as part of standard British English, so it's best to avoid it in formal writing.

**till** see UNTIL

**time**

There are accepted ways of writing down the time. For whole hours, you can use words or figures: *one o'clock* or *1 o'clock.* In formal writing, it's usual to use words.

For hours with fractions of an hour, it's usual to use words: *half past one*; *a quarter to three.*

For hours with minutes, it's usual to use figures: *1.30*; *2.45.* (American English uses a colon instead of a full stop: *1:30*; *2:45.*)

There are differences between the words used to describe the time in British English and American English. 2.45 is *a quarter to three* in British English, but in American English *a quarter of three.* 3.15 is *a quarter past three* in British English, but in American English *a quarter after three.*

**tinge** *verb*

If something is **tinged** with a colour, it has just a slight amount of that colour: *The evening sky was pale blue, tinged with red.*

❶ When you add -**ing** to **tinge**, you can either drop the **e** or keep it: **tinging** or **tingeing**.

**tire** see TYRE

**toboggan** *verb*

To **toboggan** is to ride on a toboggan, which is a sort of sledge.

❶ When you add -**ing** or -**ed** to **toboggan**, you don't double the **n**: **tobogganing, tobogganed**.

t

**tortuous** *adjective* and **torturous** *adjective*

Something that's **tortuous** is too twisty and turny, so that you can't easily follow it: *I couldn't follow her tortuous logic.*

Something that's **torturous** is like torture: *I spent a torturous afternoon listening to the ghastly details of her operation.*

**total** *verb*

If something **totals** a particular number, it amounts to that number if you add everything up: *The number of deaths on the roads over this Christmas totalled 27.*

❶ When you add -**ing** or -**ed** to **total**, you double the **l** in British English (**totalling**, **totalled**) but not in American English (**totaling**, **totaled**).

**toward, towards** *preposition*

**Toward** and **towards** mean exactly the same – 'in the direction of'. **Toward** is the more commonly used form in American English, **towards** in British English.

**traffic** *verb*

People who **traffic** in something buy and sell it, usually illegally: *Did you know he traffics in drugs?*

❶ When you add -**ing** or -**ed** to **traffic**, you put a **k** after the **c**: **trafficking**, **trafficked**. And **trafficker** is spelt with a **k** too.

**trait** *noun*

A **trait** is a way of behaving that a particular person has: *A tendency to blame others for anything that goes wrong is one of her less endearing traits.*

🔊 It can be pronounced either /trayt/ or /tray/. Both are acceptable in standard British English, although some people find the 'French'-style /tray/ pretentious. In American English it's pronounced /trayt/.

t

**tranquillity** *noun* and **tranquillize** *verb*

**Tranquillity** is a condition of great peace and calmness: *A jet screeching overhead ruined the tranquillity of the afternoon.* ❶ In British English it's spelt with two **l**s, but in American English you can also spell it with one: **tranquility**.

To **tranquillize** someone is to make them quiet and calm, usually by giving them a drug. ❶ **Tranquillize** (or **tranquillise**) is the British spelling, but in America the usual spelling is **tranquilize**.

### trans- *prefix*

**Trans-** is added to words to give the meaning 'across' or 'on the other side'. For example, *transatlantic* means 'crossing the Atlantic' or 'on the other side of the Atlantic'.

🔊 Most British people pronounce it /transs/ or /tranz/ (rhyming with *vans*), but it's also quite common to say /trahnss/ or /trahnz/. All these pronunciations are perfectly acceptable.

American speakers say /transs/ or /tranz/.

### transfer *verb*

To **transfer** something is to take it to another place: *Our export department is being transferred to our London offices.*

❶ When you add **-ing** or **-ed** to **transfer**, you double the **r**: **transferring**, **transferred**. But the adjective **transferable**, which means 'able to be transferred', doesn't have a double **r**.

### transitive see VERBS

t

### translucent *adjective* and transparent *adjective*

Things that let light through can be called either **translucent** or **transparent**. The difference is that you can see clearly through **transparent** things, but you can't see through **translucent** things. So clear glass is **transparent**, but frosted glass is **translucent**.

## transmit *verb*

Things that are **transmitted** are passed on to someone else: *It's not known how this disease is transmitted.*

❶ When you add **-ing** or **-ed** to **transmit**, you double the **t**: **transmitting**, **transmitted**. The noun **transmitter**, meaning 'equipment that sends out a radio or television signal', has a double **t** too.

## transpire *verb*

The verb **transpire** has two meanings. It can mean 'to become known': *He'd told the police he'd been out of the country at the time, but it later transpired that he'd been near the scene of the crime.*

It can also mean 'to happen': *They say he turned up uninvited at her party, but I never heard what transpired after that.*

⚠ This second meaning is quite common, but it's not completely accepted as part of standard English, so it's best to avoid it in serious writing. Use *happen* instead.

## transport *noun* and transportation *noun*

**Transport** means 'taking people and things from one place to another': *The transport of freight by air can be very expensive.* It also means 'vehicles for doing this': *The company will provide transport between the airport and your hotel.*

In both of these meanings, American English usually uses **transportation** rather than **transport**. ⚠ This use of **transportation** is increasingly coming into British English. It hasn't become completely established in standard British English yet, though, so in serious writing it's best to use **transport**.

**trauma** *noun*

Doctors use the word **trauma** to mean a bad injury, and psychologists use it to mean a severe shock which has bad emotional effects on a person. In ordinary use it's come to mean any severely upsetting experience: *We had a bit of a trauma yesterday when Jennifer came home and announced she'd broken off her engagement.*

The first syllable of **trauma**, and of the adjective **traumatic**, is usually pronounced /traw/ (rhyming with *straw*), but some people say /trow/ (rhyming with *how*). Both are acceptable in standard English.

**travel** *verb*

To **travel** is to go from one place to another.

When you add **-ing** or **-ed** to **travel**, you double the **l** in British English (**travelling**, **travelled**), but in American English you usually don't (**traveling**, **traveled**).

**troop** *noun* and **troupe** *noun*

**Troop** and **troupe** are both pronounced /troop/ (rhyming with *loop*), but they mean slightly different things.

A **troop** is any group of people or animals (*a troop of monkeys*), especially soldiers or scouts. In the plural (**troops**) it means 'soldiers'.

t

A **troupe** is a group of actors, acrobats or other performers.

**try** *verb*

You can **try to** do something or **try and** do something: *Try to be more careful in future. Try and be more careful in future.*

You can use **try to** in any construction: *I'm trying to find the loo. He tried to lift it,* etc. But **try and** only works with the actual word **try**. You can't, for instance, say ⚠ *I'm trying and find the loo.*

**Try and** is perfectly good English, and quite acceptable in most situations, but in very formal writing it's better to use **try to**.

## tumour, tumor *noun*

A **tumour** is a diseased growth in the body.

**Tumour** is the British spelling, **tumor** the American.

## tunnel *verb*

To **tunnel** is to dig a tunnel: *They planned to get out by tunnelling under the wall.*

❶ When you add **-ing** or **-ed** to **tunnel** you double the **l** in British English (**tunnelling**, **tunnelled**), but not in American English (**tunneling**, **tunneled**).

## tyre, tire *noun*

A **tyre** is a rubber ring round a wheel. **Tyre** is the British English spelling, but in American English it's usually spelt **tire**.

# Uu

**uninterested** see DISINTERESTED

**unique** *adjective*

In its original meaning, **unique** means that there's only one of something: *This vase is unique – there are no others like it.*

When it's used in this way, there's no point in using words like *very* or *most* with it. Either there's only one of something or there isn't. ⚠ *Most unique* suggests that there are others, which goes against the meaning of **unique**. And ⚠ *very unique* makes it seem as though you can have different degrees of being one.

Some people think that you shouldn't use *any* adverbs with **unique**. But that's not so. It's perfectly natural in English to say things like *absolutely unique* and *totally unique*, which simply emphasize the unique quality of what you're talking about. And there's nothing wrong with *almost unique* or *nearly unique*, which mean 'extremely rare, if not quite unique'.

**Unique** has also come to mean 'remarkable, amazing'. In this sense, there's no harm in putting *very* or *most* in front of it (*I think he's the most unique man I've ever met*), ⚠ but the usage isn't completely accepted in standard English, so it's best to avoid it in serious writing.

**unravel** *verb*

If you **unravel** a mystery, you solve it. If something knitted **unravels**, it comes undone.

❶ When you add -**ing** or -**ed** to **unravel** you double the **l** in British English (**unravelling**, **unravelled**), but in American English you usually don't (**unraveling**, **unraveled**).

## **until** *preposition, conjunction* and **till** *preposition, conjunction*

**Until** and **till** both mean 'up to the time when': *I waited till it got dark, then I left.* They're equally acceptable in standard English, although in very formal writing it's preferable to use **until**. **Until** generally sounds better at the beginning of a sentence, too: *Until I met him, I'd no idea what a nice man he was.*

▲ It's best to avoid *until such time as*, which sounds very wordy. All you usually need to say is *until*.

❶ Remember the spelling – it's ✔ **until** (not ▲ *untill*) and ✔ **till** (not ▲ *til* – or *'til*).

## **upward** *adverb* and **upwards** *adverb*

**Upward** and **upwards** both mean 'to a higher place or point': *As I entered the room she glanced upward.*

Both are acceptable in standard English, although **upwards** is rather commoner in British English, and American English prefers **upward**.

## **usable, useable** *adjective*

Something that's **usable** can be used: *It was too dark to take usable photographs.*

❶ **Usable** is the usual spelling, but **useable** is also acceptable.

## **used to** *verb*

If you **used to** do something, you did it in the past, but you no longer do it: *I used to think classical music was boring.*

u

To make **used to** negative, you can either put in **not** (*I used not to like classical music*) or **never** (*I never used to like classical music*), or you can say **didn't use to** (*I didn't use to like classical music*). All three are perfectly acceptable in spoken English, but in serious writing you should use **used not to**.

In speech, **used not** is usually shortened to **usedn't** 🔊 /**yoo**-sənt/. But remember when you write it that it's **usedn't**, not ⚠ *usen't*.

⚠ *Didn't used to* isn't acceptable in standard English.

To use **used to** in questions, you either put in **did** (*Did you use to find classical music boring?*) or you switch round **used** and its subject (*Used you to find classical music boring?*). They're both acceptable ways of asking the question, but also they're both rather awkward, and in careful writing it's better to find another way of expressing it, without **used to** – for example, *Did you once find classical music boring?*

⚠ *Did you used to* isn't acceptable in standard English.

# Vv

## **vain** *adjective*, **vane** *noun* and **vein** *noun*

If you're **vain**, you're too proud of yourself. And if you do something **in vain**, it's unsuccessful: *We protested, but in vain – they went ahead and chopped down the tree.*

A **vane** is a thin piece of metal, wood, etc. that's moved by the wind or water – for example, a *weather vane* shows which way the wind's blowing.

A **vein** is a tube that carries blood around the body. It's also a line on an insect's wing, a leaf, etc., a long thin deposit of mineral in a rock and a mood or way of doing something: *She spoke in serious vein.*

## **valour, valor** *noun*

**Valour** is a formal word for courage, especially courage in battle.

❶ **Valour** is the British spelling, **valor** the American. But the adjective **valorous** 'brave' is spelt without a **u** before the **r** in both British and American English.

## **vapour, vapor** *noun*

**Vapour** is wetness in the air, like steam or mist.

**Vapour** is the British spelling, **vapor** the American.

## **variance** *noun*

If something's **at variance** with something else, it's different from it: *Mrs Macleod's account of what happened is at variance with yours.*

❶ Remember, it's ✔ **at variance with**, not ⚠ *at variance from* – and it's ✔ **at variance**, not ⚠ *at variants.*

**vein** see VAIN

## verbs

Verbs refer to actions or states (*go, break, seem*). All verbs can have a subject. Some verbs only have a subject: *I went.* They're called **intransitive**.

Some verbs can have a subject and an object: *I broke the cup.* They're called **transitive**. Transitive verbs can be either **active** or **passive**. In the active form, the person or thing that does the action is the subject of the verb: *I broke the cup.* In the passive form, the person or thing that the action is done to is the subject of the verb: *The cup was broken by me.*

Some verbs have a subject and a complement, which is a noun or adjective that refers back to the subject: *She seems angry.* They're called **copulas**.

Some verbs are used in front of other verbs to show whether the action is in the past, present or future or to express ideas like possibility or permission: *She has arrived. You can stop now.* They're called **auxiliary verbs** (*has* and *can* are the auxiliary verbs in the previous sentences).

## very *adverb*

Before ordinary adjectives and adverbs, you use **very**: *He's a very nice man. It's going very slowly.*

Before past participles ending with **-ed**, you use **much**: *Your help was much appreciated.*

Some of these past participles have become adjectives, so you can use **very** with them: *I was very pleased to get your letter.*

**vicious** *adjective* and **viscous** *adjective*

A **vicious** /**vish**-əs/ person or action is spiteful or unpleasantly violent: *He aimed a vicious kick at my ankle.*

A substance that's **viscous** /**vis**-kəs/ is thick and sticky, and won't pour easily.

**vigour, vigor** *noun*

**Vigour** is energy or forcefulness: *She may be 80 but she's still full of vigour.*

**Vigour** is the British spelling, **vigor** the American. But the adjective **vigorous** is spelt without a **u** before the **r** in both British and American English.

**viscous** see VICIOUS

# Ww

**wagon, waggon** *noun*

A **wagon** is a four-wheeled horse-drawn cart, or an open railway carriage.

❶ **Wagon** is the usual spelling, but in British English **waggon** is also used.

**waist** *noun* and **waste** *noun*, *verb*

A person's **waist** is the narrow part in the middle of their body.

**Waste** is stuff that's not needed and thrown away. It's also using something in a way that doesn't get the most out of it: *What a waste, using that good wine for cooking with!* **Waste** can be a verb too: *Don't waste all your money on computer games.*

**wait** see AWAIT

**waive** *verb* and **wave** *verb*

If you **waive** something, such as a rule or a claim, you agree not to insist on it: *In the light of his outstanding results, we're going to waive the regulation that no one under 11 can join the chess club* (= we're going to let him join).

To **wave** something, such as a flag, is to move it to and fro: *When you see me wave my handkerchief, start moving forwards.* To **wave** is also to move your hand to and fro.

**wake, waken** see AWAKE

**wallop** *verb*

To **wallop** something is to hit it hard: *If you don't shut up I'll wallop you.*

❶ When you add -**ing** or -**ed** to **wallop**, you don't double the **p**: **walloping**, **walloped**.

**-ward** *suffix* and **-wards** *suffix*

The suffixes -**ward** and -**wards** are both used in words describing the direction that something is going in: *As you go past the library, the road branches leftwards.*

In adjectives, you use -**ward**: *He left without a backward glance. The homeward journey was long and tiring.*

In adverbs, you can use either -**ward** or -**wards**: *You have to leave the room backward/backwards, bowing low. It was evening, and everyone was going homeward/homewards.* In British English, it's more usual to use -**wards**, but American speakers use mainly -**ward**.

**was** see WERE

**wash up** *verb*

For British people, to **wash up** is to wash the plates, glasses, pots and pans, etc. after a meal. But in America it means something different. If you have some Americans staying with you, and you ask them if they'd like to help you wash up, they may look shocked. For Americans, to **wash up** is to wash your face, hands, etc. – what British people would usually describe as *having a wash*. When talking about washing the plates, etc. after a meal, Americans say *washing the dishes*.

**waste** see WAIST

## **we** *pronoun*

**We** means 'I and other people'. It sounds very pompous to use it to mean just 'I'. Some people do this when they write: ⚠ *In our first paragraph, we showed that sweet corn grows best amongst other plants.* If it's only you that's writing, it's much better to use **I**.

It also sounds very stiff and formal to refer to yourself as if you were someone else: *The author wishes to point out that ...* Again, it's better to use **I**.

Use **we** as the subject of a verb, even when it's only part of the subject: *We British seldom complain in restaurants* (**we** is part of the subject of the verb *complain*). But as the object of a verb or preposition, use **us**: *Complaining in restaurants is rather embarrassing for us British.*

If you can't remember which one to use, try leaving out the other part of the subject. That should show you which one you want: *We seldom complain. Complaining in restaurants is embarrassing for us.*

## **weave** *verb*

When **weave** means 'to make cloth by joining threads together', its past tense is **wove** and its past participle is **woven**: *Her wedding dress was woven out of the finest silk.*

When it means 'to go on a zigzag course', its past tense and past participle are **weaved**: *The motor cyclist weaved in and out of the traffic.*

## **weird** *adjective*



Something that's **weird** is very strange and sometimes a bit frightening: *It was weird the way he could make his head appear to sink below his shoulders.*

❗ Remember the spelling: it's ✔ **weird**, not ⚠ *wierd.*

**well** see GOOD

**were** *past tense* and **was** *past tense*

**Were** and **was** are the past forms of the verb **to be**. Usually, **was** is used in the first and third person singular, and **were** is used everywhere else.

But there are some cases where **were** can be used instead of **was**. When you talk about things which might be true, or which you wish were true, or which could be true in the future, or which are not true, and the clause begins with *if, as if, as though* or *suppose*, you can use **were** instead of **was**: *If I were a bird, I could fly away to a foreign country. If it weren't so dark, I could see your face. Suppose she were to fail – what then?*

It's quite common, especially in speech, to use **was** instead of **were** in sentences like this: *If it wasn't so dark, I could see your face.* ⚠ But this is not completely accepted as part of standard English, and in writing it's best to use **were**.

When the order of the subject and the verb is turned round, you have to use **were** instead of **was**: *Were it not for your help, I could never have done it.*

**wet** *verb*

The verb to **wet** has two past forms – **wet** and **wetted**: *He's wet/wetted the bed again.* You can use either, although in the passive it's better to use **wetted**, so there won't be any confusion with the adjective **wet**: *The top surface should be slightly wetted.*

**wh-**

There are lots of English words that begin with **wh-**: for instance, *whale, wheat, which, whoosh, why.* 🔈 In America, Scotland and Ireland, the **wh-** is usually pronounced /hw/. In England, it's usually pronounced

/w/. Some English people think that /hw/ is 'better', but they don't necessarily always remember to use it, and /w/ is perfectly acceptable in standard English.

In *who, whole, whom, whore* and *whose*, **wh**- can only be pronounced /h/.

## wharf *noun*

A **wharf** is a place where ships are loaded and unloaded. Its plural can be either **wharves** or **wharfs**.

## what *adjective* and *pronoun*

Do you use a singular verb or a plural verb after **what**? If **what** only refers to one thing, you use a singular verb: *What we saw was a huge pile of bones.*

If it refers to more than one thing, but the things are thought of collectively, as a single unit, it's usual to use a singular verb: *What they need is food and shelter.* But you can also use a plural verb.

If it refers to several things, which are thought of as separate things, you use a plural verb: *In the photo, they're holding what appear to be guns.*

In questions, should you use **what** or **which**? It's usual to use **what** in general questions, and **which** when you're asking someone to make a choice out of a limited number of things. For example, if you ask someone *What books have you read?*, they'd probably think you were asking about all the books they'd ever read. But if you ask them *Which books have you read?*, you're thinking of a definite set of books, and you want to know the books in that set that they have read.

W

⚠ In standard English, it's not acceptable to use **what** after nouns and pronouns. You have to use **who/whom, which** or **that**. Say ✔ *the car which* or *that I saw* (or just *the car I saw*), not ⚠ *the car what I saw.*

## whence *adverb*

**Whence** means 'from where' (*the land whence she came*), so logically you shouldn't use **from** with it. However, language doesn't always work logically, so phrases like *the land from whence she came* are relatively common. Some purists object, but **from whence** is now generally regarded as part of standard English.

**Whence** is anyway a very formal word. You're most likely to find it in old poetry, and also in legal documents and the like. In ordinary writing, *the land she came from, the land that she came from, the land which she came from* and *the land from which she came* are preferable.

## whereby *conjunction*

**Whereby** is a very formal word. It means 'by which' or 'according to which': *We run a system whereby all contributors receive a guaranteed annual income.*

Some people use it with a much wider range of meanings, such as 'in which' or 'with which': ⚠ *Now I'm in a position whereby I can't afford to take a job.* This isn't accepted in standard English, and you should avoid it in serious writing.

## which *pronoun*

If you use **and which** in a sentence, check that you've already used **which** earlier in the same sentence. It's not acceptable in standard English to write sentences like ⚠ *She has a goat living in her garden and which she gets milk from.* If you want to put **and which** later in the sentence, you have to have another **which** before it: ✔ *She has a goat which lives in her garden and which she gets milk from.*

To find out whether to use **which** or **that**, look at the entry for THAT. And to find out whether to use **of which** or **whose**, look at the entry for WHOSE.

## while *conjunction*

**While** can mean 'during the time that': *Thieves broke in while I was out.* It can also mean 'although': *While we appreciate your problems, we must insist on immediate payment.* ⚠ Try to avoid using it with the second meaning if people could confuse it with the first – as in *While he's only a boy, he's just right for the part.*

## whisky, whiskey *noun*

**Whisky** is a strong alcoholic drink made from malted barley. When it's made in Scotland it's spelt **whisky**, but when it's made in Ireland and the USA it's spelt **whiskey**.

## wholly *adverb*

**Wholly** means 'completely': *They are wholly responsible for this mess.* 🔊 You can pronounce it either /**hole**-li/ (saying the two **l**s) or /**hoh**-li/. See also under HOLEY.

❶ Remember the spelling – there's no **e** between the two **l**s (it's different from *solely*, where the *e* of *sole* is kept).

## whom *pronoun*

In formal English, **whom** is the form of **who** used as the object of verbs and after prepositions: *Whom did you see?; a man whom I dislike; the person to whom I spoke.*

In ordinary spoken English and less formal writing, **whom** can sound rather stiff and pretentious. When it's the object of a verb at the beginning of a clause, you can leave it out altogether: *a man I dislike.* It's also quite common to use **who** instead (*a man who I dislike*), but this isn't generally accepted in standard English. When it's in a question, you can't leave it out, so it's all right to use **who** instead: *Who did you see?*

W

With prepositions, it sounds less stiff and formal to leave out **whom** and put the preposition at the end: *the person I spoke to.* In questions, it's much better to say

*Who did you speak to?* than *To whom did you speak?*, which is uncomfortably formal.

⚠ Don't use **whom** as the subject of a verb. In sentences like *Tell me who you think is the best footballer of all time,* **who** is the subject of the verb *is*, not the object of the verb *think*, so it's right to use **who**, not **whom**.

## whose *pronoun, adjective*

**Whose** is the possessive form of **who**: *Whose scarf is this?* (= who does it belong to?)

⚠ Don't get it confused with **who's**, which is short for **who is** and **who has**: *Who's that woman over there? Who's forgotten their lunch?*

When you're talking about things rather than people, it's better to use **whose** (*The programme, with whose production I was connected, was a great success*) than the long-winded **of which** (*The programme, with the production of which I was connected ...*).

## wilful, willful *adjective*

Someone who's **wilful** is very determined to do what they want.

**Wilful** is the British spelling, **willful** the American.

## will see SHALL

## wind *verb*

There are two verbs **to wind**. The one rhyming with *find* means 'to move in curves or circles'. Its past form is **wound**, which rhymes with *found*: *She wound the bandage round her finger.*

The one rhyming with *tinned* means 'to make someone out of breath'. Its past form is **winded**: *He was winded by a punch in the stomach.*

**-wise** *suffix*

You can put -**wise** on the end of a word to describe the way something happens. For example, if someone moves like a crab, you could say that they move *crabwise*.

The suffix is also used to mean 'from the point of view of', as in *Moneywise we are doing better than last year.* ⚠ It's quite common to do this, but it hasn't become completely accepted as part of standard British English, so it's best to avoid it in serious writing. For example, you could write *As far as money is concerned, we are doing better than last year.*

**withhold** *verb*

To **withhold** something is to refuse to give it: *He threatened to withhold his permission unless we promised to be back before dark.*

❗ Remember the spelling: there are two **h**s, not one.

**woman** see LADY

**wonder** *verb*

People sometimes say *I shouldn't wonder* when they mean that something wouldn't surprise them: *I shouldn't wonder if he was late* (= I think he probably will be late). It's not acceptable in standard English to put a negative word in the last part of the sentence – ⚠ don't say *I shouldn't wonder if he wasn't late.*

In sentences like *I wonder who that can be*, put a full stop at the end, not a question mark.

W

**won't** *verb* and **wont** *noun*

**Won't** is the way we usually say **will not**: *He won't be back until Thursday.* Sometimes, when we're being very emphatic, we say **will not** (*I will* not *allow this noise!*), but usually it's **won't**.

You can use **won't** in writing, too, but in very formal writing it's best to use **will not**.

**Wont** is a formal word for 'what someone usually does': *He had his nose in a book, as was his wont.*

**woollen, woolen** *adjective*

Things that are made from wool are **woollen**: *a woollen jumper.* **Woollen** is the British spelling. American English uses mainly **woolen**, but can also use **woollen**.

It's the same with **woolly**, which is British and American, and **wooly**, which is only American.

**word classes** see PARTS OF SPEECH

**word order** see INVERTED WORD ORDER

**worship** *verb*

To **worship** is to give praise, love and respect to a god.

❶ If you add -**ing** and -**ed** to **worship**, you double the **p** in British English (**worshipping**, **worshipped**), but in American English you usually don't (**worshiping**, **worshiped**).

**would** see SHOULD

**would have** *verb*

*If I had known you were coming, I would have arranged to be here.* When we say **would have**, it usually comes out as 🔊 /wuud əv/. The word /əv/ sounds just as much like **of** as like **have**, but remember, it's ✔ **would have** – it's not acceptable in standard English to write ⚠ *would of.*

Remember how the first part of that sentence goes: *If I had known you were coming, I would have arranged to be here.* It's ✔ *If I had known*, or *If I'd known*, but not ⚠ *If I would have known* or *If I'd have known.*

For more on **would** see under SHOULD.

## wreak *verb* and wrought *adjective*

To **wreak** means 'to cause something bad or unpleasant': *The fog wreaked havoc with our travel plans.* Remember, its past form is **wreaked**.

The adjective **wrought** refers to metal that has been shaped by hammering: *wrought iron.* ⚠ It's not acceptable in standard English to use **wrought** as the past form of **wreak**.

## wreath *noun* and wreathe *verb*

A **wreath** 🔊 /reeth/ is a circle of leaves or flowers or a curving line of mist or smoke. The plural **wreaths** can be pronounced /reeths/ or /reedhz/.

To **wreathe** 🔊 /reedh/ something is to wind round it like a wreath and cover it: *The valley was wreathed in mist.*

## write *verb*

In American English, if you send a letter to someone, you can say that you 'write them': *I wrote my sister and asked her to come and stay.*

In British English, you have to put in **to** after **write**: *I wrote to my sister and asked her to come and stay.*

## writing style see CLEAR WRITING

W

# Xx

## **xenophobia** *noun*

**Xenophobia** means dislike or distrust of foreign people. It's pronounced 🔊 /zen-ə-**foh**-bee-ə/, but is spelt with an **x**.

# Yy

## **you and I**

Use **you and I** when it comes before a verb, and means the same as *we*: *You and I shouldn't quarrel about this.*

But after a verb or a preposition, when it means the same as *us*, use **you and me**: *They've sent you and me separate invitations. Between you and me, I think he's mad.*

## **your** *adjective* and **you're**

**Your** means 'belonging to you': *Is that your bag?*

**You're** is the way people usually say you are: *You're standing on my foot.* You can use it in writing too, but in formal writing it's better to use **you are**.

## **yours** *pronoun*

**Yours** means 'the one belonging to you': *Is this bag yours?*

❶ Remember the spelling – it's ✔ **yours**, not ⚠ *your's*.

# Zz

## z

Z is the last letter of the alphabet. 🔊 In British English it's pronounced /zed/, but Americans say /zee/.

## zoology *noun*

**Zoology** is the scientific study of animals. 🔊 The first syllable of **zoology**, and of related words like **zoological** and **zoologist**, is usually pronounced /zoo/, as in *zoo*. Some people say /zoh/, rhyming with *go*, and think that this is more correct, but it's perfectly acceptable to say /zoo/ – /zoo-**ol**-ə-ji/.